D0461006

GOD
WILL MAKE
A WAY

DR. HENRY CLOUD
DR. JOHN TOWNSEND

GOD
WILL MAKE
A WAY

INTEGRITY®
PUBLISHERS
Nashville

GOD WILL MAKE A WAY

Copyright © 2002 by Henry Cloud and John Townsend.

Published by Integrity Publishers, a division of Integrity Media, Inc., 5250 Virginia Way, Suite 110, Brentwood, TN 37027

HELPING PEOPLE WORLDWIDE EXPERIENCE *the* MANIFEST PRESENCE *of* GOD.

All rights reserved. No portion of this book may be reproduced, stored in a retrieval system, or transmitted in any form or by any means—electronic, mechanical, photocopy, recording, or other—except for brief quotations in printed reviews, without the prior written permission of the publisher.

Published in association with Yates & Yates, LLP, Literary Agents, Orange, California

Cover and Interior Design: David Uttley
UDG | DesignWorks
www.udgdesignworks.com

Unless otherwise indicated, Scripture quotations are taken from the Holy Bible, New International Version, copyright © 1973, 1978, 1984, International Bible Society. Used by permission of Zondervan Bible Publishers.

Other Scripture quotations are taken from the following sources:

The New King James Version (NKJV), copyright © 1979, 1980, 1982, Thomas Nelson, Inc., Publishers. Used by permission.

The Living Bible (TLB), copyright © 1971, by Tyndale House Publishers, Wheaton, Illinois. Used by permission.

New American Standard Bible (NASB), copyright © 1960, 1977 by the Lockman Foundation.

The King James Version of the Bible (KJV).

Library of Congress Cataloging-in-Publication Data
Cloud, Henry.
    God will make a way / Henry Cloud and John Townsend.

ISBN 1-59145-008-X (hardcover)
ISBN 1-59145-043-8 (international paperback)
ISBN 1-59145-124-8 (SS)

    1. Suffering—Religious aspects—Christianity.   2. Hope—Religious aspects—Christianity.   3. Trust in God—Christianity.   I. Townsend, John Sims, 1952–   II. Title.
BT732.7.C57   2002
248.8'6–dc21   2002032721

Printed in the United States of America
04 05 06 07   RRD   9 8 7 6 5

DEDICATION

TO ALL THOSE
WHO ARE LOOKING FOR GOD
AND THE WAY
THAT HE PROVIDES FOR US.

CONTENTS

Contents

ACKNOWLEDGMENTS

A s always, we are grateful to a number of people—personally and professionally—who helped us in the development and writing of this book:

Byron Williamson, President of Integrity Publishers, for his vision for this project and his shared desire to make the spiritual life practical. Without his responsiveness to both our needs and the needs of the organizations and ministries with which we work, this project would have had no legs.

Joey Paul, Publisher of Integrity, for helping to shepherd the editorial process in a way that hopefully makes our ideas usable to readers. His tireless efforts and availability when we needed him is very much appreciated.

Rob Birkhead, Marketing VP of Integrity, for his creative direction on the book cover and interior design, as well as the marketing and promotion campaign.

Sealy Yates, our agent, for his faithful stewardship over all of our work. Without him our publishing would certainly have been different and probably not as fun.

ACKNOWLEDGMENTS

Maureen the Queen, Jodi, Kevin, Raul, and Grace—our home team at Cloud-Townsend Resources who were there for the process of this book coming to fruition. We so appreciate the fervor with which you strive to bring God's principles to so many people. Your passion for growth is contagious and motivates us to always do our best.

Janet Williams, our resident Zookeeper who juggles all the pieces for us. Without her, we might be lost at sea.

Steve Arterburn and Mike Marino, who make things work at New Life Live. You are part of how God makes a way for many people.

Dennis Beausejour, director of Answers for Life, a special thank you from Henry for your partnership in ministry and the passion and commitment that drives you to take a loving God to the neighborhoods of America.

The Answers for Life Staff, for their commitment to growth and to helping tell many people that God Will Make a Way. You model how He does that.

The Stakeholders of Answers for Life deserve a special thanks for joining with us in our mission. Your friendship and efforts are much appreciated.

Liz Heaney, our editor, for her clarity, direction, and support.

Don Moen, for his inspirational song, "God Will Make a Way," whose title and message are shared in this book.

And to *Mike Coleman, the President of Integrity Media, Inc.,* for his vision and support of a new publishing endeavor, Integrity Publishers.

PROLOGUE:

WE ALL NEED A WAY

I was almost four years old when the pain began. I (Henry) vividly recall the day it started, a Sunday. We had been at church, and the Sunday school teacher had to summon my parents to get me out of class because my leg hurt so badly. She had tried to help all she could, but there was little else for her to do. What we were soon to learn, however, was that there was little that my parents could do either. The pain would not go away.

From what my parents tell me, and from what I am able to recall, the next few months were pretty tough on everyone. When the pain got so bad that I began waking up in the middle of the night crying, my parents took me to the hospital. Unfortunately, the doctors did not exactly know what to do either, and I was hospitalized for weeks while they tried to figure it out. All they knew was that I was complaining of pain in my leg, but they could find nothing wrong. Since there was no external injury, something had to be wrong internally. But everyone was at a loss.

Finally, they sent me home and began to figure out the next step. I now know they were considering some pretty drastic options, including the possibility of amputation. Mercifully, my parents and the doctors kept me in the dark about the potential seriousness of my condition.

For my mother, this was one of the most difficult times that she'd ever been through. Daily, hourly, she had to watch as her little boy suffered, while she stood by helpless to relieve my pain. Both she and my father were deeply afraid that something was very seriously wrong and that it would go undetected until something horrible happened. At first, my mother could only cry and plead with God to help.

My parents did not attend healing services or expect miracles to happen every day. Yet they were people of faith, having learned in their own journey that, when your back is up against the wall and you pray and seek his help, God will make a way through the trial. So it was not unusual for them to lean on God for help in a tough time. This situation was particularly tough, though, because it involved their being powerless to help their own child. As a parent of two young girls, I can only now begin to identify with the pain they must have been feeling as they watched me suffer.

My parents prayed every day even though their emotions were in tumult. They did not understand why a happy, healthy little boy would suddenly be looking at the prospect of losing a normal life. It didn't seem fair. What had they, or I, done to deserve this? Yet as they prayed, they felt a certain steadiness inside, despite the fear. And they also began to sense that they should just be willing to do whatever they had to do—and that somehow, if they acted and did all they knew to do, God would come to their assistance and make a way for them. Then something truly unusual happened.

My mother and a friend had taken me to another doctor's visit, during which they were going to consider all the available options. As we sat in the waiting room, and time passed, my mother felt her fear growing. The doctor was not showing, and she just did not know what to expect. Still we waited . . . and waited. Then it happened.

Suddenly, my mother felt something inside of her, almost as if a voice said, *Take him to New Orleans.* At first, she felt a little startled, then a little weird. The impression was not audible, but she was so confident about what she had "heard" that she turned to her friend and said, "We have to go. I must take Henry to New Orleans." Grabbing me by the hand, she got up and walked out, with her friend trailing behind, stunned.

Take him to New Orleans meant only one thing to my mother. It meant that she should take me to Oschner's Clinic, the famous training hospital in New Orleans, Louisiana. At that time we lived in Vicksburg, Mississippi, a small town about 225 miles north of New Orleans. We had fine doctors and hospitals, as small towns go. But when something serious and/or unable to be diagnosed would come along, many people would seek the renowned specialists at that well-known institution. So when she heard *New Orleans,* my mother knew that God must be making a way for us there.

I wish I could have been a fly on the wall when she went home to tell my father that they had to pack up and leave immediately, and *why* it was so important to get me to New Orleans. I can just imagine his perplexity, because they'd spent two months working with very fine physicians in Vicksburg, and this would mean starting all over, with new doctors, in a distant city. How did she convince my dad, a no-nonsense businessman? How does one explain a seemingly irrational move like that to a spouse? I do not know, but somehow the compelling voice that she had heard gave her the fortitude. After making a bed for me in the backseat of the car, the three of us set off for New Orleans—going on pure faith.

When we checked in at Oschner's Clinic (and this is the miracle of it all), we were randomly assigned to a new doctor on their staff, Mary Sherman, a pediatric orthopedist. Dr. Sherman was very friendly as she examined me, and then she handed me over to the x-ray technicians.

I still remember those big, loud, scary machines that they had back then. I don't know if it was because of the machines or just the mystery of all that was happening to me, but I was scared. I knew that I was hurting a lot, confined to a wheelchair, and no longer allowed to walk, and my life was very different. I think also that I could sense my parents' uncertainty and fear. I knew that things were not okay.

Later, in Dr. Sherman's office, she told us that she had diagnosed what was wrong with me. I had necrosis—soft tissue that was dying—in my hip joint. Although this rare condition was serious if not properly treated, she knew exactly what to do. I would have to be in a wheelchair and on crutches with leg braces, but within a year or two I would be back to normal. How did she know?

The miracle was that Dr. Sherman had recently been trained in her residency under the two doctors in the U.S. who had extensive experience with this particular rare disease. *This made her one of only a few doctors, at that time, who knew how to diagnose my disease this early and provide the necessary treatment.* If God had not intervened and impressed my mother to take me to New Orleans, it is unlikely we would have found a cure in time. He had supernaturally led her to the one doctor who could help.

My mother and father discovered that God continued to make a way during the next few years, as they learned how to deal with a disabled child. They found that he provided coaches to do the tricky balancing act of helping me yet requiring me to take responsibility for myself. Every step of the way, God provided for us. If you ask my parents today, they will tell you that all eighty-seven years of their lives have been just like that as well. No matter what the crisis, God has made a way.

◆ THE WAY IS NOT ALWAYS AS EASY TO SEE

Life's crises do not always turn out as well as mine did. In my case, God provided the specific doctor I needed, and I did not lose my leg. I was healed. I don't pretend to know why such help does not always come in every situation. Every one of us has times when we lose, and we hurt, and we find ourselves asking, "Where is God in all this?" Often, it's not easy to see where God is when the road gets hard.

Yet what countless stories like mine tell us is that there are many times and many surprising ways that God shows up and changes even the *most* hopeless situations. One of the most powerful, though difficult, lessons we all need to learn on our spiritual pilgrimage is that even when bad things happen and we do not understand why, we can trust God to be present and working on our behalf. As an adult, after witnessing many tragedies and experiencing some of my own, I know that even when the worst things occur God is present and caring. I believe that death and suffering were never supposed to be a part of the human story. Yet countless times I have witnessed God enter a heartbreaking situation and, by revealing his presence, love, strength, resources, and specific guidance, create a path through the most painful wilderness.

What we need to do is learn how to recognize when God is present and at work. The thing is, we never know how he is going to show up. The Bible tells us that God often reveals himself to people in the most unexpected ways. The words of Don Moen's song "God Will Make a Way" (Integrity's Hosanna! Music, 1999) say it well:

> God will make a way
> When there seems to be no way
> He works in ways we cannot see
> He will make a way for me
> He will be my guide
> Hold me closely to his side
> With love and strength for each new day
> He will make a way

"Wait a minute," you may argue. "Not all crises turn out as well as yours did, even for people who trust God. Some people don't get well. Accidents happen and people die. Where is God in situations like these?"

Yes, in my case God provided the doctor I needed, and I was healed.

But you're right, sometimes the outcome is not as positive or pleasant. A single mom loses her teenage son in a terrible car accident. An executive runs off with his receptionist, leaving his wife and three children heartbroken and alone. A woman drops dead of a heart attack just as she and her husband are ready to enjoy retirement. A minister succumbs after a long and painful illness and many prayers for his healing. And you have your own stories of disappointment, pain, or tragedy where miraculous intervention didn't happen—or at least hasn't happened so far.

Consider the biblical account of Job. Here is further demonstration of just how difficult it is sometimes to see God at work. But Job's story also shows us the secret to finding a way through tough times. You'll recall that Job's friends gave him answer after answer for the tragedies in his life. But do you remember God's response? God's response was not really an answer at all; it was an encounter. God met Job face to face. Most people will tell you that in the midst of the most unspeakable suffering, they don't want an explanation; they want your presence. The ultimate answer, then, to the problem of pain is a person. It's God himself.

What John and I often hear from people struggling through seemingly hopeless situations is precisely that. They don't want philosophy or theology as much as they want the reality of God. And you know what? Their story, and the testimony of millions throughout history, is simply this: *God still shows up in very powerful ways.* God makes a way even through death and suffering by revealing his presence. Like Job, we never know when, where, or how he is going to show up, but he will.

At times in my own life, God has made a way for me by sending just the right people, the ones who could tell me the next step to take in finding him or who could help me work through some major losses and pain in my life. Without them I don't know what I would have done. But the key is that I will never have to know. Because when I reached out to God for help, he provided them. And they were able to bring to me and teach me exactly what I needed at that time.

The key, I have learned, is to reach out to God for help. When we do this, God has some pretty surprising ways of getting us the help we need—even when things look really bleak. And even when the problem is of our own making.

◆ MANY FEEL HELPLESS AND HOPELESS

John and I do a daily, national radio show during which people call in to talk about some very difficult life issues. Recently, we received a call from Marian, a middle-class career woman who was on the verge of losing it all, even her husband and children. In a not-so-smart moment, at the suggestion of a friend, she had "just once" tried crack cocaine. Drug use was totally out of character for this Midwestern mother, but, because of the power of chemical addiction, she was not able to do cocaine "just once." The drug had instantly gripped her, and this respected working mother had suddenly found herself to be something that she never would have imagined—an addict. Can you think for a moment how incredibly conflicting that must have been for someone who had previously thought that addicts were people who hung out in alleys or rundown tenements? We told her that, unfortunately, she was in the grips of a powerful substance.

Helpless, hopeless, and feeling terribly guilty, Marian decided to turn to God. In her effort to reach him she had been going to church, thinking that finding God meant making a commitment to being good, stopping the drug use, and attending church. As Marian told her story, I was immediately concerned that she was not finding God at all. Instead, she was finding "church" by trying to clean up her act and be a good churchgoer. She thought that finding God meant trying to do the "God thing," meaning, go to church, be a religious person, and change your life. It was not working. Nothing was changing. Now, believing that not even God would help her, she was more desperate than before.

I interrupted her and explained that she was not finding God, but religion instead. Religion is about trying to be better people than we are and using "God language" and even a "God address"—

like a church—in which to do it. But God does not depend on our willpower and commitment to transform a hopeless situation. He can raise people from the dead and create life where there is none. If Marian were finding God, or if God were finding her, then she would have found some kind of help, strength, and presence beyond her own efforts. I did not hear evidence of any of that. Instead, she seemed like a half-dead person trying to reach out and shock herself back to life with electric paddles. That is not how God makes a way.

God's way, I explained, is through grace—that is, by his *providing what we cannot provide for ourselves.* I did not hear much in Marian's situation that sounded like grace. I said I wanted to see her in a program, surrounded by other addicts through whom God could provide his understanding of her inability to stop without help. I wanted to see her needs addressed by people who understood the patterns of addiction and God's ways out of that misery. I wanted to see people expressing the love and support that God has for her and to provide her the strength to make it through another day. And I wanted to see God intervening directly with his power. Yet none of that was in the picture. All I heard from her was religion.

We finished by asking Marian to reach out for God to break through her old way of doing things—by human willpower—and to meet her where she was. And we prayed for her, for God to do a miracle. She did not know a treatment facility that would understand her or her faith, or be able to help her overcome her addiction, but she said she was open to God's help. That's when the miracle began.

The first part of the miracle was this: We knew just the place for her. It was perfect for what she needed, a drug rehabilitation center called Calvary Center in Arizona. But she did not have the money to pay for it. So we prayed, feeling as if God was going to make a way. I cannot explain it; it was just what we felt.

Then the miracle continued. Within minutes, the phone was ringing. People from all over the country called to say they felt as if they were supposed to pay for Marian to get treatment. It was incredible. At one point, we thought that her treatment had been paid for, but then

8

it became apparent she was going to come up short of funds—$5,400 short, to be exact.

We were surprised. We had all felt that this was a "God thing" and he was in it, but it seemed that things were not working out for her. Then the rest of the incredible miracle came. A woman called who, a few years before, had received an inheritance from which she'd never given God a tithe. Now she felt God was moving her to give a gift for this woman's treatment.

"How much is the tithe?" she was asked.

"The inheritance was $54,000," she replied. "I would like to give $5,400." We were ecstatic! It was the exact amount needed. God had indeed made a way for a woman who could see no way to get the help she desperately needed. Within a short time, Marian was in treatment, and as of this writing, she is doing great.

Maybe you're like Marian. You've been to church before, but you didn't find much of a connection with God, and you didn't see him work in your life. You thought that going to church was the thing that would get him to act on your behalf. We love church, and we encourage you to be a part of a local congregation. Yet, for whatever reasons, sometimes people do not find God when they go. It might be that the church you went to does not really know him, or it might just be where you were spiritually when you went there. Or the church could just not be a good fit for you.

Yet, as God demonstrated with this woman, he can find a way for you wherever you might be. Little did that woman know that her call from the Midwest to a radio studio in California would land her in a treatment center in Arizona, paid for by people from several other states. God is never limited in how he can make a way or what that way might look like.

◆ But I'm Not an Addict, and I Haven't Lost Anyone

You may be thinking, *But I'm just a normal person, with only the normal kinds of life stresses and problems. I don't have a big life crisis.* You may be wondering how God fits into your life. How will he make a way if you don't feel as if you have lost your way?

The fact is, if you think that your life is perfect and cannot get any better, then you are right—you don't need any help. You have already arrived at heaven. I think that is great. Unusual, but great. In reality, I've never seen a person who felt that his or her life was perfect, and I know some pretty successful, happy, and accomplished people. Even if you believe you have arrived, then God can *still* make a way for you to give to others. Ask him today whom he can send you to, and, believe me, he will give you a mission.

Chances are that few people who are reading this book have reached a place in life where they are beyond the need for God's help and grace. Chances are that you are a normal person, living a reasonably normal life.

Let's talk about normal. What is normal? As psychologists, we can tell you that being normal is not "having it all together." In fact, most normal people often feel there is still something missing in their lives. There is a distance between where they are and where they want to be. We call that the "gap." This longing usually expresses itself in one or more areas of your life.

1. *You want your relationships to be closer.* Chances are you have a relationship in your life that is good but could be better. Maybe you are languishing in a relational gap between you, a loved one, or a friend. It may be a relationship with your child. Or you may be longing for a closer relationship with an extended family member, such as a parent or an adult sibling.

Or perhaps the gap is in your marriage. Your day-to-day life with your spouse is okay, but you don't enjoy the depth of intimacy you anticipated when you were dating and first married. You know there should be more, but your dreams of growing closer over the years and being soul mates have not materialized as you had hoped.

2. *You want to be in control of your life.* This gap is personal, between where you are in life and where you want to be. It's about your personal goals, the way you think and act, and the way you feel emotionally. Maybe for you it's about accomplishment. You don't feel that you are living up to your potential or fulfilling your dreams. You wonder why your gifts and abilities aren't providing the achievement you expected. As a result, you feel disconnected from any passion for life.

Others stuck in this gap have personal patterns they are unable to change, ways of thinking, behaving, and living that defeat their best efforts. For example, a person may not be able to lose weight because he or she is locked into a destructive eating pattern. Still others experience the personal gap emotionally. They are reminded daily of the gap between how they feel and how they really *want* to feel.

3. *You want to satisfy your spiritual hunger.* Maybe you are experiencing a gap between yourself and God. You yearn to recapture the wonder of that childlike faith you had when you were younger, to be connected with the God you knew as loving, accepting, and wanting the best for you.

You want to restore your spiritual passion. But you want to restore your spiritual passion without the judgmentalism and weirdness that a lot of "religious people" have. You long for a spiritual reality with like-minded, real, and authentic people with whom you can share a relationship with God.

Or maybe you have been searching for a God who is more than a vague, New Age awareness. You want something more than calming music, mindless meditation, and a sense of oneness with nature.

However your longing expresses itself—relationally, personally, or spiritually—if you are in the gap, feeling stuck between your disappointing circumstances and your hopes and dreams for life, we have good news: God will make a way for you if you call on him. But here is where things sometimes get difficult. Most people cannot see God's way for them because they have difficulty believing there *is* a way.

◆ EXERCISE FAITH IN THE WAY

The main obstacle to finding God's way through the crises and gaps of life is failing to believe a way exists. Don Moen's touching lyric promises, "God will make a way where there seems to be no way." But how do we find that way? How can we transcend the trials and tragedies of life? *It starts by believing God indeed will make a way.* It's a matter of embracing and exercising faith in God.

Most of us don't have difficulty simply believing *in* God. But for some reason we are reticent when it comes to really trusting God. We think, *Will he come through for me? Can I depend on him? Will he make a way for me?* Trust is the bridge over the raging river. Trust is how we access God's way for us. Trust is acting on your belief that God will make a way.

You will never benefit from your faith in God until you step on the bridge and start walking across. Trust is both an *attitude* and an *action.* Your first small step must be followed by another, and another, until you realize that God has indeed made a way for you to know him personally. The more you act on your faith in God, the more you will see of his way for you.

When God makes a way for you through your trials, it is an active, not passive, process. God is active on your behalf, even when you cannot see it. And he calls you to be active also. At times, this may seem like a paradox to you. *Am I doing it? Or is God doing it?* The answer to both questions is "yes." God will do what only he can do, and your job is to do what you can do. That's when faith really shines.

Marian could not kick her crack habit or find the money for treatment. God had to do all of that. But she acted in faith by praying to him to do something, and when he moved on her behalf, she said "yes." This is just as much an exercise of faith as her prayer.

As you begin this exciting journey, we want to encourage you. The God who made a way for my parents when I was four is the same God who is available to you now. He is the One who made a way for a Midwestern mother addicted to crack, living a life that she would not have chosen in her wildest dreams. And he is the God who we personally have seen make a way over and over again in our own lives, even at times when there was not a crisis but only the next problem to solve. He watches over all of the earth, with an ear attuned to all who desire him. As the psalmist said, "The LORD is near to all who call on him, to all who call on him in truth. He fulfills the desires of those who fear him; he hears their cry and saves them" (Psalm 145:18–19).

We don't believe you are reading this book by coincidence, any more than Marian tuned into our radio program that day by coincidence. And just as Marian's faith made her well as she followed God's directions, we believe that you will have the same experience when you exercise your faith in God by following the eight principles as presented in the chapters to follow. Just as you would exercise faith in a doctor by following his advice to get well physically, by following God's instructions you can get well emotionally and spiritually. God is looking for you. So join us for an exciting journey as we see the many means by which God will make a way in your life.

I

THE PRINCIPLES OF THE WAY

1

PRINCIPLE ONE:

BEGIN YOUR JOURNEY WITH GOD

I (Henry) was sitting on an airplane, feeling especially grateful that I had a few hours to sit back and do nothing that required effort, thought, or any kind of emotional investment on my part. I was wiped out, so I was hoping for a seating companion who was equally as tired and did not want to talk. But on this particular day, it did not happen.

"Are you coming or going?" the man next to me asked. My first thought was that I would like to be going—to a different row.

"I'm on my way home from a working trip," I answered, hoping it would end there. But it didn't.

He went to the next level. "What do you do?"

I decided to give him the answer that's a big conversation-stopper for a lot of people. "I write books about God." There was a good chance he'd decide I was some sort of religious weirdo and make the move to another row himself.

"Oh really!" he said, seeming excited. "That's great."

"Are you into God too?" I asked.

"Oh, no. Not me," he replied quickly. "But I do place great value in it. In belief, I mean. I think *belief* is a really good thing."

Now I felt a bit intrigued. "What do you mean by 'belief'? Belief in what?"

"Well, God, or anything else," he answered. "I've noticed that when people believe in something it seems to help them. Sort of settles them down, I think. Gives them a sense of purpose or something like that."

And then he said the thing that really grabbed me and got us started on a conversation that lasted the rest of the flight. "I don't think it really matters what they believe in. Just the fact that they believe in *something* is what helps."

"You don't think it matters *at all* what it is people believe in?" I pressed.

"No, I really don't. All that matters is that they believe."

Actually, in one sense what he said was true. Research—and just commonsense observation—affirms that a person with a set of beliefs and a strong sense of "faith" is more grounded than a person who is perpetually confused and does not know what he or she believes in.

But what I would assert to my traveling companion, and to you as well, is much better news than that. It is not that *"belief* will make a way." It is that *"God* will make a way." Belief, or faith, is the step of trust that we take from *our* side, connecting us to the real God who makes the way.

You may recall the story of Abraham from the Bible. We're told that he had no idea where he was headed, but he believed that *God* knew. He didn't just believe in *belief* and head out across a desert, leaving all that was familiar to go to some distant land of "promise" in some attempt to "keep the faith." No, it was much more personal than that, and with a much more specific design. Abraham believed, or trusted, in a God *who knew exactly where he was taking him and who was more than able to lead.* Faith was the "way" from Abraham's side to connect to the God who knew the way and had the power and ability to get him there.

Abraham knew who he was following. Centuries later, the writer of Hebrews recorded: "By faith Abraham, when called to go to a place he would later receive as his inheritance, obeyed and went, even though he did not know where he was going. . . . He was looking forward to the city with foundations, whose architect and builder is God" (Hebrews 11:8, 10).

So when we talk about faith, trust, and belief to carry you through, we mean it in a very specific way. Faith, trust, and belief are not just exercises of positive thinking. They involve a relationship with a very real person who knows the way for us to live and who promises to lead us in it.

◆ BY DESIGN

Very often I hear people telling others what the man in the plane was advocating. They say, "Just have faith," or "Keep on believing." They sincerely want to give a friend hope and courage to get through a rough time or to reach a goal. But the problem in life is that we *all*, in some situations, come to the end of our own abilities, strength, knowledge, and experience. And at that moment, just having faith in faith, or belief in belief, or even faith in ourselves is not enough. We need more.

We need someone on the other end of that expression of faith. We need help to know what the next step is, what the next piece is. We need someone to give us the key to unlock the door that will lead us through whatever mystery lies before us. We need someone greater than ourselves to tell us what to do when we don't know what to do.

The fact that you and I need someone greater than ourselves is not a weakness. Some say that our need for God is a "crutch" and that only weak people need God. But that's not true any more than our need for air or food is because we're weak. We are *created* and *designed* to reach outside of ourselves to find the things that we need each and every day. One of the biggest oxymorons is the term "self-made" man or woman. No man or woman ever "made" him- or herself. The psalmist understood this when he wrote, "It is [God] who has made us, and not we ourselves" (Psalm 100:3, NKJV). I also love what he goes on to say at the end of the verse: "We are His people, and the sheep of His pasture."

Life is designed in a way that tells us we are not *supposed* to be able to make our own way. We did not make ourselves to begin with, nor did we design life and how it's supposed to work. So what I would say to my friend on the airplane is that it does matter what you believe. More specifically, it matters whom you believe *in*. Don't believe in faith—instead, use your faith to believe in God.

When we put our faith and trust in God, we've done the one thing that a human can do to accomplish superhuman things. We have reached past human strength and knowledge. We've touched infinite strength and infinite knowledge.

The message of the psalmist, along with the testimonies of many who go before us, is this: We begin to find our way when we realize that we are not God. We are not limitless. We do not have all the answers, because we did not make ourselves or life itself. So the fact that we do not know it all and are not able to figure it all out is okay. Second, since God made us, he wants to show each one of us how to live the life that he's given us.

Do you believe this to be true? He is your Shepherd. Life is his pasture, and he will guide you through it. He will show you the way. Indeed, *he will actually make a way, wherever you find yourself.*

Begin your journey with the first step of realizing that since you are not God, you are naturally going to run into the limits of your finite abilities to solve your problems or to create the life you desire. And since he is God, and he wants to be your Shepherd, you have the opportunity to live life in a relationship with the One who designed you and your life, and therefore he knows best how you can live it. That is the first step to finding out how God can make a way for you.

◆ WHAT WE NEED . . . AND WHAT HE PROVIDES

Here's an important question you need to answer: What do you do when you don't know what to do?

The sad truth is that many people do one of two things. First, we do the same thing again. We just try harder to make a relationship work, or to succeed in our careers, or to break a harmful or useless habit. Chronic dieters think, *This time it will be different,* because "this time" they're making a more sincere and heartfelt commitment to getting healthy and losing weight. People in a difficult relationship—even after one more blowout fight, or even one more separation—think, *This time it will change. Somehow we can make it be better.*

This approach reflects a popular definition of insanity: *Doing the same thing over and over again but expecting different results.* If you have tried your best, tried all you know to do, and tried it again and again, you know how insane it is. Going at a problem you haven't been able to resolve with your own limited knowledge and strength is pretty crazy, isn't it? If it didn't get you the results you wanted the first three or four . . . or ten or twenty times, why do you think it will give you your answer *this time?* Yet most of us keep trying, hoping things will turn out differently.

The second thing most of us do, at some point, when we've tried and tried with the same results, is we *stop* trying altogether. Understandably, we get tired and give up. We say, "This relationship will never work," or "I can never lose weight," or "I'll never reach my goals and dreams," or "I'll never be able to get over depression."

So the result of trying to do life within our own limitations of strength, knowledge, and resources, is futility and hopelessness.

Fortunately, in God's economy, getting to the end of ourselves is the beginning of hope. Jesus said, "Blessed are the poor in Spirit" (Matthew 5:3)—meaning that when we realize we have no more resources, we're ready to ask God for help.

The very great news is that when we ask God for help, we have instantly transcended our own limitations. We have stepped over to the side of a God who has infinite ways to grace us with all the resources we really need. Maybe you're wondering what God's resources are. Here are just a few:

◆ Strength and power
◆ Knowledge and wisdom

- Opportunities and resources
- Guidance and direction
- Healing and comfort
- Forgiveness and acceptance
- Skill and ability
- Love and community
- Hope and courage
- Values and principles

If you're hesitant, doubtful, or just plain resistant about making the step away from your own resources to God and his limitless resources, consider this. Throughout history, people have found the same thing to be true in science, philosophy, and their own experience—that is, our outside lives are manifestations of our internal lives. We understand that our soul and our spirit, the inside parts of ourselves, are what drive our ability to love and to create the lives we desire. The paradox is that the things inside of us are also the very things that we cannot create for ourselves: *They must be given to us from outside ourselves.* We must get them from God. Gifted people are indeed that: *gifted.* Through God, you can be gifted too.

Here is the very heart of what we're saying in many different ways throughout this book: *No matter what limitation or circumstance you find yourself up against in life, there is a God who can empower you and gift you to go past what you thought was possible.* It may be to help you through a hard time, deal with a difficult relationship, or even to make a dream come true. Whatever it is, our experience, and the experience of people throughout history, is that God can be trusted to provide more of what you need than you ever thought possible. Sometimes, through some very unexpected means, he will make a way for you.

When you're at the end of yourself, that's the time he can do his best work. That is why Jesus tells us, "Blessed are the poor in spirit." If you have a need, there is good news! You can have God on your side.

◆ How He Provides

What do you have to do to get past your own abilities and tap into the power, strength, and resources of God? It seems so good, maybe your assumption is that this is only for the really special, or really good, or really unique people. You may feel that this kind of life either does not exist or exists only for a few.

The Bible attests to a different truth. God's power and resources are not for special people at all. In fact, they cannot be earned by any human effort, ability, or goodness. They can only be received as a free gift. They can only be accessed through *humility*—that is, by realizing we are just humans in need of our Creator. Throughout the Bible God said one thing over and over: "Come to me and I will give to you."

How does God give to us today? The same way he always has: by coming to us and asking us to come to him. As Jesus said, he stands at the door of our life and knocks, and if we let him into our hearts and into our daily needs he will lead us to life in all of its fullness (Revelation 3:20; John 10:10). He seeks us each and every day. All we have to do is say "yes."

So the first step of how God will make a way in your life is to say "yes" to his invitation to give you all the things that you cannot provide for yourself. Instead of seeking those things, he tells us to seek *him* instead. As we do that, he will provide the "way" that we need. As Jesus said, "Seek first his kingdom and his righteousness, and all these things will be given to you as well" (Matthew 6:33).

Throughout the course of this book we'll expand on all the different things that God will give you to make a way out of wherever you are. As you read you'll be able to find the specific steps in the path you need to take. But without the first step—saying "yes" to God—the principles we offer you here will just be another set of rules or concepts that you try to live out in your own strength, subject to your own limitations. To make them work, you first have to be connected to Someone larger than yourself. You have to be connected to more than mere "belief." You have to be connected to God.

To begin your path, no matter where you are right now in your life, take the first step. Say "yes" to God's offer to make a way for you through his power and not your own. Ask him, even if you have taken this step before, to make a way for you.

He will.

As you're about to see, sometimes the way God makes for us is truly miraculous. Many other times, though, it's a way that involves a lot of work, growth, and change on our parts. Sometimes, it's not even the way we thought we needed to go, but it's a different and even better one. No matter how simple or how challenging our spiritual journey from here proves to be, when God makes a way, it's real and powerful, it gives meaning, and its results last.

When we connect to God and follow his ways, a whole new world can open up.

2

PRINCIPLE TWO:

CHOOSE YOUR TRAVELING
COMPANIONS WISELY

I (Henry) ran into my friend Joe—and man, was he angry! Someone had just given him a piece of advice that cut straight to his core, and he did not like it one bit.

Joe was in the process of building a new business, and he'd been working hard at putting all the pieces together. He wanted to be successful so badly he could taste it. Joe had always done well as an employee of a large sales organization but definitely had the talents and abilities to go out on his own. So, as he was working on beginning that process, he decided to get some input from a very successful businessman who had started his own company many years ago. This was the person who delivered the advice Joe did not want to hear.

As Joe told this world-class businessman all of his plans and the dreams that he had for his new company, he expected to get a download of wisdom in response. He was hoping for some savvy "how-tos" that would make it all happen.

Instead, the older man responded, "I will tell you how I began my business—and it's my advice to you, as well. I put together a small support group that met every week. We prayed together, confessed our struggles and sins to each other, reviewed our plans, but most of all, just supported each other. That's how I built my company."

"Sure," Joe jumped in, "but what about the initial funding? How did you approach the banks?" He rattled off a few other questions.

"Those things are not the most important, not at the beginning. Getting your support team in place *is* important," the successful businessman repeated.

No matter how Joe pressed him for business start-up secrets, he remained steadfast in what he wanted Joe to see. Over and over, the man repeated, "Surrounding yourself with spiritually tuned, well-grounded people is the single most important first step."

As I said, though, Joe was hopping mad when he told me how this guy had wasted his time offering such "useless" advice. Joe didn't want to get close to spiritually wise people; he wanted to be successful. He wanted to build something, make money, and accomplish his goals. What did surrounding yourself with spiritual people have to do with financing and sales?

Within two years, Joe was broke. Not only that, he was also broken. He had decided that the man's advice would just take valuable time away from "working his plan." He could not see that getting grounded with good people should have been the first and most important part of his strategy.

Joe's story illustrates one of two big reasons that people do not find God's way for them. They believe that solving the problem they're facing is the most important priority, thinking that the task itself—such as getting a career going, overcoming an addiction or bad habit, or solving a difficult relationship—is the most important thing.

But it's a proven fact that the work of solving a problem is *secondary* to getting your team together. People who try to do it on their own rarely make it—and when they do, they usually cannot sustain the effort. Like Joe, they succumb to their own limitations.

Every day as psychologists, John and I see people who are trying to do a better job at life. But they're trying to do it without the kind of support they need from others. That's one of the biggest reasons people fail—trying to go it alone.

There's also another reason that some do not find the way that

God is making for them. It is not the absence of good people on their team but the *presence of not-so-good ones*. Not only do they lack people who will get them closer to their goals, they have people who are *getting them further away* from their goals.

These nonhelpful people are not necessarily bad people. In fact, they can be some of our best friends and buddies. Yes, we all need some fun-loving "crazies" in our lives, because life would be boring without those kinds of people around. I love my nutty friends, even those who do not get me closer to finding my way. They're fun, but at the same time I don't depend on them for help. *The reality is that some friends and acquaintances are not able to do the things that our community is supposed to for us.* They like to have fun all the time and avoid facing the growth issues in their own lives. If they avoid their deeper issues, then you can bet they're unable to help you with yours. Sure you can have fun with them, but they're not going to help you grow and find the way that God has for you.

In fact, it can get worse than that. You might have people who do more than just not help you to move forward. You might have people who are actually taking you backward.

Susie was a woman who had recently been making progress in her life, finding the new way that God had for her. When she returned to counseling from the Christmas holiday break, she seemed different. She was a little negative about herself. I could feel that the energy of growth she'd had in the fall was gone—as if a light had been dimmed.

She began by talking all around the important issues—about some things that she wanted to accomplish. But I did not want to go there. I could not get away from the "feel" that Susie had around her. It was as if a cloud had followed her into the room. What was also very apparent was that she did not seem to notice the feeling surrounding her that I was noticing. She was just going about "solving life," as if nothing was different. But I could not ignore it.

So I asked Susie about her holidays. Over Christmas, she'd spent a lot of time with her family, primarily her mother and sister. She'd also gone out a few times with an old boyfriend. Nothing horrible had happened with any of them, at least not on the surface. Yet below the surface, a lot had happened.

Susie's mother was a negative person, and so was her sister. Both of them were especially negative toward Susie. They were not overtly abusive, but they tended to put her down in subtle ways. It had always seemed to Susie that she could not gain their approval, no matter what she did. She'd told them about her counseling, sharing some of the things that she was learning. They'd responded, "Oh, counseling never helped anyone. It's just a waste of time." The reality was that Susie had made great gains in her counseling throughout the previous year.

Slowly, they spread their negativity over every part of Susie's life. When she told them about the classes she was taking and how she was looking at a career change, they gave a dozen reasons that she was going about it wrong. When she told them about her growth in the area of relationships—particularly how she was looking for men to date who shared her newfound faith—they had their own views about her choice of men and what she'd "always" done wrong in her dating life. They didn't see her spiritual life as something having value.

The key point, however, is that all of this happened *very* subtly. They were not loud or overtly mean. Being with them was more like being in a room with a gas leak. After a while you find you're getting a headache, but you didn't notice it coming on and you don't know why you feel that way.

Interestingly enough, the same thing had happened with her former boyfriend—though he was a little more aggressive in his putdowns and devaluations. He could alternate charm with darts in a way that she'd forgotten.

While I saw no reason for Susie to have seen her old boyfriend, I didn't think she should have avoided her family. However, I did tell her in no uncertain terms that while family is important, she needed to be careful about allowing them into her vulnerabilities. Her dreams, growth, and heart were to be shared with those who could be on the side of life and light, not darkness and destruction. I encouraged her to love them and see them but to be wise about sharing with them the things that need protection and nurturance. She was not going to find it with them; in fact, what she would find would take her backward, not toward where she wanted to go. So there are two "traveling companions" dangers: the absence of good supporters and the presence of those who hurt our cause. What we need to know is how to pick the best people to be on our personal team.

Here are some things to look for in the kinds of support you are going to need.

◆ CHOOSING YOUR TEAM

I grew up playing competitive golf, and when I was a youngster Jack Nicklaus was king of the sport. The "Golden Bear," as he is called, dominated the PGA tour for a number of years. From my vantage point, he was the greatest golfer who ever lived.

Then one day my view of Jack Nicklaus abruptly changed. I heard that he periodically traveled home to Ohio to see his teacher, Jack Grout. Nicklaus needed some help with his swing, the announcer said. I was stunned. *Jack Nicklaus, the reigning king of professional golf, still needs a teacher?* I thought. *Jack is the best. Why does he need a teacher? Who could teach him anyway, since no one is better?*

In my kid-sized view of life, I assumed that, if you were very good at something, the last thing you needed was a teacher. Teachers were for people who didn't know what they were doing. I have learned a lot since then. People who rise to become the best they can be in their sports or their professions usually don't get to the top alone. They seek help from a teacher, counselor, or spiritual adviser.

There are many people who want what God has for them, but unfortunately, just like a kid who thinks he doesn't need a teacher, they fail to take advantage of the gifted, loving, and wise people he puts in their path. Part of God's program to make a way for you is to put good people around you who are gifted to help you get where you need to go. Some of these people will just show up in your life, sent by God at just the right time. Others you have to seek out on your own. Some will be professionals. Others may be neighbors or friends at church.

As the Bible tells us, when we love and support each other, we are actually handing out the resources of God himself: "Each one should use whatever gift he has received to serve others, faithfully administering God's grace in its various forms" (1 Peter 4:10). Part of God's program to "make a way" for you is to put around you good people whom he has gifted with the resources that you need to get where you need to go.

Here are some of the things others can give to you, which are really God's gifts, as you avail yourself of them:

Support. When we're going through change or trying to reach a goal, it's as if we're pushing our way uphill. By definition, we are handling something, either good or bad, that's more than day-to-day life. We do not have these resources in and of ourselves, and God gives us this strength through the support of others. From overcoming illness, to loss, to reaching a dream, all of these activities require more strength and stamina spiritually and emotionally than we possess on our own.

Love. The Bible also says, "Above all, love each other deeply, because love covers over a multitude of sins" (1 Peter 4:8). No matter what's happened to you, what you've done, or what you have to do now, *you need the safety net of love.* Love takes the sting out of life, and knowing that people are on your side—that they are *for you*—will make it possible for you to do what you have to do.

Courage. What you have to do is not going to be without risk and fear. Sometimes the task looks like it has dangers that we cannot face. We need people to tell us what the apostle Paul said to his friends who were in great danger: "So keep up your courage . . . for I have faith in God that it will happen just as he told me" (Acts 27:25). Even if you're someone who has great faith, you will experience times of fear, times when what you're up against just looks too big. We all need God's people on our side during those times to remind us to have courage. We also know that the mere presence of a support team adds courage in and of itself.

Feedback. As we will discuss more fully in the next chapter, we must have feedback from others. That's because we need it to correct us if we're going to get where we want to go in life. Over and over, the Bible tells us that people are one of the sources of God's correction to us: "Like an earring of gold or an ornament of fine gold is a wise man's rebuke to a listening ear" (Proverbs 25:12).

Wisdom. We just do not possess all the knowledge and wisdom that we are going to need. God speaks those things into our lives through wise people.

Experience. What a blessing it is to have someone on your team who has been where you are and who understands. In times of trouble or times of growth, we need the experience of others who have been there before.

Modeling. We can't do what we have never seen. One of God's most powerful ways of making a way for us is to give us people who can be role models for us. The Bible says, "We do not want you to become lazy, but to imitate those who through faith and patience inherit what has been promised" (Hebrews 6:12). In any area of life—whether marriage, work, or personal growth—we have to see others who are doing what we want to do. We learn best when we're able to watch and learn. In the same way that a child grows through imitating parents, we grow through watching others who serve as role models in various areas of life.

Values. Your values are what guide you. But the thing is, values are not built in a vacuum. They develop in the context of community. We learn new values from others, and we're supported in keeping our values and refining them through the people we associate with.

Accountability. The temperature gauge tells an engine if it is okay, as does the fuel gauge. A company gets an audit to let its directors know what needs to be corrected. In the same way, we need to be held accountable. We need to be "audited" by others to know how we are doing and what areas need more focus.

Most times in the Bible when God makes a way for someone, he sends at least one other person to help. At times it was a prophet, like Nathan, who guided and corrected David. Other times, it was a relative, like Jethro, who instructed Moses how to create the first government over Israel. Sometimes it was a friend, like Titus, who encouraged the apostle Paul when he was depressed. Certainly, there are supernatural times when God sends an angel, a vision, or even Jesus himself to speak to someone. We hear about those things happening all over the world, even today. But, by and large, God's main program for us is to have loving and supportive friends who will be there to help us make it through whatever life decides to throw our way.

Ask yourself today what kind of team you have put together to help you along the way. The wisest man who ever lived, King Solomon, put it like this:

> Two are better than one, because they have a good return for their work: If one falls down, his friend can help him up. But pity the man who falls and has no one to help him up! Also, if two lie down together, they will keep warm. But how can one keep warm alone? Though one may be overpowered, two can defend themselves. A cord of three strands is not quickly broken.
>
> —ECCLESIASTES 4:9–12

Who comprises your "cord of three strands"? Who are the people who are there for you, on your side, pulling for you, and not afraid to tell you the truth? Which friends are available to comfort you when you are down, show you more about God than you already know, and confront you when you are headed for trouble? Who can you count on to teach you when you don't know what to do, lead you to help when you need it, cry with you when you lose, and then celebrate with you when you win?

Your group can be informal or structured. A structured supportive environment has several elements that, if you will openly submit to them, will change you inside and bring God even closer. Here is a list of what to look for in any growth context in which you are seeking help, training, or repair of some area of life:

◆ A safe place to bring your struggle
◆ A leader who is loving, honest, and experienced in the issue
◆ Information and truth that pertains to the issue
◆ Accountability to God and others
◆ Regularity of schedule, such as meeting times and dates
◆ Requirements for people to take personal responsibility
◆ Risk-taking experiences
◆ Loving but direct feedback and confrontation
◆ Support and encouragement
◆ Goals, tasks, and homework assignments
◆ A way to use failure to learn and grow, rather than feeling discouraged and condemned by it

You may think this sounds like a lot of work. It is work. Yet it is very worthwhile.

On a practical as well as a spiritual level, my friend Joe would have benefited from doing this kind of work before he started. You'll recall that he was counseled to put such a team in place around him. Had he done so, I believe he would not have ended up where he did. Instead, he would have reached and surpassed the goals that he had for himself and for his business. Left to himself, however, he was no match for the challenge. The same is true for all of us. We need wise and loving support.

There are basically two kinds of people in the world: those who are growing personally and those who are going nowhere and stagnating. Welcome as traveling companions people who are pursuing God and his way for them, because they are constantly growing. They will help keep you on the way that God has made for you. Do not entrust your heart to those who are stagnant or doing things that destroy love, life, and accomplishment. They can kill your dreams and turn you away from God's way.

Some of the people you need may already be in your life. If they are, thank them for their ministry to you. Also, tell them that you need them in order to make the next steps on your journey. Ask them if they will be available to you for accountability, feedback, or support. They will probably feel very valued and touched that you asked.

If you find there are not enough of these good and supportive people in your life now, then get active and find them. You might need to join a structured support group to provide the team that you need. Either way, one thing has been proven over and over again: *The people with the best team, win.* Make sure you are one of those people.

PLACE HIGH VALUE ON WISDOM

Jan's husband found her in the garage, slumped on the floor with the bottle of pills in her hand. He knew she'd been depressed, but he had no idea that it was this bad. Nor did anyone else in her life. Jan was a very accomplished woman who had a lot of friends. No one would have guessed she was suicidal unless she had told them, and she was not about to tell anyone.

Depression was one thing; suicidal hopelessness was another. *How can I tell anyone that I've sunk down so far?* she reasoned. *What would they think?* And past that, *What could they do to help me anyway?* She felt as if she'd tried everything that she had always been taught to do to deal with life. Hadn't she read all the right books and listened to all the right sermons and teachers? Wasn't she well educated? As for talking to anyone about this, she'd been to counseling once years ago, and it had not been helpful. And if a counselor could not help, what could a friend do? Besides, she did not want to burden any of her friends with her problems. It seemed that the pills were the only answer.

Thankfully, her husband intervened and took her to the hospital. I (Henry) interviewed her and was saddened by how low Jan was feeling. "I have no hope at all," she told me, with a blank stare. "None.

And I know nothing will ever change for me. I'm just stuck down here in this depression. And no one gets it."

Jan was voicing the way deep depression is by its nature. There is no hope.

"I'm so mad he found me," she went on. "It could have all been over by now." By this, I knew she was still intent on dying. What stood out to me, though, was the amount of certainty she had that things would never change and that she'd never feel any better.

As I talked with her, I was amazed at how far apart our perspectives were. She had no hope, but I was filled with hope for her. She was certain that the only way for things to get better was to die— while I was certain that she would get well!

When I told Jan I could see her getting well, she looked at me as if I were an alien. Undaunted, I said there would certainly be difficulties in the process and that recovery would not be easy. Yet, I affirmed, she was not beyond hope, even though she felt that way. I assured her I knew from experience and training what was causing her depression and what to do about it. "Just from the little I've learned about you in this short time," I said, "I know you can do it." But she was not ready to believe my assurance.

"I don't want to be in this hospital," was all she could say.

"Yes, I know," I said. "But you are. And we need to keep you here until you feel better."

"No, I don't want to stay here," she protested, much more adamantly. "I will never feel better. So just let me go."

"Sorry, I can't let you go," I refused. "But I do believe you will get better. I know that you can't see that right now. From your perspective at the moment, there is no way out. In that sense, you're right. But from my perspective, given what I know, there is a way. You just can't see it yet.

"So," I continued, "you'll just have to hang with us and see for yourself."

As is the case with truly suicidal people, my encouragement didn't have any effect. And her answer was what I expected. Dully, she responded, "I don't have much choice, do I? You guys have locked me up. So I guess we'll just see."

◆ WISDOM MAKES THE DIFFERENCE

Years of clinical experience have taught me something very valuable about life and how God makes a way. What I learned came through a scenario that repeated itself and went like this: Someone who checked into the hospital or came to see me for counseling would be totally without hope. Actually, that's an understatement given some situations I have seen. Whether they were struggling with a marriage disaster, an addiction, a difficult child, the end of a career, or a long-term depression, I have met many people who truly believed there was *absolutely nothing that could make their situation better.* Their subjective experience told them they were at rock bottom, with no hope of things changing.

But my experience has taught me to see things differently. What I can see is this: While many people feel there is no hope, I can feel, *with total certainty,* that what they are experiencing will be resolved.

One person is certain that it's all over. Another is certain that the victory is guaranteed. What's the difference? In one word: *wisdom.*

Don't get me wrong—I'm not claiming to be a wise man or to have special intelligence. Far from it. But if wisdom is skill and knowledge applied to living, then I do know some principles of wisdom by which people can resolve seemingly insoluble problems. It just comes from years of experience in treating hurting and hopeless people, seeing what works and benefitting from experienced teachers.

The point that I am making is this: When we possess the wisdom needed for a particular situation, we gain hope, and even certainty for the resolution of the problem. *I knew that a person was going to get well if he or she did the right things.* And the reason that I knew was that there were true and tested principles of God's ways that would make them better.

Take depression as an example. I knew that if someone worked on the proven dynamics that cause depression, the depression would be healed. For example, if your heart is isolated and you learn how to connect with others, the depression that comes from emotional detachment goes away. Or if you're depressed because you feel powerless and you learn how to stop being manipulated, the depression leaves. Likewise, if depression is the result of unresolved grief or hurt and you resolve that pain, the depression gradually vanishes. If depression stems from a biochemical problem and you take the right medicine, you will get well. And on and on, depending on whatever the dynamics are.

But one thing was sure: If the depression was something that I had seen resolved before, and there were tested treatments that I knew worked, I had hope from the *wisdom* that good teachers had passed on to me. I knew that the person would get well. My point is actually the same one that God makes in the Book of Proverbs, when he says that hope comes from wisdom: "Know also that wisdom is sweet to your soul; *if you find it, there is a future hope for you,* and your hope will not be cut off" (Proverbs 24:14; emphasis ours).

Many times we feel hopeless because we do not know what to do next. When we add to that the sense that maybe nothing *can* be done, things do indeed seem hopeless. And the way we look at things creates the way we feel about things.

But the reality is that God has no limit when it comes to solutions. He can and *will* make a way. Sometimes, as he tells us, the path to that way is *helping us to gain wisdom as it applies to our situation.*

Proverbs is a wonderful book of the Bible, and it gives us a clear look at how much God values wisdom. Here are some wise insights you will want to firmly hold on to in various difficult situations:

◆ *If you're struggling with difficult or hurtful people:* "Wisdom will save you from the ways of wicked men, from men whose words are perverse" (Proverbs 2:12).

◆ *If you're wondering whether it's worth the effort to seek out answers to your problems:* "Wisdom is supreme; therefore get

wisdom. Though it cost all you have, get understanding"
(Proverbs 4:7).

◆ *If you're wondering about the best things that you could do to take care of yourself:* "He who gets wisdom loves his own soul; he who cherishes understanding prospers" (Proverbs 19:8).

Over and over—and these are just a few of the many examples—the Bible tells us that one path God uses to make a way is to give us wisdom. Our task is to find out what we do not know about what we are going through and what will help. So here are a few things to remember about the process of gaining wisdom.

◆ Wisdom and Truth Come from God

The first place we need to look for wisdom is directly from God himself. When we're in trouble or faced with a situation in which we do not know what to do, we can ask God. He *will* give us the wisdom we need. Consider this truth from the New Testament:

> Consider it pure joy . . . whenever you face trials of many kinds, because you know that the testing of your faith develops perseverance. Perseverance must finish its work so that you may be mature and complete, not lacking anything. *If any of you lacks wisdom, he should ask God, who gives generously to all without finding fault, and it will be given to him.*
>
> —James 1:2–5; emphasis ours

In every tough situation, the *first* thing we need to do is ask God.

Recently I was talking to a woman who was going through a divorce after thirty years of marriage. She said this: "It's been horrible. But I've learned something incredible. Each day, with each new situation—from wrangling over finances to custody of the children—I would find myself totally not knowing what to do. But when I'd ask

God, he would always tell me somehow. One way or another, the answer I needed would come. I've learned that he will tell us what we need at the point we need it. Also, I've learned that he does not seem to tell us ahead of time, but *just in time!"*

As this woman had learned so well, God will give us the wisdom we need if we ask him for it.

◆ GOD USES THE WISDOM OF OTHERS

There are many situations you and I do not know how to handle. Some are serious situations, in which big things are at stake. But the reality is, *someone* knows how to resolve our problem. Our job is to find that someone.

First, we should pray and ask God to help us in our search. Second, we should actively seek those who have experience in whatever it is we're struggling with. I have a friend in my life whom I call whenever I have a financial difficulty. He has wisdom when it comes to money matters, and so I lean on him for help in that area. The fact is, we do not have all the answers and others often do.

Learn to seek out friends who have the understanding you need.

◆ SEEK STRUCTURED WISDOM

At times, a phone call to a friend will not give us the wisdom we need. We need help from a more *formal* source. By "formal," I mean someone who is skilled in the form of help we need.

Dealing with a clinical depression is a good example. Clinical depression is serious and most often requires someone with psychological training to help. Often, John and I get calls on our radio program from those whose loved ones are caught up in an addiction. They've tried to deal with it themselves or by talking a few times with a counselor—and nothing's working. We get so frustrated when we hear that. We find ourselves almost screaming at them to get with a specific counselor who has dealt with hundreds of alcoholics or sex addicts. Most counselors without that experience do not know what to do with an addict. The help that addicts need almost always has to come from a structured substance-abuse program.

The areas in which we struggle have usually been addressed, and there is some sort of formal help available if we look. There are grief programs, divorce recovery programs, couples groups, financial debt relief counselors, résumé writing courses, job interview coaches . . . and on and on. There is no need for you to reinvent the wheel. It's sad, to me, when I see people staying stuck and not seeking wisdom and help—when it's so widely available! And today, cost does not have to be an obstacle because there are many fine programs available through churches and government agencies.

Recently, I was leading a seminar and talking about our need to get active in seeking God's purposes and dreams for us. Dreams that come from God, I explained, are never based in wrong or selfish motives. Only if they're based in good motives are they truly God's dreams for us, and in that case we can count on him to make a way for them to come to fruition (James 4:2–3). So, I said, if a dream truly comes from God, through our heart, he will make a way for it to be realized.

A woman asked, "What if you have a dream and there is no money to realize it, and God has not provided it?"

"What's your dream?" I asked.

"I want to go back to school and become a musician. But I can't afford it, and God is not providing the money."

"How many granting agencies have you applied to?" I probed. "How many scholarships have you sought? How many people who have heard you sing and minister with this gift have you asked to support you in reaching this dream?"

She blinked. "None."

You see, she had just assumed that the money was not there. And she assumed, because she had prayed a few times and cash did not show up miraculously, that God was not providing. I was suggesting that God does provide sometimes through formal, structured scholarships and through financial aid counselors who could help her get what she needed.

I then told her, "Go and seek *that* kind of help, from the people who know how to get grants. Apply to a zillion places. If you've done that and *still* get no help, then you can say God has not provided and the door to that dream is closed. But not until then."

Remember, God tells us to seek wisdom. "Ask and it will be given to you; seek and you will find; knock and the door will be opened to you. For everyone who asks receives; he who seeks finds; and to him who knocks, the door will be opened" (Matthew 7:7–8).

For years we have interviewed and hired psychologists and psychiatrists and counselors. All of them had formal education. But there was a noticeable difference in the candidates whom we really wanted. They had gone way past their education to seek wisdom from experienced people in structured places other than schools. They had attended continuing education seminars, read books, listened to tapes, and participated in workshops. So it was no accident that they were so far ahead of the pack from the others who did not do those things.

The same thing is true of the people we counsel. The ones who do the best are the ones who go beyond the help we provide and seek out structured learning and wisdom-gaining experiences. They go to groups, workshops, watch videos on growth and relationships, and listen to teaching tapes. The wisdom that you need for your situation is available if you seek it. Here are some sources:

- Pastors
- Churches equipped with programs for many different needs
- Community colleges
- Seminars
- Books and tapes
- Workshops
- Retreats
- Professionals
- Self-help groups

◆ TEST THE VOICES OF WISDOM

As we seek wisdom, it's important to be sure the people who offer wise counsel know what they're talking about. There is a lot of wisdom for sale out there. Actually, the Bible says we should make it a goal to get wisdom, even though the cost might be high (Proverbs 4:7). But you can also waste your money buying "wisdom" and experiences that are worthless.

To draw an example from a different venue, how many people do you know who have actually gotten flat, rippling abdominal muscles from an "ab machine" that costs "only $69.95" and "does the work for you"? None, right? On the other hand, how many people do you know who are in shape because they work out regularly? Do you really know anyone who has gotten rich by buying some "get-rich" program from television? However, chances are that you do know people who have been coached by experienced people in finance or learned a career skill and became financially grounded.

Do not believe every so-called expert or put your trust in quick-answer "solutions." Check the track record. Get a good referral from someone who is familiar with a counselor's work. Talk to a pastor who sends people to various counselors. Ask your friends, your doctor, or some other trusted person for a knowledgeable referral. Make sure that you are not being sold a bill of goods that has no value but one that has a history of good results. Remember, just because someone says that he or she is an expert does not make it so.

◆ NOT A RANDOM UNIVERSE

God has put you in a universe that has order. There are principles that govern relationships, work, the way you feel, and the like. Things work or don't work because of laws that have been in place since God first created everything. And speaking on the matter of wisdom, the Bible says this: "By wisdom the LORD laid the earth's foundations, by understanding he set the heavens in place; by his knowledge the deeps were divided, and the clouds let drop the dew" (Proverbs 3:19–20).

Part of the way God has laid out for you through your dilemma has probably already been made! It's quite likely all laid out for you already. Your job is to find that way by seeking the wisdom that applies to your troubled situation.

One thing is sure: We can depend on God's ways to work. So ask him for help, seek wisdom with all your strength, and then when you find it, apply it with all that you are.

LEAVE YOUR BAGGAGE BEHIND

Glen was excited about his new job—as excited as I (Henry) had ever seen anyone. His new position was with the marketing department of a family-owned company that sold medical supplies. He was hired to build relationships with doctors, hospital administrators, and other key influencers in the medical community that the sales force could follow up on. To an outgoing guy like Glen, having a job that primarily involved building relationships with people was a dream come true.

In the first few weeks, he thought the course of his whole life had changed. Talented and bright, Glen had always thought that he could be a success. He was extremely well liked, and with his brains and personality, he seemed like a shoo-in for any job that required creativity, intelligence, and people skills. Yet it hadn't happened. The truth was, at thirty-seven, he wasn't much further along than he'd been in his late twenties. But *this* job, he assured me, was going to change that.

He could not believe how perfectly suited he was for the position. His first assignment was to take a group of orthopedic surgeons to play golf and befriend them for a couple of days while they were in town. "Can you believe it?" he asked his wife. He continued to tell her about how well it went, how he kept them all laughing, and how he knew that the sales group was going to score big with them because of what he had done. He could just see the future forming right in front of him, corner office and all.

Glen continued with some other meetings, and what had always been true was true there as well: People loved him. Things looked bright. Then one day, about the third week, he got a call from accounting, reminding him that he hadn't turned in his receipts or expense report. "Oh yeah," Glen apologized. "Sorry. I got held up with a new deal the boss is working on. He has me running all over the place. I'll get what you need up to you later today."

As soon as he hung up the phone, he got back involved in work and forgot. Then, for the next few days, he would think about his promise—and every time he'd tell himself, "I'll get to it later." But, as was a familiar pattern with Glen, "later" did not come. The phone call from John, his boss, did. "Glen, I just got a call from Raymond, the CFO. He said some paperwork they're waiting on from you is holding them up. They need it in order to finish some analysis. What's the deal? Why aren't you getting that to them?"

"Sorry," Glen apologized. "I've just had too much to take care of. I'll get it to them right now."

"Good. I hate it when those guys are breathing down my neck," John responded. "It doesn't help my cause, since I'm trying to get our budget increased. Please don't do this to me again."

"Don't worry, John. I won't," Glen reassured him. There was a little sting in Glen's gut when he placed the receiver down. "That seemed a little heavy-handed," he muttered. "What's the big deal about a bunch of paperwork? Don't they understand how important what I'm doing is for the company?" He even felt a little angry at being underappreciated.

Later that week, Glen was supposed to turn in an important research report to top management for the annual meeting of the board of directors. Once again, he did not submit the report on time. And once again, his boss was on the phone. This time he was irate.

"Where is that information, Glen? We really need it for the board meeting."

"Sorry, John. I had to go do a presentation for a hospital yesterday and couldn't get to it. I'll work on it now," Glen explained.

John was concerned about what seemed to be an emerging pattern with Glen, so he decided to talk to him about it. He needed to tell Glen that the times that he had not followed through had been a problem for other people, and he wanted it to get better. He liked a lot of the people-work that Glen was doing, but his irresponsibility in turning in necessary information was getting in the way. As a seasoned manager, John knew that all the people skills in the world did not make up for sloppiness. He also wanted to get off on the right track with Glen. John liked him and was really impressed with his intelligence and relational strengths.

The meeting did not go well. What John thought was going to be constructive give and take, turned into an emotional roller coaster ride. Glen reacted with anger and some sarcasm.

"Why does everyone seem so petty about the details, when I'm doing such great things in the big picture? I can't believe you are making such a big deal out of this," Glen griped.

John just listened.

Glen continued. "I'm hurt by your criticism and feel put down."

"I don't mean to put you down," John responded gently but with authority. "These issues are important to all of us reaching our goals. This is not personal. I appreciate what you are doing. This is about solving problems."

John left and hoped that Glen could understand. As a manager with a lot of experience, he had remained firm and had not allowed Glen's reaction to get him sidetracked from the issue. Yet Glen's reactions had caused John to make a prediction: *Glen is not going to make it long-term.*

Sadly, John's prediction came true. As Glen got more feedback and input, he resisted more and started resenting John and the other managing partners. He griped about the management to his peers, and that caused even more trouble. Eventually, Glen's poor administrative performance, as well as his divisiveness, could not be outweighed by his talents and contributions. Regretfully to all the managers who had had such great hopes for him, he was let go.

For Glen's managers, he shortly became just a memory. They would never see him again, nor would Glen's character issues affect them. Yet Glen's problems would continue to plague his wife and three school-age girls through two more jobs and job losses. His family had to move and start over twice, until Glen finally figured it out and God made a way for him.

What was the way that God made for Glen? *God made a way for him to finally move past his past.*

◆ CHECK IN YOUR BAGGAGE

There is a concept in life called "finishing." Here's how it works.

We all have relationships, experiences, and lessons in life that are sometimes painful, difficult, and, for whatever reason, hard to process. As a result, we walk around with certain feelings, patterns, and conflicts that do not really relate to the present but to people and events from a previous time. Because those things are not "finished," they get in the way of present situations, present relationships, or present goals. And the sad thing is, this "baggage" that we carry around does not go away until it is dealt with, or "finished."

What happened with Glen was not new at all. It was an old pattern in his life that was reenacted one more time, around a new goal, in a new place, with new people. For Glen, it was all about his relationship with his father.

Glen's dad had been a strong, overbearing man. Glen felt he could never please him. It seemed that no matter what Glen did, he was not quite good enough for his father. He always felt put down and unappreciated. He would try his best to please his dad, but to no avail.

As a result, Glen was deeply hurt and developed a sensitivity to

48

criticism, for good reason. In many ways, his dad was just mean. So Glen felt "one-down" in comparison to others. As he grew older, he did what most of us do: He worked hard to overcome those feelings. He performed well and tried hard. And because he was very talented, he often did well, until some significant authority figure (like John, or a coach, or another boss) criticized him in some way. Then he would characteristically feel "one-down" to that person—not good enough, unappreciated, and hurt. In short, all the things he once felt in his relationship with his father, he would feel in present-day relationships with authority figures whom he wanted to please.

Trying to overcome his feelings had not worked, because Glen had never *dealt with* his feelings and patterns from the past. As a result, all of those feelings and patterns were still very much present and active inside him. They were just waiting for a chance to be expressed, like in a relationship with a new authority figure. Then, once again, he would feel hurt and begin to resist the things that his boss would ask of him as a way of passive protest. The more he would resist, the more he would get criticized. It was a vicious cycle, and ultimately he would lose his job.

The saddest thing about Glen's behavioral patterns was that his bosses generally did not intend to put him down. But because of the sensitivity and hurt that had never been healed, any criticism, even *constructive criticism,* could feel that way. He would go into a time warp and begin to feel just as he'd felt as a kid. Sadly, he'd act like a child also, and not many companies like to employ children. So he would lose his job, and his wife and daughters would suffer. His patterns of resisting authority, being indirect, and not fulfilling his boss's expectations would catch up with him.

Glen did not understand the concept of "finishing." God has wired us with a very predictable path for processing life, no matter what our circumstances. With his help, we can work through former hurts and patterns we developed in previous painful situations. But if we haven't dealt with the baggage we bring to any given situation, then those hurts and issues will interfere and may wreak havoc with whatever new situation we find ourselves in. In a very real sense, *our past will become our present.*

If hurtful things have happened to your heart and you have not yet dealt with them, those old events will continue to produce what we refer to as "issues" in your life. God promises that from our heart, all sorts of things happen. The issues that we find ourselves dealing with day to day come from inside, as the Book of Proverbs reveals: "Keep thy heart with all diligence; for out of it are the issues of life" (Proverbs 4:23, KJV).

Glen had hurts in his heart that were affecting him. When he received correction from a boss in the present, he felt as if he were dealing with his unreasonable father. He needed to "keep his heart," so that he could be free from the past and have a new present.

◆ RESCUE YOUR HEART FROM THE PAST

So how does God make a way for us to leave behind our old baggage from the past? Here are six steps you can ask God to help you take.

1. *Agree that you have a problem from the past, and confess it.* I have seen people, with God's help, overcome just about every sort of past imaginable. Yet no issue can be overcome until we admit that it exists.

Recently on our radio program, a woman called about her lack of desire for sex with her husband. She had been very sexually attracted to him throughout their engagement. But when they married and began to have intercourse, she'd "go numb," as she put it, and have no desire. "In fact," she said, "I even feel repulsed by sex. It's really bothering me. I love him and he loves me. I'm so tired of this." Then she said something very revealing: "And there's absolutely no reason for me to feel this way."

The truth is, we never feel any way—whether anger, or passion, or "numb"—for no reason. When I pressed her on this point, though, she remained adamant. From this I knew there was some reason that she *needed* to believe there was no reason for her lack of sexual feeling toward her husband.

"Karen," I decided to press, "I know that you don't feel there is any reason for you to have this problem. But if I asked someone who knew you well why you feel this way, what do you think they'd say?"

Her response was immediate. "They would say it has to do with the sexual abuse I experienced. But I don't think that has anything to do with it. I just don't see the connection."

"What happens inside you when your husband wants to be intimate?" I asked.

Karen thought for a moment. "I don't know. I just feel detached. Like I want to get away."

"Did you know that's exactly what happens to someone during sexual abuse? The victim 'detaches' from the experience. And since the experience is sexual, they are also detaching from sexual experience. That's exactly what you're saying happens to you now."

The point is that until she could acknowledge that the significant and damaging events she'd experienced in her past had a major effect on her *now*, she could not work through them. *And as long as she could not work through those experiences, they continued to be present, not past.*

God's word for "agree" is the word that is translated "confess." To confess something means that we agree that it is *true*. When it comes to baggage that is bothering us, we must recognize that things have gone wrong, either to us or by us, and agree with God, or "confess," that they happened and affected us deeply.

2. Get healing and express grief. The next step is to receive the care and healing we need to deal with whatever has happened to wound us. If your heart has been broken, then you have to allow others to give you God's care and love to help mend that broken heart. He tells us to "weep with those who weep" (Romans 12:15, NASB), which gives us the healing and support from others that we need to start healing from our hurts. Glen needed some loving people to talk to about how his father had hurt him and to validate that his pain was warranted. Karen, likewise, needed someone to mourn with her and to help process the fear and hurt that accompanies sexual abuse so that it could lose its power.

God's process of helping us get "finished" with pain, hurt, and loss usually involves grieving as well. Our past losses and hurts can be healed as we allow ourselves to attach to them the sadness that's warranted. Simply put, we need to *grieve*. It is a critical step in God's process for healing hurt. In the Bible, Solomon, the wisest man, said it this way: "Sorrow is better than laughter, because a sad face is good for the heart" (Ecclesiastes 7:3).

If Glen and Karen could allow themselves to face their grief—to have "a sad face"—then his sensitive heart to criticism, and her frightened heart from abuse, could begin to heal. They could take in the love that God and others would have for them, love that people from their past did not give. Then they would be able to be more in the present and less in the pain and feelings of the past.

3. *Receive forgiveness.* Many times, the pain that we drag into new situations is the pain of failure from the past. If you are feeling guilty or ashamed of things that you have done, you can have difficulty going into new relationships or situations because you feel "bad" or "unworthy." To tackle life with gusto, we have to be free from guilt and shame associated with previous failures and shortcomings. Leaving our baggage behind means that we have to know we are totally accepted, forgiven, and loved.

That kind of forgiveness and love is the kind of love that God has for all of us. All we have to do is ask for it and receive it. He promises that he will totally forgive us for anything and everything that we've ever done, no matter how bad we might feel it is. He will take all of our failures and totally erase the record: "For as high as the heavens are above the earth, so great is his love for those who fear him; as far as the east is from the west, so far has he removed our transgressions from us" (Psalm 103:11–12). All we have to do is ask: "If we confess our sins, he is faithful and just and will forgive us our sins and purify us from all unrighteousness" (1 John 1:9).

To be cleansed and set free from the guilt and shame of your past, just ask. God will make a way to a new start. He will wipe the slate totally clean and not remember your mistakes ever again (Hebrews

8:12). You can have a totally fresh start. The entire story of the Bible is about the fresh start that Jesus accomplished for everyone who wants it. He took *all* our guilt and shame upon himself. As a result, we can all be totally free from all guilt and condemnation (Romans 8:1). All we have to do is accept his payment for us, and we can be forgiven.

The past can lose its grip on you, but not if you continue to deny it. It loses its grip when you confess it to God and then are forgiven. Then your past can be truly gone. You can leave your baggage behind.

So if you feel bad about anything, ask God to take it from you. He has made a way for all of us to start over, and he does so each and every day. All we have to do, whenever we fall, is ask. His forgiveness and grace is always there, always giving another chance for whoever asks.

Confession is also God's way for us to get over feelings of alienation from each other. When we sin, or fail, we tend to think that others will not accept us; so we feel isolated and alone. Sometimes we can feel this is true, even if we know that God has forgiven us. God tells us to do the same thing with each other that we did with him. He tells us to confess to each other so we can be healed: "Confess your faults one to another, and pray one for another, that ye may be healed" (James 5:16, KJV).

One of the most powerful ways that God makes a way out of our past failures is for us to talk to each other—and to pray for one another. Then we find out that the alienation we feel from past failures does not have to be there at all. Our failures lose their grip in the light of acceptance and prayer.

4. *Forgive others.* If you talked to Glen about his past, you would find out that he was carrying a lot of baggage around in his heart. It would not take long in a conversation about his employment history to find out that a lot of people had "done him wrong." He had real problems letting go of the ways he felt others had let him down.

Because of his resentment and lack of forgiveness, Glen was still tied to all of those offenses. In a very real way, everyone who had ever hurt him was *still* hurting him every day. They were very alive in his memory, and these memories were eating away at his soul. His past was very present. The baggage that he carried into each new situation was heavy. As a result, he was suspicious of every new authority and was somewhat of a ticking time bomb.

This is a kind of spiritual cancer at work. Things that we cannot let go of eat away at us from the inside. But it is not so in the life of God. As we read earlier, God "remembers our sins no more." He lets things go. He forgives. He does not hold a grudge. And as a result, he is free from everything that everyone ever does to him. Once he deals with it, it's over. As the popular saying goes, he's "free to love again."

God wants to make a way for all of us to be free to love again as well. All of us have been hurt, and he understands that. So he has provided a way for us to be free of past debts that are owed—the same way that he takes care of our debts: forgiveness. When we forgive others, *we* are free.

To forgive does not mean that we deny that someone has hurt us. Nor does it mean that we have to necessarily trust them again or allow them into our heart again. That all depends on whether they've seen the error of their ways and repented. If we are going to trust them again, it's important that they have become trustworthy. But forgiveness is not about the future and whether we are going to open up and be vulnerable again. It's about letting go of what has already happened. It's about acknowledging the things that were done to harm us and the debt that we are owed.

As long as we feel like someone "owes us," we're tied to him or her by the offense committed. That's why the Bible uses the word "forgive," which means "to cancel a debt." When we forgive, we are saying the person no longer owes us, and we are releasing that person. Once we have forgiven, the debt is over, and we no longer feel obligated to punish the person or to retaliate. However, when we hold a grudge, we're always in a mode of punishment toward the offender.

Forgiveness frees us in both directions. It frees us from having to try to collect something that we can never collect, and it frees us from having to seek justice and make things right. It's the ticket that gives us the freedom to go forward. God has made a way for us to experience the same kind of freedom that he has, through forgiving others as he does.

If you look around, you can tell the difference between the kinds of people who hold grudges, and those who are able to let things go. The forgivers are much better to be around and go through life with much lighter hearts. No wonder, for they are carrying less baggage!

5. *Examine your ways.* We've talked about hurts—but a significant part of the baggage of the past has to do with patterns of behavior that we learned from those hurtful situations. As a young boy, Glen learned that authority—any authority—was unreasonable and impossible to please, and that he was powerless to do much in that kind of relationship. As a result, he developed a strategy for dealing with his father. He passively avoided him and resisted doing what was asked. He also avoided talking to his father directly about their conflicts but would go behind his back to find solace and comfort. As a result, he never learned how to solve problems and get past them. That's why a late expense report, which was a small oversight, could grow to be something that could end his career.

Perhaps there is some pattern of dealing with life, people, relationships, risk, and even love itself, that is causing you problems now. You learned how to operate and negotiate those issues in a certain environment where God's ways were not practiced. So those dysfunctional patterns may be holding you back from all that he would like for you to have now. That is okay. God has been in the business of making a way for people to get out of crummy situations for thousands of years. He led his people out of slavery in Egypt and then gave them new "ways"—or patterns—for dealing with life. And later, he told them to turn from the ways of their fathers, their previous generations, and their captors. If they would examine those ways and learn new patterns of behavior, he would make a way for them.

Isn't it time to examine your patterns? If your life has taught you, for instance, that love is only going to hurt you and that you must avoid it, you will only remain stuck in emotional isolation until you examine that pattern. If you have learned not to let people get close, examine that pattern to see when it is limiting you. If you've learned to avoid conflict, examine that pattern to see how it's actually weakening you and prolonging conflict. If you've learned to avoid any risk in an attempt to maintain control of everything, examine how that is keeping you from the possibility of a new and exciting future.

The list of self-defeating patterns we can develop is almost endless, but the principle is the same: *Patterns we have learned in the past can be baggage ruining our present.* Examine your ways of dealing with relationships that might be tying you to your past, and allow God to make a way to a new future.

6. *See the new you through new eyes.* Another kind of baggage we carry around is the view of ourselves that we learned in past relationships or situations. Glen learned that he was not good enough. Karen learned that she was an object for someone to use. He would be hurt, and she would be afraid. Both emotions are very understandable, for that is how God made us—*we find out who we are through the people who love us or, sometimes, through the ones who don't.* In other words, how we see ourselves is a relational perspective. We "borrow" the eyes of others when we are growing up, and we continue to do so later when we're in new relationships. This is why you sometimes see people "blossom" in new relationships. They are finally seen and valued as God created them. It's also why you see some other people loathe themselves, because it's how they've been seen and treated in the past.

Included in the baggage we all need to unpack are the various false views of ourselves that we learned in past relationships. Why not take the time right now to do an inventory about how you see yourself? Ask yourself, *Is the way I see myself realistic? Is it balanced with strengths and weaknesses, of things I value and areas where I need to grow? Do I see myself as loved?*

God has designed us to learn who we are by who loves us. We need—deeply need—to see ourselves first of all as loved by God and having great value to him. Then we can begin to see ourselves as the people who love us can see us. In this way we begin to unpack the baggage of old views that are holding us back.

◆ BE FREE TO BE YOU

If the Bible tells any story at all, and if believers around the world have any story to tell, it is the story of a God who frees us from enslavement to the past. He has been releasing people from the weight of painful, old baggage since time began. One thing we know is that he does not want your past to hold you back. Holding on to hurt, unforgiveness, or other dysfunctional ties to the past will certainly affect your present realities. And unless you deal with them, they will affect your future as well. But God has made a way out, and a way to unpack your bags of grief, pain, unforgiveness, guilt, shame, or even old patterns of relating.

Ask him to show you his ways of unpacking your heavy baggage so you can begin to travel light. If you follow his guidance, you'll begin to experience more happiness, better relationships, and more fulfillment than you ever thought possible.

PRINCIPLE FIVE:

OWN YOUR FAULTS AND WEAKNESSES

*S*haron—*I am leaving. I'll call you with my new number. We'll need to discuss the kids and finances. I'm sorry things aren't working out. Rob.*

Numbly, Sharon looked around the kitchen. Pictures of herself, her husband Rob, and their kids filled the walls. She felt surreal and disoriented, as if something foundational had suddenly crumbled from under her feet. Waves of hurt, fear, and sadness overwhelmed her.

To gain some kind of equilibrium, she tried to take stock of things. She believed in God but couldn't fathom where he was right this moment. She loved Rob with all her heart. He was her soul mate and life partner. All those years ago, when they'd met, both of them felt God had brought them together. She was sure of it. All the signs had been there. And he was a great father to their kids. How could it all come down to this?

Sharon was aware that she and Rob had not been doing well and that he was miserable in the marriage. In the last few months he had become shut down, distant, preoccupied, even cold. She didn't feel she could reach him. They would sit beside each other in church, not holding hands like they used to, feeling a million miles apart. To make things more difficult, Rob had been spending more and more time at work.

She was also aware of the stress they'd been through recently. Rob's company had presented him with an option to relocate to another part of the country, which would give him a much better position with the firm. If he didn't take it, he risked being laid off. When the issue had arisen, the couple and their close friends had made the decision a matter of a great deal of prayer, thought, and discussion. Finally, it was clear to them that moving was the best decision. Leaving their home, church, and close relationships had been very difficult. Now, in their new place, Rob had been trying to adjust to his work. They'd spent weeks moving in, enrolling the kids in school, getting to know the area, meeting the neighbors, and finding a church home in which they felt they belonged. In fact, the church was where my wife and I (John) met them and why I know their story.

When Rob would start to distance himself or shut down from her, Sharon would notice it and be concerned. She'd ask if anything was wrong. Most of the time he'd say "no," and she'd say she would pray for him. Over a period of months, they had coexisted in a polite death of a marriage.

Sharon attributed most of their struggle to the move. Yes, the relocation had taken its toll. But the fact was, long before the move there were serious seeds of discontent in their marriage. And Sharon's lack of awareness about these signs of discontent was the most serious part of the issue.

You see, Sharon had a certain spiritual blindness that she had never allowed God to touch, help, or heal. *She was one of those people who have great difficulty taking responsibility for their life.* In Sharon's mind, whenever a problem arose, it was always the fault of someone other than her. She would blame others, excuse herself, and not admit to her part in the problem.

This is not a rare condition. In fact, we all have it to some degree, and it's been around since the beginning of time. When Adam and Eve pointed the finger at each other and the devil, blame began.

When the Israelites became uncomfortable in the wilderness, blame continued. So while Sharon had a severe case of spiritual blindness, she was in good company.

She wasn't a bad person—in fact, she was a good person at heart. She loved God, her family, and her friends, and she wanted the best for all of them. She worked hard to be a helpful wife, mother, and friend. And when things went well, they went very well. But when problems arose, things went very badly. Most of the time, the blame went to Rob, since he was the person closest to her.

For example, when she was overwhelmed with the kids, it was because Rob worked too much to help. When they had financial struggles, it was because he didn't make enough money. When she wanted long, involved talks with him and he was dead tired, she attributed his resistance to his lack of concern about her feelings. When he disagreed with her opinion and became firm, he was controlling her. And the worst moments came when he mentioned something she did that caused him distress. That's when Sharon would lose it, blow up, and accuse him of being critical and judgmental of her.

Now, Rob certainly had his share of responsibility also. He would attempt to change to please her, but when he'd realize that nothing he did was enough, he would simply give up and disconnect. Or he'd try to address Sharon's lack of responsibility, but she would deny it and he would then avoid her. Or he'd try to be thick-skinned and strong, not letting her know how much she hurt him inside. All in all, he gave up too quickly.

The truth was, their relocation merely reinjured an already wounded marriage. Sharon blamed the problems of the move on Rob, even though she had been a 100 percent partner in prayer in the decision. She told him that she was disappointed in his job track and blamed him for not trying to find something better back home. Nothing he tried would satisfy her. There was not enough love, time, or support to make her happy. Whatever was wrong was always entirely his fault.

In fact, even before the breakup occurred, Sharon had talked to me about their marriage and her problems with Rob. I'd been around them as friends long enough to be aware of some of the dynamics. I went so far as to tell Sharon I thought that, though Rob certainly wasn't perfect, he needed a break from being at fault for everything she felt was wrong and that it seemed she had difficulty owning her part in their struggle. Generally, when I said something like that, Sharon would respond with, "But you don't understand what kind of man he is!" And then the conversation would go nowhere. After a few futile attempts to communicate with her, I'd dropped the issue.

I am glad that God didn't think Sharon and Rob's situation was futile. In fact, when things are darkest, God shines his light the brightest. I now believe, in retrospect, that in this couple's case God let the darkness get really dark. I think perhaps it was his way of making things very clear to Sharon.

◆ SOMETIMES IT TAKES A SHOCK

Sometimes we need a shock to wake us up to the truth.

Sharon had refused for months to consider that her constant blaming was at the root of their marriage problems. She could not see that her behavior hurt Rob so much that it made him doubt that he was loved by God or anyone, and it depleted his heart of life, love, and energy to work things out. Certainly Rob should have done something other than abruptly leave. But the shock of Rob's goodbye note caused the first small breakthrough. Suddenly he wasn't there to blame for the way she was feeling. And Sharon had no clue what to do, where to turn, or what decision to make. Should she call Rob and try to talk him into returning? Should she get an attorney? What was she supposed to tell the kids?

Fortunately, as I mentioned, Sharon loved God. So, as people from ancient days until today have been doing, she did the one thing anyone should do when they are lost and cannot find their way. She reached out to God by praying and asking him to help. Nothing happened—at least not right then. Reality didn't shift. There were no signs, signals, or voices to heed. But Sharon didn't give up on God. He was her only hope, so she kept praying.

Reflecting on the story Sharon told me, I'm reminded that, often, God allows us to wrestle for long periods of time as we reach out for him. At one of the most painful times of his life, Jesus prayed three times without any noticeable response from God (Matthew 26:39–44). It is as if God is helping us to truly own our pleas, wishes, and desires—to want them deeply, from the heart, rather than casually or offhandedly.

Sharon continued to pray, to search, and to listen for an answer. Within a few days, something began to happen in her heart. Like a plant seed sending a tiny shoot out of the ground, Sharon began to feel something inside—emotions that had to do with Rob. As she explained it later, rather than feeling her usual disappointment and hurt toward her "abandoning" husband, she began to feel *his* hurt. Specifically, she stopped feeling the pain he'd caused her and instead felt the pain that *she'd* caused *him*. She remembered conversations they'd had that, previously, she'd seen as examples of his failings. Now she recalled things she'd said—statements of blame in which she had made everything his fault. She remembered that Rob had tried to point out her part in the problem, but she had simply ignored what he had to say.

Sharon remembered one night in particular. In a rare vulnerable moment when he was feeling lots of job stress, Rob had asked her to cuddle with him in bed for a few moments before they went to sleep. Like a little boy who needed some reassurance, he was asking for comfort to get through a rough spot. She had been so angry at him that she'd said, "Maybe if you handled your job better you'd be a man and not need this." Then she had rolled over, turned her back on him, and gone to sleep.

Now, with a clearer perspective, Sharon could not believe how hurtful she'd been. She deeply felt the rejection and injury that she had caused Rob. Along with that, she felt such remorse and anguish for his hurt.

The jolt she'd gotten from Rob, coupled with God's grace in showing her the truth about her actions, had done their work.

◆ THE TRUTH CAN STING—BUT IT SETS YOU FREE

This process in which God gently opened up Sharon's heart went on for some days. It was not pleasant. She was constantly facing her lack of ownership for her own failures and the neglecting of her responsibility toward Rob. She didn't like herself very much during this period of God-given clarity. It reminded me of a statement in the Bible about the way we sometimes feel toward ourselves when we become aware of our failings: "Then you will remember your evil ways and wicked deeds, and you will loathe yourselves for your sins and detestable practices" (Ezekiel 36:31). Still, she kept praying for God's help and strength to bear the truth. And she desperately wanted his solutions.

At the same time, Sharon told me, she began feeling something else that was more positive. She was discovering a deeper sense of appreciation and love for Rob. Now that she was shouldering her rightful share of the blame for their problems, it was as if there was more room inside her to see his good parts—all those great things she'd married him for.

Things began tying together in her head. God's little messages began making sense. The feedback that I and a few other of her friends had given, the crisis of Rob's leaving . . . and now these internal stirrings all seemed to be saying the same thing: *Go to Rob and make it right.* Sharon didn't know exactly what "make it right" meant, but she called him.

When they met, she told him what had happened to her as best she could and then sincerely apologized for the many years of heaping blame on him and for not acknowledging her own problems and failures. Though it was hard, she didn't say anything about how disruptive his sudden departure had been. She wanted it to be clear that this conversation was about her failures and nothing else. As she said later of the experience, "It was the most difficult conversation of my life."

For his part, Rob was stunned. On his way to the meeting he'd prepared himself for more angry blaming. But when Rob realized that Sharon was truly remorseful, he was *sure* God must have done something to change her. It was then he began to open up his bruised and untrusting heart to her, his first love. Rob was immediately willing to try to connect with Sharon again, and she with him. Within a few days he was back in the home, where he had always wanted to be.

The story doesn't end there. Sharon had had a sort of spiritual rebirth in which she'd realized she needed to learn how to take ownership of her own failings. The thing about birth, however, is that new life doesn't appear on the scene fully grown, but small and immature. With some counseling, Sharon realized that if things were truly going to be different, she would have to do more than take ownership for the pain she'd caused Rob; she would have to take responsibility for the *patterns* of her life. She would have to enter into a process of changing her behavior. It is one thing to say you are sorry you stepped on your dancing partner's feet; it is another to take some lessons so you don't keep doing it!

Sharon says, "I began to 'own' things like disorganization, self-centeredness, and unrealistic expectations of Rob . . . not to mention my defensiveness. It was a good thing I was praying all during this time, because God had to keep softening my heart. I really did not want to see the things about myself I really needed to see in order to grow up."

Sharon's new inner habits had good repercussions far beyond her marriage. She stopped blaming her kids for being kids. Instead, she took ownership of how her sometimes inconsistent, sometimes critical parenting style affected them. Her friendships improved, because she stopped alienating certain people with her behavior. She apologized to them and asked them to give her honest feedback when she was out of line. Sharon even stopped being angry at God for allowing the relocation and humbly told him how grateful she was he'd given her a second chance to do her marriage the right way.

There was also a side benefit to how God made a way for Sharon. Her newfound and God-given ownership of her failings made it safer for Rob to own up to his shortcomings. He stopped shutting down, living for work, and retreating inside his head. He started admitting to her when he was having problems or when he had let her down. Finally, these two started down the right path toward becoming the couple they had always dreamed of being. Sharon and Rob's marriage is certainly not a finished work. Both of them have growing to do. Yet as God has made a way for them to take ownership of their lives, they have seen profound changes in their parenting, work, and friendships. Now they even minister to other couples in significant ways. It is truly a different day for them.

When Sharon reached out to God in the kitchen that day, she thought God would show Rob the error of his ways. She was surprised that God answered her prayer by showing her that she needed to learn to shoulder the burdens of ownership of her life. But that is simply the cost of finding the way God has made. He creates it, but it is our responsibility to walk it. As Jesus said, "If anyone would come after me, he must deny himself and take up his cross daily and follow me" (Luke 9:23).

As I reflect on Sharon's story, part of me wishes that at that moment in the kitchen, lightning had flashed and a trumpet had sounded, while an angel appeared to tell her exactly what the next steps were. That would have been a great illustration of how God makes a way for people, and it would have encouraged us all in our journey of faith. I deeply believe, and have personally experienced, that God sometimes does rip apart the fabric of space and time to thunder into our everyday world with his grace and power. He is truly God, and he is supernatural, miraculous, and divine.

Yet another part of me is glad that this is not what God did with Sharon, but that he instead gave her an inner awareness and deep convictions over a period of time. Why am I glad it happened that way? Because, for one thing, Sharon's story helps us remember that we will never be able to predict what God's path or approach will be. We will never be able to create a formula for what he will do next in our lives. It also reminds us that the greatest miracles are often those he brings about in the quiet of the human heart.

◆ IMPLEMENT THE PRINCIPLE OF OWNERSHIP

Sharon's story illustrates an important principle at work: the principle of ownership and responsibility. Basically, ownership is a stance a person takes toward life, goals, and issues that says, *My life is my problem. Whatever I want, need, or desire, God has a part for me to play in getting it. Whatever dreams God gives me or problems I need to resolve, I can take part in furthering my goals.*

Some may say that this sounds like self-effort and willpower, not God power. Nothing could be further from the truth. God takes more responsibility than anybody. He is the one who takes the ownership to make a way for us when we don't know what to do. He constantly provides deliverance and protection for us. As the psalmist declared, "The LORD is my rock, my fortress and my deliverer; my God is my rock, in whom I take refuge. He is my shield and the horn of my salvation, my stronghold" (Psalm 18:2).

So God sees us as partners, or colaborers, with himself, in making the way. He does his job, and we do ours. The apostle Paul said, "Therefore, my dear friends, as you have always obeyed—not only in my presence, but now much more in my absence—continue to work out your salvation with fear and trembling, for it is God who works in you to will and to act according to his good purpose" (Philippians 2:12–13).

What does "work out your salvation" mean? It means that now that God has delivered and saved us, we are to take responsibility to live a life that reflects him and his ways: daily dependence on God, trust, love, honesty, and all the things that are of him. And while *we* are doing that, *he* is doing miraculous, divine things to achieve his ends.

Sharon's story is a good example of being a colaborer with God. What did God do? He sent friends, let Rob move out but not file for divorce, and opened Sharon's heart to her blindness. What did Sharon do? She searched, listened, remained open, did not give up on God, and finally became responsible to the light he was pointing her way. In the end, the principle of ownership is a matter of spiritual discernment. We all need to learn that God prepares a way, and we take ownership to put our feet on the path and walk it.

◆ TAKE OWNERSHIP, FAULT, AND BLAME

Some people struggle with the fact that they are not always the cause of their problems. This often hinders them from taking full ownership. A man whose company lays him off because of the economy may feel that he is owed another job because the layoff wasn't of his doing. Or a woman with a controlling husband may get stuck in feeling helpless because he's the problem, not her.

No one would disagree that we aren't the cause of all our problems. It is one of the truly tragic realities of living in a fallen world. The innocent are wounded. However, ultimately, in terms of solving the issue, fault is irrelevant. So here's a much more helpful way to look at it: *The person who cares about the problem owns the problem.*

When we take responsibility for our lives in this way, we're empowered to make changes. Ownership empowers us to *act*—to use our various skills to make plans, tackle a hurtful situation, or right a wrong. People who "own" their problems are people who can take initiative. The jobless man goes on executive search interviews. The unhappy wife seeks help, whether or not her husband is interested.

Ownership also gives us *freedom.* You are no longer a slave to the past, to false hope, to wishing someone would change, or to discouragement and passivity. You are free to try out answers, take risks, and take steps.

Ownership is, in fact, a *blessing.* It feels uncomfortable at first but pays off later. The other side of the coin, which is blame, is the opposite—a kind of curse. It feels good at first, but in time it ruins us. Technically, when we blame, we project all the responsibility for a problem onto something or someone else. And it keeps us in bondage. That's why every one of us needs to be aware of, and deal with, any tendencies to find fault, blame, excuse, minimize, or deny our responsibility in any given situation.

There is a time in which some blame can help us. But what I mean by "blame" here is the process of assessing the responsibilities in a given situation. In a sense, we should go through a kind of spiritual audit process to figure out who contributed what to the problem. This is not the same as accusing someone, and it makes us much better prepared to solve the issue. Assessing this type of blame can instruct us about what we need to forgive. At the same time, if we did have a part in the problem, we are to confess, ask forgiveness, and repent.

Assessing responsibility can mean a man with an alcoholic wife may need to "blame" her for drinking rather than thinking he did something that caused her to drink. At the same time, he may need to "blame" himself for not speaking up and taking a strict stand when he should have. Essentially, a period of assessment can help us to ferret out the roots of a problem. Remember, though, the problem and its solution are the real issues—not who caused the problem.

◆ LEARN WHAT TO OWN

If you want God to make a way in your life, own your own faults and weakness. God blesses ownership. Here is a brief list of things for which you can begin to take responsibility, and in this way be a co-laborer with him:

- ◆ *Your own unhappiness.* Begin to ask God for help in taking ownership of whatever pain or discomfort you experience. Then ask him to help you find relief.
- ◆ *Specific issues.* Determine the root cause of your problem. Is

it a relationship disconnect, a faith journey, a job issue, or a habit that won't go away?

♦ **Needed resources.** You must lead the way in finding the resources you need to solve your problem. Get help, support, comfort, and advice. Search until you find people who have answers and can give you encouragement.

♦ **Weaknesses and obstacles.** Identify the areas in which you don't have the strength you need to meet the challenge, and then begin to develop those areas.

♦ **Accountability.** Submit yourself to a few people who will keep you on task with your project of resolving your struggle or meeting your goal.

♦ **Support team.** Seek out friends who are full of compassion and comfort but who will not let you shirk your responsibility for taking the next step in resolving your issues. (And avoid, like the plague, people who will keep you stuck by helping you feel like a victim!)

♦ **One day at a time.** Address the issues of today rather than obsessing about yesterday or hoping for rescue tomorrow. People who take charge of their lives know how to live in the present.

Finally, resist the temptation to take *all* the blame for everything. Your struggle is not for you to bear alone. God has his part, and he will gladly act on your behalf. Neither your shoulders nor mine are wide enough to carry it all.

The good news is, when we take ownership, life works better. That's because when we do things his way, he is there, helping us to carry the burden. As Jesus said, "My yoke is easy and my burden is light" (Matthew 11:30).

EMBRACE PROBLEMS AS GIFTS

W hen my friend Gary called to ask if we could meet for breakfast, I (John) sensed something was troubling him. I hadn't seen him for a while, so I looked forward to the meeting. When we greeted each other at the restaurant, Gary abruptly announced, "I've been fired."

Fired? I was shocked. Gary was not some inexperienced young man fresh out of college and trying to establish himself in the workplace. He was a seasoned, upper-level management professional in a large manufacturing firm, a position he'd held for many years. He liked his job and had planned to make it a lifetime career. He also had a wife and three children who depended on him. "Gary, I'm so sorry," I responded. "What happened?"

He explained that a personnel restructuring at the upper levels had left him with a new boss. Gary and Dan did not hit it off well. Gary was orderly and methodical, and Dan was more intense and challenging. Dan pushed Gary to take more risks, explore new ideas, and try different approaches with the people he managed. Gary knew these concepts were valid, but he thought Dan was missing the importance of diligence, responsibility, and helping people do their jobs better. Gary also thought Dan was rather unreasonable in his expectations.

Gary tried to fit into Dan's system, but he was unable to meet his boss's goals and expectations. After protracted and painful attempts to remedy the issue, Gary was let go.

"What can I do, Gary?" I asked, assuming he wanted my encouragement and perhaps a couple of leads for a new job. His answer surprised me.

"John, I want you to pray that I will learn whatever it is God wants me to learn in this situation."

"What do you mean?" I probed.

"This whole experience has sort of derailed me," he said. "It's never happened to me before, and I have no idea what's next. But I know God is behind all of this. I am sure this was no accident, though I have no clue as to what it all means. So I figure the best way to deal with my crisis is to begin with God and move on from there. At this point, learning what God wants me to learn seems like the best approach."

Gary's words made perfect sense to me. I told him I would be glad to pray for him.

We stayed in close touch for the next few months as Gary picked up the pieces of his shattered career. During that time I gained great respect for my friend. He didn't wallow in self-pity or blaming. Rather, every day, he questioned and investigated God's way for him. At the same time, he conducted an energetic and relentless job search that landed him a good position with another firm. He's still there today and doing fine.

Had Gary concentrated all his energies on the job search during this time, no one would have blamed him. He had a family to take care of and bills to pay. By anyone's standards, it would have been a good thing to do. *But it would not have been the best thing.* The "best thing" was that Gary asked God to teach him something.

You see, even though Gary knew he was smart enough to find *a way* out of his dilemma, his faith directed him to search for whatever lesson, change, or growth was behind his loss. He knew that the best thing is to see problems as windows to the face of God and to stand at that window until God shows us the light that illuminates our hearts. Gary wanted to walk through his dilemma *God's way.* That was because Gary's faith in God told him he could trust God to take care of him.

As Gary searched, asked, prayed, read the Bible, and talked to people, God did answer. At first, what Gary learned made him uncomfortable. Over time, God showed him that Dan was basically correct in his evaluation. Gary resisted risk and change. He feared failure and loss of control, even in his relationship with God. He had oriented his life, work, and faith to play it safe. There wasn't a lot of room for risk, creativity—or, for that matter, for the power of God to work on Gary's behalf—in the way Gary had structured his habits and beliefs.

Once Gary understood his problem, he went to work in changing and growing. It required a lot of effort, but in the end he was a new man. Today, he is still the same responsible and dependable person. But when I'm with him, he seems more alive inside. There is more to him than the next project. Gary now tries new things. He's more open to experience. And he has discovered that he has a talent for helping other businessmen grow and develop in the same way. Through his church he volunteers to mentor men who need career assistance, and he loves doing it. Gary used his problem to find God in a new and better way.

◆ A MATTER OF PERSPECTIVE

Like Gary, we all have problems. They are part of life. But how we solve our problems divides us into two groups: *those who end at the problem* and *those who go beyond the problem.*

The first group of people has a tendency to stop dead in their tracks when they hit a crisis, and that's where they stay. All they want is to get rid of the problem as soon as possible. The second group, like Gary, finds something useful in problems. But doing that requires an act of grace from God because our tendency is simply to deal with the problem itself and move on.

Whether the problem relates to career, relationships, health, emotions, or loss, we all tend to focus our energies on putting out the fire and making sure it doesn't flare up again soon. It may be a recurring chest pain that you hope will go away, a disconnect in your marriage that you have learned to cope with, or an eating problem for which you are trying various remedies and plans. It's a problem, it's painful, and you want it gone. So that's what you concentrate on.

There's nothing wrong with trying to solve the problem and alleviate the pain. But the way *out* of our problems shouldn't be our first concern, because God sees our difficulties very differently than we do. In a very real sense, they are his gifts to us, for they bring us to him and his ways. He wants to develop much more in us than our ability to put out fires. He has many, many lessons and a new life for us as we learn how to go through problems.

The word *through* is important here, for God is not as concerned with getting us *out* of problems as he is in getting us *through* problems. Because of that, God often approaches our problems very differently than we do. We might compare it to the difference between the way a physician and a patient view pain. You come to the doctor in pain. You want a shot or a pill, something to make the pain go away, and you want it *now*. But your wise physician knows your pain is a sign of a deeper problem. He prescribes even more pain: surgery and physical therapy.

It's your choice. You can demand immediate relief, knowing that your physical problem will recur. Or you can go through the healing process and resolve the problem once and for all. That's the same kind of choice you face when dealing with life's problems and crises. God loves you completely and wants the best for you. But like your physician, *he is less concerned about your immediate comfort than about your long-term health and growth.*

This is why we read in the Bible, "Consider it pure joy, my brothers, whenever you face trials of many kinds, because you know that the testing of your faith develops perseverance" (James 1:2–3). God's way is not out of your problems but *through* them. That's how we learn from our difficulties and find God's way.

So instead of looking for a way out of your problems you may want to consider two other places to look that will get you through them: *upward* and *inward.*

◆ THE TWO DIRECTIONS

First, we look *upward.* A problem that you cannot solve is, by definition, beyond you. If you could have fixed it, you probably would have. So whatever the struggle, all of your attempts to resolve it are not enough. Problems bring us to the end of ourselves. They exhaust our resources, our strength, our will, and our patience. It is not pleasant to be at the end of ourselves. We feel helpless, lost, afraid, and unsure of where to turn. If we stop here, feeling sorry for ourselves or bemoaning how helpless we are, we are truly stuck in a mess. But we can choose a different course.

We can allow our problems to turn us *upward.* We can shift our focus off the issue itself and onto how God sees the issue. Problems give us an opportunity to look beyond our small world, our familiar answers and trusted habits, and peer out into the unknown, where God is waiting. When we're at the end of ourselves, that's the place where God truly is. Like a lost child searching for the voice of his parents, we search the heavens and reach out for the One who knows the problem, the solution, the lessons, and the ways. The limitless God is always there for us.

Now, our tendency is to play it safe. Needing and depending upon an unpredictable God is not a comfortable path. We would rather keep things under our control. Yet God knows that approach dries up our souls, and he works against that. He wants us looking upward to all his opportunities and resources. Often the way God acts is like a cloudburst raining down on a stagnant stream that's been clogged with debris. As the great deluge moves with great force into the debris, it breaks up the clog, and then the flow begins again. Fresh, pure water renews the life of the stream. I want you to look at it this way: When we look upward, we open up to God—and God also opens himself up to us.

Next, we look *inward*. The transformation we go through does not end with our taking the upward view to God. Once the problem drives us to him, God then takes us through a journey into ourselves, to demonstrate what he wants us to learn. He is constantly teaching, encouraging, guiding, healing, and directing as he helps us understand what's going on inside us—that is, in terms of our attitudes and reactions. When we ask him to show us the inner workings of our own hearts, it's as if he starts shining a bright spotlight into the recesses of our hearts, lighting up hurts, wounds, weaknesses, and opinions that need *his* touch and *our* submission to him.

For example, I speak to lots of single people, and I find the inward view very relevant for what they are dealing with. Most of them deeply want to marry. Most, however, have experienced some relationship that was an emotional train wreck for them. As a result, they have formed various attitudes. Some address the problem by shutting down. Among these, some live feeling sorry for themselves. Others blame the whole opposite sex, saying, "There are no good men [or women] left out there to marry." Others take the attitude that being with someone—anyone—is better than being alone. They solve the problem of not having a spouse by dating someone they're drawn to for some unknown reason and marrying that person. None of these people is taking the inward route.

Some singles do, however, go the inward route. They ask God to help them look inward. They learn what happened in the train wrecks of past breakups and disappointments. They ask him to show them if they contributed to the relationship's problems or if they allowed themselves to be drawn to the wrong person. They ask him what they need to change in order to pick the right person. Allowing God to open our eyes and give us the inward view of ourselves bears a lot of good fruit. Eventually, these people are much wiser in whom they pick to love.

There is another point to make about the importance of taking the inward view. It's very possible that when we look inward, God reveals that we have certain central issues that are like attitudinal foundation stones. They form reactions that occur in not just one but many areas of life. Many of my counseling clients discover that they are carrying deep inside an issue that relates to much more than the problem that got them started in the journey. Many times, in fact, it becomes like a theme running throughout their life. For example, Gary, who we met at the beginning of this chapter, found that he was fearful of risks and anything new. As we saw, this affected his work. But Gary was surprised, as he looked inward, to discover that he was also fearful of taking risks in relationships as well. Though he couldn't see this at first, Gary played it so safe his wife and friends sometimes felt shut out of his life. While he cared and was kind to them, he avoided the risk of being vulnerable and exposing how he really felt about things.

As we have been seeing, God does help us identify themes, or patterns, in our lives. And as we patiently let him show us the truth, we are able to see how these themes affect much more of our life than we ever imagined.

♦ SEEING PAIN AS NORMAL

Problems are also a gift in that they help us *normalize* pain—that is, they help us to expect pain to be a regular part of life. Much of our existence involves pain, either the minor discomfort of small problems or the pain of catastrophic losses. By nature, we do not like to experience problems or pain as part of life. We wish life to be different than it is. So when pain and struggle occur, we protest, deny, or argue that these things should not be. But life is difficult, and all our resistance does nothing to alter the reality of pain.

When we resort to protesting and denying pain, we are actually getting into an argument with God. God does not say, "Life should have no pain or struggle." We do. But since God sees ultimate reality as it is, the only response from us that makes sense in life is to lose that argument. Only then can we win.

When we give up protesting about pain and problems, we begin letting go of things that we can't keep anyway. We learn what choices, paths, lessons, and opportunities are ours, and we enter the place of acceptance. We accept that pain is part of life. We accept that we don't have all the answers. We accept that problems will always be around us. We accept that there are some problems that will remain mysteries until we are face to face with God. That acceptance helps us live in God's reality, which in turn allows us to adapt and change to the way things really are. It also allows us to relax and become flexible, so that God can more easily direct us through our problems.

◆ IDENTIFYING WITH SUFFERING

Problems are a gift in yet another way: They help us identify with the sufferings of God. God is not one who shrinks from problems, nor does he avoid the difficulty they cause him. Though he could arrange things differently, he has chosen the path of suffering for himself. He deals with problems, even when they hurt him.

Ever since Adam and Eve, we have been a problem for God. He only wants to love and guide us—and yet we have walked away from him since time began. He doesn't want to destroy us and start over, because he is attached to us. Sadly, when he tries to be close, we often shake our fist or attempt to be God ourselves. This creates problems for God in that what we have done with his love is not what he ever desired.

Most of us forget that God has a heart. He feels things deeply, especially about us. Our stance toward him can hurt him. When his people lost their love for him, his response was, "My heart churns within me" (Hosea 11:8, NKJV). When Jesus saw Jerusalem's hardheartedness, he ached to gather its people as a hen covers its chicks under her wings, but they refused his love (Matthew 23:37).

God's response to his problem is to face it and take responsibility for doing something about it. He does not avoid, deny, or misunderstand the meaning of the problem. Even still, he suffers during the process. While he is redeeming, restoring, forgiving, repairing, and healing us, he suffers from what we put him through. When we learn how God addresses problems this way, we learn to identify, or associate ourselves, with his suffering. Throughout the ages, spiritual people have studied how identifying with his pain helps us to be closer to him, to see reality as it is, and to take a right approach to life and its problems.

This is why we can learn much through our problems, as we allow ourselves to come closer to God's suffering, especially through Jesus, "the author and perfecter of our faith, who for the joy set before him endured the cross" (Hebrews 12:2). When we identify with God's sufferings, we are deepened and matured. Often, people who have been down this path will report that whatever the problem was that started the process ultimately was not nearly as important as what they learned about suffering God's way.

Become a part of this kind of life. Don't ask God to get rid of problems. He is not that way, and he knows that is not best for you. Much of life is moving from problem to problem. See problems as the next steps of growth for you, embrace them, and move along—looking upward and inward—with him.

◆ BEYOND SUFFERING INTO GROWTH

Sometimes we have a tendency to approach problems as if they are simply an exercise in learning endurance and patience. That is, we see ourselves exclusively as blameless sufferers who are learning a lesson in how to bear up under pain. While there is much to be gained by learning patience, that's a limited view of the situation. Go further than merely tolerating bad times.

Begin to wonder, and be curious. Ask God about your own control issues, about idealized expectations of him and life, about brokenness, selfishness, and the like. Like Gary, you will often find things to grow from, change, heal, or repent of that can provide new life for you.

P R I N C I P L E   S E V E N :

TAKE LIFE AS IT COMES

I (John) have a bone disease called *osteopenia*, meaning that my bones are too porous. Osteopenia, a precursor to the better-known osteoporosis, can lead to easy fracturing and slow healing of the bones. A couple of years ago I broke my back in a hot-air balloon accident in Kenya, and the doctors theorized that my back wouldn't have broken if I did not have this condition.

Since my diagnosis, I've spent a good bit of time investigating treatments and cures. My mother has osteoporosis, and the disease has not been easy for her to live with. If I can avoid it at all, I do not want to grow old with brittle bones.

There is some good news, though—the medical world has learned to do many things to help my condition. Experts recommend certain supplements and daily weight-bearing exercises that induce the bones to strengthen themselves. My doctor has put me on a regimen built around these factors.

I'm glad to know that, by following this course of action, things can improve for me. The question is, Will the things I'm doing actually work? It's important to measure the treatment's effectiveness, so every year I get a particular set of x-rays taken so the doctor can measure if my condition is improving or deteriorating. Bones change very slowly, so more frequent x-rays are not helpful. Yet I have no way of measuring how I'm doing until each year is up.

To live for these long periods of time with the unknown has taken a little getting used to. As I write this chapter, for instance, my next x-ray is six months away. I try to keep up with the supplements and exercises—but I'm in the dark about how I'm really doing. It would be nice to be able to have more immediate feedback, the kind a dieter gets by stepping onto a scale. I'd love to be able to monitor myself more closely. At this point of the development of medical science, however, the ability to do that does not exist. All I can do is stick to the regimen and hope things will get better.

Waiting is difficult. I have to say, though, that the situation I find myself caught in has offered me some benefits. For one thing, it's showing me so clearly that I am not the master of time. Time is its own master and has its own pace and process. Here is a reality that we would all do well to accept: *When God makes a way for us, that way will generally take time.*

Though I deeply believe in God's ability to perform miracles and in his instantaneous, supernatural activities with us, I also believe that the normal way God deals with us involves a sequence of events—a process that God directs and that we are to follow. This requires some patience on our part.

Even though waiting may take patience, time is the field in which God has chosen to operate to get things done. Consider this. He created the universe in stages. It took the Israelites forty years to enter the Promised Land. Hundreds of years passed before the promised Messiah was born. There are many, many more examples of how, all through the pages of the Bible, God factors time into the way he works to care for us. What is it about time? Why does God take time, when we'd love instant answers, change, and deliverance from our dilemmas?

Here's what I've witnessed again and again: *Time allows God's healing ingredients to be applied to our situation.*

It requires time, for example, to make us accessible to God in all the ways needed to bring about change. We need thorough and repeated exposure to his love, truth, grace, and help. We don't generally learn things the first time we hear them. And wounded hearts take time before they're ready or able to make use of the help they are being offered. Even our physical body teaches us that healing and change take time. For instance, you take an antibiotic for an infection over a period of days. With time, the medicine can affect every part of the infected system. Time also allows the antibiotic to interact repeatedly with the infection, so that it is systematically weakened and eventually destroyed.

From these examples, we can see that time is a blessing and not a curse.

◆ But I Want It Now!

Letting time pass is not easy. Time often brings out in us that childish part that *demands* to have things fixed right now. We feel stretched, discouraged, frustrated, and ready to give up. There are many ways in which we try to work around the reality of time's measured pace. For example, some people will feel a desperate need for immediate relief from a painful crisis. Others have a belief that God will always bring instant deliverance if they have enough faith. Some people feel out of control when they can't speed things up. Still others tend to be impulsive and can't tolerate any sort of frustration in getting what they need.

However, those people who can submit to time's restrictions generally find better results than those who protest or try to get around it. When we insist on shortcuts and quick fixes we tend to repeat the same problems over and over again, getting nowhere.

A helpful way to understand why we need to develop patience is to remember this: *If a goal is meaningful, it will require time.* In other words, those things that have immediate payoffs and results tend not to be as important in the larger view of life. However, those things that require more time tend to be more meaningful and significant. To illustrate the point, there are people whose financial dreams are built on winning the lottery. Then there are those who spend years training, getting experience, learning, and executing a well-designed business plan. These are the people to whom the Bible refers when it says, "The plans of the diligent lead to profit as surely as haste leads to poverty" (Proverbs 21:5).

What makes it hard to wait, I believe, is that time has a sort of "underground" nature. By that I mean God is often making a way for us when we cannot even see his hand at work. During that time when it seems nothing is happening on our behalf, it's a gift of faith to be able to trust that God *is* at work in our relationships, our families, our work, and even in our own hearts. Consider this parable that Jesus told:

> This is what the kingdom of God is like. A man scatters seed on the ground. Night and day, whether he sleeps or gets up, the seed sprouts and grows, though he does not know how. All by itself the soil produces grain—first the stalk, then the head, then the full kernel in the head. As soon as the grain is ripe, he puts the sickle to it, because the harvest has come.
>
> —MARK 4:26–29

This story teaches that for God to make a way, we need to undertake two tasks. The first is to *sow whatever seed he gives us.* This might mean admitting a truth, confronting a problem, or giving up something to God that we've been holding onto. Our second task is to *wait without trying to rush God's pace.* He has a task also. He makes a way by taking the ingredients of growth and producing something good in our lives.

Tolerating the pace of time is a big part of healing in relationships. Many years ago, I let a friend of mine down and hurt his feelings in a big way. The relationship was strained and, though he forgave me for what I'd done, he became distant for a while. I remember trying to fix things as quickly as I could so our friendship could get back to normal—but it just did not happen that way. My friend needed time to allow himself to get close to me again.

Rather than try to force things, we both prayed that God would make a way for things to get better. I worked on changing the things I'd done to hurt him so it wouldn't happen again. We also stayed in the relationship and kept talking to each other about matters when they came up. Things were slowly getting a little better, but I was still unsure.

One night we were having dinner and I made an offhanded remark that—the moment I heard it leave my lips—reminded me of what I'd done originally. I froze inside, wondering if I had triggered the same hurt all over again.

My friend noticed my anxiety and apparently knew what was going on inside me. He said, "Look, I didn't even think about what you said until I noticed your expression. I'm over it—now it's time for you to get over it."

As in Jesus' parable above, time allowed God to keep our relationship exposed to healing elements until it was fully healed and we could both move on.

If there is any one thing that helps us tolerate time's passage, it is *getting actively involved in the process of development God has us in.* It helps a great deal to become actively engaged in the tasks, experiences, learning, trials, and relationships that are part of his path for us. When we're engaged in whatever God is doing in our life, we are, in a sense, experiencing eternity. For eternity is where God is. Interestingly, the more engaged we are, the more timeless the journey seems.

I see this all the time in my children. On Sunday night, they'll often talk about how much they dread the thought of going to school on Monday. Yet when I see them Monday after school, they can't stop talking about all the things that happened at school that day. Likewise, when we're disengaged, time drags on. The more we are in time, the more we forget it.

◆ TIME ALONE DOES NOT HEAL

On the other end of the spectrum, it's important to know that time's passage is not enough for God to make a way. Some people think that all they need to do is be patient and wait, and then God will bring about something they desire. This is not true, and many people who believe that time heals all things find themselves stuck in a holding pattern in life. They wait for God to change things, or for another person to come around, or for their feelings to be transformed, and they're disappointed when the change doesn't occur.

This is because time is simply a context in which God's healing ingredients interact with your situation. All the other elements that God uses to make a way are still necessary. People don't wait for a sprained ankle to heal. They get the brace, do the stretches and physical therapy, and carefully apply heat and massages. Time, by itself, is never enough. Make sure you surround yourself with all the love, truth, support, advice, safety, and accountability you need to do your tasks in the way God makes. Time alone is often time wasted, while time, with the healing components added, will produce deep and long-lasting results.

◆ EACH SEASON HAS ITS ROLE

Time has some close relatives: We call them *seasons*. Not all periods of time are the same. They have different uses and meanings in God's scheme of things. It helps to understand the nature of the varying seasons, so we can understand our tasks and expectations to help time do its work. As the Bible's great wisdom teaches us: "There is a time for everything, and a season for every activity under heaven: a time to be born and a time to die, a time to plant and a time to uproot" (Ecclesiastes 3:1–2).

Here is a way to look at the seasons of growth you will need to use and adapt to in order for God to make a way. They relate to any situation or context of growth and struggle we might be experiencing.

Winter. Cold weather and hard ground make this season appear dead and unproductive. However, winter is a very important time. You clear out dead things, debris, and stones that are in the way of future growth. You mend and repair broken fences and machines. You set up and plan for the future.

You may want to use this season to prepare for the work ahead, say, getting your schedule and affairs in order to have time and space for your goal. You may want to research which resources you need, such as good churches, groups, and experts. Winter lets you settle in and get ready for growth.

Spring. This is a time of new beginnings and fresh hope. You plow and aerate the soil, providing fertilizer, water, and a controlled climate. You wait a little while and then care for the fragile shoots that begin to appear like magic. You keep watch over the field so that birds and animals don't devour them.

In the springtime of your growth you'll begin to get involved in the plans and commitments you made last winter. You may start studying a related topic or join a group that is working on the issue. And when you are seeing those initial changes beginning to peek out from the soil, you may need to protect them from people and circumstances that might trample on them and snatch them away.

Summer. Growth is very apparent, and the field is increasingly lush with bigger and stronger plants. You're in a maintenance mode, making sure that what was begun in spring continues. The ingredients for growth are still as necessary as summer rains, and so is the need for protection.

In the summertime of your growth, you are diligent to keep going. Don't be lulled into stopping because some good changes began last season. *Stay with the program for the full harvest next season.* Keep working on the same tasks and the same relationships, because you're building on the work God has begun in you.

Fall. This is the time of the harvest, when you reap what you have sown! You experience the benefits of the work and spend time picking the fruit, using some today and storing some for the upcoming times of cold and dark.

In the fall of personal growth, you will see changes in your emotions, behavior, relationships, career, and the like. They are not just cosmetic changes but are truly the product of internal transformation. In that particular area of life you are a new person. So it's a time of celebration and gratitude to God. It's also a time of giving back what you have been given, in service to God and others.

We are by nature people who look for all four seasons to be harvesttime. We desire results now and are easily disheartened when they do not readily appear. It is not easy to submit to the tasks of the season you're in, waiting for the fall season. But those who adapt to the season, rather than demanding that the season adapt to them, will reap in due time. The others will, regretfully, keep making the same mistakes and enduring the same failure and pain.

◆ Take Hold of These Great Truths

Time and "seasons" are the context in which God makes a way for us. Take hold of the great truths that they teach us. Learn their ways, and use them to make something in your life better—sometimes better than it was before the time of change and growth even began.

We can always be sure of this: As we walk through time, doing our part and allowing the seasons of life to work great changes in us, the God who inhabits eternity walks at our side, doing his deeply transforming work.

Of this we can be sure: *We are never left on our own!*

PRINCIPLE EIGHT:

LOVE GOD WITH ALL YOU ARE

Years ago I (John) was on the Sunday service response team in the church I attended. When the pastor preached, he would invite people to come to the front if they needed prayer or spiritual help. The response team assisted these people in whatever way we could.

I have to say, it was very meaningful to be part of helping those who had felt God tug at something inside them to take the next step of faith. Often I was present at some truly sacred moment in a person's life. One Sunday, Nancy came to the front in tears about an issue involving her teenage son, Scott. The boy was rebellious, doing drugs, and had major problems in school. He resisted any advice or help from Nancy. He ignored her concerns or made excuses so that she wouldn't bug him. As any mother would, she wanted her son to find God and to have his life straightened out. So I prayed with her and tried to offer encouragement.

A few Sundays later Nancy came up to me again with the same concerns. A few weeks later she was back again. And then once again. Finally, she asked if we could talk about her situation when there was more time. We agreed to meet for lunch.

Nancy, as it turned out, was a single mom who worked two jobs to make ends meet, while trying to raise her son. She told me it was a big step for her to ask for prayer in church, as she was shy. She also wondered if maybe she was making a bigger deal of things than she should. I reassured her that having a child who is struggling is no small matter.

Then I asked her a slightly discomforting question. I said, "What does it *mean* for you to come up to the front of the church and ask someone to pray for you?"

Nancy thought for a moment and then said, "Well, I know that God is the only answer for Scott and me. I suppose when I walk up to the front of the church it's my way of letting God know that I am serious about my faith—that I really love him, that I will do anything he wants if he'll give us help."

"I could not agree with you more," I assured her. "I believe you really love God. And when we seek him and love him, he responds to us by showing us a way that is his way.

"But," I continued, "I want you to think about something. I think it's possible that you are not loving God enough for him to help you."

Nancy was a little confused. "I don't think I understand you. I am giving him my whole life when I come up to the front. I am not holding back from him. There is nothing else to give."

I replied, "I'm not at all questioning the sincerity of your commitment to God. But I'm wondering if you have parts of yourself that—maybe without being aware of it—you've left out of your relationship with him. You may not even know that you are holding some part of you back from him, or you may not know it is important. It's a little like missing the details in the big picture. Loving God involves more than committing your life to him. Your life is a lot of different things, not just one thing. Loving God means bringing *all* the aspects of your heart, personality, and emotions to the relationship so that he can work with you and help you."

She was not clear on what I meant, so I offered this illustration. "Suppose you have a stomach pain that doesn't go away. You see a doctor who diagnoses you with an irritated stomach lining and puts you on medication. But suppose that you forgot to tell him you're allergic to some food that you ate last night that always gives you stomach distress. Even with the medication you're taking, what do you think would happen to the stomach pains?"

"I would still have them," she said.

"That's right," I went on. "You were totally serious and totally committed to getting well, but this particular part of your system—your allergy—was not involved in the treatment. As a consequence, you won't get the results you need. All of you must to be present to be healed."

"So if this is what I am doing, which part of me is not showing up in my situation?" Nancy asked.

"From the little we've talked about so far, here's one thing I've noticed—your fear. I think you're afraid that if you begin setting some strict limits with Scott, you may lose his love forever. You're also afraid of being more open with other people about how difficult things really are, maybe because you think they'll see you as a bad mother. And I think you might be afraid that God will allow Scott to self-destruct if you don't do something. Fear is a large part of your life. And it sounds like you're handling all this fear by yourself.

"So, fear is one thing you don't bring to the relationship with God," I said. "I believe that you genuinely love him. One thing I would add to your loving him is all the many fears you have to deal with. I think that would be a good place to start."

Nancy did some thinking about our conversation. She began seeing how much and how often she had not brought her fears to God and his resources. She had thought it was not okay or that it was a sign of weakness or a lack of trust. She had been afraid to be afraid, so to speak.

Fortunately, Nancy began facing her fears. She asked God for help with them, and she talked to people who helped her deal with them. In time, her life began changing, as she became less afraid to do what it took to help Scott. As she let God have her fear, he gave her something much better—the renewal of her son.

◆ LET LOVE LEAD

God loves you unconditionally and desires to make a way for you through your difficult situation. Like Nancy discovered, finding his way is also a matter of love on your part. Loving God as fully as you can, with every fiber of your being, is the only true and meaningful beginning point. Loving God is so important that Jesus identified it as the first and greatest commandment: "Love the Lord your God with all your heart and with all your soul and with all your mind. This is the first and greatest commandment" (Matthew 22:37–38).

Jesus was referring, of course, to the ancient and great first principle in the Old Testament law (Deuteronomy 6:5). Loving God is the greatest command because it serves as an all-encompassing principle that covers all the other rules of life. It places us in the universe the way he designed us to be. If we love him, connect to him, and follow him, we'll end up doing the things that he wants which are best for us. After that, the rest of life tends to emerge in the right order. Other rules, principles, and commands are not ignored; rather, they are fulfilled. In fact, Jesus said that all the law and the prophets hang on the two commands to love God and others (Matthew 22:37–40). If you love God, it follows that you will value what he values and see things the way he sees them. When you love God, you enter his world of spiritual reality, transcendence, relationship, responsibility, freedom, and much more.

Therefore, when you are in a bad situation in life and can't find it within yourself to know what the next step should be—*love God*. It is impossible for us to misstep when we begin with that command.

As Nancy discovered, however, loving God is simple, yet complicated. That's because there are many parts to our internal makeup, and each part needs to learn how to love God. We have been "fearfully and wonderfully made" by God (Psalm 139:14), and we have complex aspects inside ourselves. This is what Jesus was referring to when he talked about our loving God with all our heart, soul, and mind.

If you're wondering what this means, consider this: Every one of us is familiar with the experience of having conflicting feelings, say, about a relationship or about desiring something that conflicts with our values. These are examples of our having different internal parts to us. Each of these parts of ourselves—heart, soul, and mind—need God, need him to know them, and need to be loved by him. These parts all exist together, connected but separate. They were all designed to love him with all their might. When that happens, they are completely connected to the Source of love and life, and receive all they need.

◆ WHAT'S INSIDE YOU THAT GOD WANTS TO LOVE?

Here is a brief list of some of the most important aspects of your inner being. These pieces of you all need to be joined to God so that they can take part in helping you find his way:

- ◆ ***Values.*** Our values are the architecture of our lives. They make up what is important to us and what is not. What is important to God needs to be important to you. For example, some core values might be that God is real, that he loves you, and that following him is the most important thing you can do. Our values direct and guide us. When we do not love God with our values—that is, when we don't derive our values from him— we are sure to go astray like a ship without a rudder.

- ◆ ***Passions.*** Our deep urgings and drives keep us feeling alive. They can be pleasant or painful. Often people are hesitant to let God into their passions. They think that they are being too subjective or immature. But when you turn your passions over to God, he can transform them into passions that work for and with him. It's good to remember that God is the Author of passion. Allow your love for God to fuel your passions.

- ◆ ***Emotions.*** Loving God with all our hearts includes our emotions. God created us with a wide range of emotions, which serve as a signal for us to let us be aware of the state of our soul. Are we afraid and in danger, joyful and feeling loved, at peace, angry, or sad? When we love God with our feelings, positive and negative, he uses them to help us grow and learn about ourselves.

◆ *Hurts.* All of us experience deep inner hurts at various times. People fail us, dreams are shipwrecked, and circumstances go against us. God will make a way when you allow him into the places of your wounds. You may avoid bringing him into your hurt, fearing that you will be hurt even more or that he'll blame you for the hurt. But remember that God is no stranger to hurt either, and he will heal those wounds when you give them to him.

◆ *Loves.* We are people who love deeply. Sometimes we love those who are good for us, and sometimes we love those who are not so good for us. When you bring your loves to God, he transforms what we love so that we begin to invest in and trust the right people.

◆ *Motives.* Underlying our choices in life are our motives, which are our deeper reasons for our actions. Some motives have to do with being caring, responsible, and free. Some motives have more to do with being self-protective, fearful, or selfish. Expose these motives to God so that he can transform them into motives like his own.

◆ *Sins.* We have all fallen short and missed the mark in life. We harbor sinful thoughts, speak sinful words, and do sinful deeds. When you bring your sins to God, he forgives freely, heals, and provides a way to work through them and find victory and freedom.

◆ *Talents.* God designed all of us with strengths and gifts so that we can take a part in helping others have a better life. Love God with your talents. Many people find that when they enter this path, God has found a way for them to help others in ways they never dreamed of.

◆ ***Preferences and opinions.*** Part of life is taking ownership of our freedom to have our own preferences and opinions in many areas. You enjoy a certain kind of church or worship style. There are certain types of people you are drawn to as friends. Don't be afraid to bring your unique preferences to God. He will make a way for you to sort out your preferences and use them to make a better life.

◆ GOD MAKES A WAY AS WE LOVE HIM IN ALL OUR PARTS

Ultimately, loving God is about a relationship. It was intended to be a complete relationship, in which all of ourselves was to be connected to everything in God that he makes available to us. Think about the dearest, closest, most loving relationship in your life. It may be someone to whom you've opened up deeply and loved unreservedly, someone you loved with every fiber of your being. You let that person know your secrets, your fears, and your deepest desires. You took risks of vulnerability with that person. You allowed yourself to need and depend on that person.

People who have experienced this type of connection with another will tell you that this sort of deep and full relationship makes them feel amazingly alive. Life is vivid. It matters and has meaning. They say things like, "Life was in black and white before, but now the whole world is full of color." Our deep and loving human relationships are a picture of how completely God wants us to love him with all our hearts.

Getting to know God in all the ways that are possible is a lifelong and all-encompassing journey. The more aspects of our life and soul we can connect to him, the more God is able to make a way for us, for whatever purposes are ahead. This can be about growth and intimacy, using our talents and gifts, success at work, or service to others. At the same time, loving God with every aspect of our inner being can unlock answers about struggles and heartbreaks too: a parenting problem, a dating relationship, a bad habit, or a faith issue.

The bedrock truth is, *God will make a way for us to the extent that we make a way for him.* That's what loving him completely is all about. It's getting our handcuffs off him and saying, "Do whatever you need to do with whatever part of me needs you." It's saying, as Jesus—who loved God completely—said, "Not my will, but yours be done" (Luke 22:42). *But it is not about what loving God does for God. It is what loving God does for us.* When we love God with all of ourselves, he has access to all the parts that need his love, grace, and support.

We are designed to flourish when we connect to and love God. Conversely, we wither away when we're not connected to him. Jesus said, "I am the vine; you are the branches" (John 15:5). That is why some people feel their souls and emotions have died. They have not been made alive by God in a long time, if ever. Others do not have dreams and desires because they have not given God a chance to renew them. Still others experience a withering of their values because they have not given themselves to things that are of ultimate importance in life. When we love God with all of ourselves he also makes a way for us in another fashion, called *unity*. The aspects of our inner beings that connect to God, depend on him, and love him also begin to work together in a harmonious unity. Like a mature and well-trained orchestra, each part does its work with the rest, and the result is one of beauty.

For example, some people are good at loving God with their heads but not with their hearts. They are good at principles and knowing what's right and prudent to do, but often their hearts feel dead or burdened. Or they have strong emotions that are hard to control, no matter what their brains tell them to do. This is one component of people who struggle with impulsive behaviors. Their hearts aren't working well with the rest of them. When these individuals began unleashing God's love into their hearts and opening up to him, their head and their heart began seeing things the same way. This makes perfect sense, because God's reality is harmony. He is never in conflict with himself. So the more parts we connect to him, the less disruption we experience in our inner selves.

Another aspect of how God makes a way when we allow our-selves to love him with every aspect of ourselves has to do with our need for healing. When we've experienced problems, pains, or hurts in life, we go into an injured state. We suffer emotional pain, rela-tional distress, faith struggles, and the like. There is no clearer indication of how much we need God to make a way than in these periods of suffering. By nature, God is a healer. He has the will and the resources to do it: "He heals the brokenhearted and binds up their wounds" (Psalm 147:3).

God's healing process works to the extent that we bring all of our inner parts to that process. Suppose a person has experienced the loss of a significant long-term relationship. Let's say someone she loves deeply is no longer in her life. She tries to pray over it, get over it, think positively, and all the things we attempt to do to get something painful behind us. Yet the intense feelings of grief remain. Sometimes this is an indication that she has not allowed God to give her hope that she can find another relationship that will fulfill those same needs. It seems disloyal to her to replace the one she loved, or she may be afraid to be close again. Whatever the reason, she avoids bringing to God her need for close human contact. When she realizes this, she understands that God heals to the extent that we love and connect to him. She is then free and able to love God with her need. God does his part and brings the right person or people to her life. It is as the Bible teaches: "You do not have, because you do not ask God" (James 4:2).

◆ We Love God—Because God *Is* Love

God is about love. He makes a way for those who love him with every-thing they have, with every fiber of their being. You can be sure that the more of yourself you make available to God, the more you can grow, be healed, and find his way. *God will make a way for us to the extent that we make a way for him.*

Whatever obstacle or setback you are dealing with, begin to search your heart carefully. Find out if the solution rests in bringing some unknown, unloved, or disconnected piece of your inner self to the light of his love, care, and healing ability.

Love God with every part of yourself—heart, soul, and mind—and watch the real miracles of your life begin to unfold.

THE PRINCIPLES AT WORK

Dating and New Romance

I (Henry) was speaking one evening at a seminar when a woman raised her hand and asked me, "When do you know if God is giving you a sign?"

"Why do you ask? What happened that you thought you were getting a sign from God?" I replied.

"Well, I was wondering if he was trying to tell me I should get back together with my old boyfriend."

"What made you think that?"

"Well, I was in the supermarket and I ran into him when I was shopping. I thought that might be a sign that God was telling me I should get back together with him."

At first I thought she was kidding. "So just because you ran into him, you think that God is telling you to get back together with him?" I think she could probably sense my surprise.

"Yes."

"Well," I said, "I think it all depends on what aisle you were in when you ran into him."

"What?" she said. "What do you mean 'what aisle'?"

"What aisle in the market. For example, if you ran into him in the pastries section, then it probably was not a sign from God. It would be a sign that if you got back together it would be really sweet and taste really good, but only for a moment. A few hours later you would have a deep crash and a sugar low. So it probably would not be a lasting thing.

"If you ran into him in the produce section, it might be a little healthier, but you can't make it on just one or two good things in a diet. For a healthy diet, you need a lot of good things. Just a few fruits or vegetables won't do the trick; there aren't enough nutrients in the relationship.

"Furthermore, I would want to make sure that you looked into his cart and figured out what aisles he had been down since the last time you were with him. What was the relationship like? Was it good?" I asked.

"No," she said. "It was horrible. He did not treat me well. It was really bad."

"Well, then," I said, "I would look into his cart and see where he had been. I would hope that he had picked up some things from the detergent section. It sounds as if he needed to clean up his act some since the time you were with him. I'd also look to see if he had gone down the health aisle and picked up some medicine. It sounds like he was pretty sick.

"If he did not have all of those things in his cart, chances are the relationship would not be any better. It was probably not a sign from God after all," I told her.

Afterward, as I thought about it, I realized that my response was a metaphor for a lot that goes on in the world of dating. People pretty much take whatever comes their way and hope that God is somewhere out there watching over them. As a result, they often end up in not-very-nutritious relationships.

◆ PREPARE TO DATE

Lots of intelligent people make really poor decisions in dating. Let's look at the kinds of problems you might be experiencing:

- ◆ ***Passive dating.*** You get only what comes your way.
- ◆ ***Valueless dating.*** You allow or participate in things you do not feel good about.
- ◆ ***Dissatisfied dating.*** You end up in relationships that are not good for you or are not what you truly desire.
- ◆ ***Hurtful dating.*** You end up in relationships that are actually destructive.
- ◆ ***Little or no dating.*** You desire to date, but nothing is happening.
- ◆ ***Repetitive dating.*** You live out the same scenario over and over again.

Dating problems abound. Some people become disillusioned and give up dating altogether. Others teach that God doesn't want you to date. Yet John and I have a different view. We think that dating is great. It can be a wonderful time of growth, fun, significant human interaction, and relationship. It can be a time of learning about your own patterns of relating and how to grow past them, as well as learning what kinds of people you like and don't like, and which are ultimately good for you. Dating is a good thing.

However, because dating is a human exercise, it can be a tightrope fraught with danger. You will be dating imperfect people, and some of them are more imperfect than others. In addition, you are not perfect either, so that complicates the picture. That is why you need to approach dating, with all of its strong passions and promises, with a great deal of thought, prayer, and wisdom. If you do, God can make a way for you to grow in your dating life.

Dating is serious business of the heart and soul, but most people do not think of it that way, nor do they prepare for dating. By and large, most of us have received very little training in *the one activity of life that influences some of the most significant and life-changing decisions that we ever will make.* Some of these decisions are unconscious, and sometimes they are made impulsively or at least without a lot of planning. A few of the things your dating life influences are these:

- Who and when you marry
- Your feelings about relationships and love, positive or negative
- Your ability to trust and believe people
- How you feel about yourself
- Who you have or keep as friends
- Whether you stay put or move to another city, state, or country
- Whether you are growing spiritually or personally

The list could go on. The point is that dating is not just a sport. *It can truly alter who you are, who you will love or not love, who you become, and all sorts of directions in your life.* For that reason, it deserves a lot more attention than it usually receives. More often than not, people date as their heart and passion dictate. While heart and passion are necessary to fuel the male-female relationship, they can be ignorant, foolish, or even self-destructive as guiding lights.

It's possible to integrate your heart and passion into dating patterns that will give you the greatest possibility of growth and ultimate satisfaction. In order to help you do that, we've come up with twelve rules for how you should approach dating.

1. *Begin with pursuing God and become the healthiest person you can become.* You probably think that in a book like this we are going to say that the best preparation for dating is "Jesus." You are right, but we do not want you to hear it in the Sunday school, "be a good boy or girl" kind of way. We want you to see it for the profound truth that it is. For it could truly save your dating life and give you all that you desire and are seeking in whomever you are dating now.

Jesus said:

Therefore I tell you, do not worry about your life, what you will eat or drink; or about your body, what you will wear. Is not life more important than food, and the body more important than clothes? Look at the birds of the air; they do not sow or reap or store away in barns, and yet your heavenly Father feeds them. Are you not much more valuable than they? Who of you by worrying can add a single hour to his life?

And why do you worry about clothes? See how the lilies of the field grow. They do not labor or spin. Yet I tell you that not even Solomon in all his splendor was dressed like one of these. If that is how God clothes the grass of the field, which is here today and tomorrow is thrown into the fire, will he not much more clothe you, O you of little faith? So do not worry, saying, "What shall we eat?" or "What shall we drink?" or "What shall we wear?" For the pagans run after all these things, and your heavenly Father knows that you need them. But seek first his kingdom and his righteousness, and all these things will be given to you as well. Therefore do not worry about tomorrow, for tomorrow will worry about itself. Each day has enough trouble of its own.

—MATTHEW 6:25–34

A paraphrase of this could read: "Don't worry about who you will date, where you will find that person, and so on. Don't the birds figure it out? God leads them to other birds, doesn't he? He puts the flowers in nice gardens, doesn't he? He knows you need a social life and a satisfying dating experience. The real thing to worry about is this: Seek him and his righteousness, and good dating will follow as a fruit. Don't worry about your future dating life, for it will take care of itself. Instead, worry about where you are with your spiritual growth today, and who you are becoming today, and what your dating looks like today. Seek him and become who he wants you to be, and your dating life will take care of itself."

You don't make good decisions about dating on the night or the day of the date. *You make them in the months and years before that date ever occurs. In fact, you make them before you even meet the person with whom you are going on that date.* Good dating comes from your becoming the healthiest person that you can become. A healthy person dates in healthy and satisfying ways and is able to attract healthy and satisfying people.

So dating begins with your being in a process of becoming the most complete, honest, loving, responsible, creative, satisfied person you can be. That kind of life comes from seeking God, allowing him to lead you into the kinds of growth that you need, and following his "righteousness" as best you can. Then, as you find the "right" way to be you and to be in relationship, the rest will fall into place.

2. Get your relationship needs met outside the dating context. There is an old saying, "Never go grocery shopping when you are hungry." The principle here is that *when we are in a state of need we do not make wise choices.* This is true for dating as well as for shopping.

Sara had come to our group because she had found herself in a succession of unsatisfying relationships. She wanted to learn how to "pick better men." She knew that she had a tendency to be attracted to the "wrong type."

When she began talking about her dating, it was mostly about the choices that she was making in regard to all these "bad men" she found herself getting involved with. Yet we all wanted to know something else. "Who do you turn to for help with your loneliness?" we asked.

"What loneliness?" she replied.

"The loneliness that you feel when you are not in a relationship," I said.

Sara went silent. It was a new thought for her. She did not see herself as empty or lonely, because she had never allowed herself to get close enough to how she felt "without a man" to know who she was on her own. Her relationships with men who were incapable of connecting kept her from being aware of how disconnected and love-starved she really was.

So we had her enter into a pact. She agreed to get to a place where her life was so full without a man that she was not distressed or lonely when she did not have one in her life. As she began to let other supportive people get close to her, know her heart, and touch her loneliness and some of her hurts, she became stronger. She also found herself dating out of a desire to find someone with whom *to share her life,* as opposed to a desire *to get a life.* She could much more easily say "no" to men who were not good for her or in whom she was really not interested. She could be more selective because she was not in a place of need.

If you are already loved, you will not be clingy and needy. You will make better choices when it comes to dating.

3. *Learn your patterns and work on them so you do not repeat them.* When people we are counseling begin to say things like, "I have a tendency to get involved in relationships that are _____ or _____," we know they are going to get better. Such statements indicate that they are beginning to take responsibility for their actions, to see themselves as actors instead of victims who are *acted upon.* They understand that these patterns in their dating life are coming out of their own hearts, their own makeup.

By and large, we create the patterns in which we find ourselves. Whatever the situation, we usually have something to do with either creating it or allowing it to be present. Of course this is not true 100 percent of the time, because "bad people happen to good people." Yet when there is a *pattern,* then we have to take a look at what part we are playing in setting that pattern.

When we begin to see our patterns, we can do something about them, before they cause serious problems. The Bible says that difficult things are sometimes good for us because they can lead to wisdom and maturity. In other words, we can change unhealthy patterns and avoid the problems that can arise from them. Unfortunately, a lot of people go through sad things over and over again because they don't recognize the unhealthy patterns in which they are engaged, and thus they are destined to repeat them. Yet, as James says, when you go through trials, seek wisdom from God and persevere in the process, and then you will become complete (James 1:2–12). The tough dating scenario will be in your past, never to be repeated.

To do this, however, you have to find out why you have this pattern. Why are you attracted to certain kinds of people? What sucks you in?

Here are a few things to consider:

◆ Your original family abandoned or mistreated you and you are simply repeating old relationship patterns.
◆ You are seeking completion for something you lack in yourself but finding another unbalanced person to complete you.
◆ You are not comfortable facing the sadness that someone is not what you want and the pain of saying good-bye and letting him or her go.
◆ You have idealistic wishes for yourself, so you pick idealized people who are not comfortable with a real relationship.
◆ You fear closeness or intimacy.
◆ Your spiritual life is not integrated, so you pick people who are also not spiritually integrated.
◆ You have unresolved parts of your personality that make only certain kinds of relationships possible.
◆ You are unable to set boundaries with people or actions that are not good for you.

Do any of these ring true for you? It's important to identify your pattern and resolve it.

Recently I was leading a seminar when a woman asked a question: "I have a tendency to pick men who I have to take care of. My fiancé now is in a slump in his work, and I want to confront it but don't know if that is appropriate. Am I being a nag or mothering him if I do so?"

"What do you mean 'a slump'?" I asked.

"He is starting his own business, but he just stays home and plays video games," she said. "He is not getting anywhere."

"Is he in the video game business?" I asked, thinking that he might indeed be working and she might not be getting it.

"No," she said, vaguely. "It is a different business."

I wanted to know if this was a pattern in his life or just something that was happening now, so I asked her about something that tends to show people's patterns financially. "What does his credit report look like?" I asked.

I hit some resistance with her, as she said that hers was not perfect either, but I pressed her. "How imperfect is his?" I asked.

She went on to paint a pretty unflattering picture of how he had managed his finances in his past. I then asked her, "What kind of business is he starting?"

"A financial services business," she said.

I was stunned. Here was an intelligent, competent woman about to make a lifetime commitment to a man whose own financial life was upside down but thought he was in a position to tell others how to manage theirs. And she was wondering if she should be confronting him about it. She then went on to say that when she brought it up, he got defensive and angry.

In response I told her, "I think this is about *you*. This is about you and what you want for your life. I would tell him something like this—'Joe, I love you. And I hope that we end up together. But here is something that is true about me. The guy I end up with is going to be someone with whom I can talk about issues without him being defensive. He is going to be someone who is responsible with money and can delay gratification, reach goals, and be responsible. He will be honest and dependable. That is the man I will marry. *I hope that person is you.* I do not know if it will be, because right now it is not. But that is up to you. If you become that person, then we can be together, and that is what I desire. But that is the description of the man I will marry. Let me know what you think.'"

Then I told her that my hunch was that she was someone who had difficulty depending on other people and probably had always been in the role of being the strong one and taking care of others. I suggested that she find a healing community where she could learn to be weak and to depend on others, and then she would not be drawn to dependent people who could not be strong for her. Her pattern was to deny her own weaknesses and then find them in others who were imbalanced in the opposite direction. To change this pattern, she had to learn how to be a more balanced person, both strong and weak.

4. Date according to a few nonnegotiable values. I do not know anyone who gets into bad dating situations on purpose. But I have known people whose lack of purpose caused them to end up in bad dating relationships.

You will be far less likely to stay in a relationship that is bad for you if, before you date, you have a clear idea of what values you want to guide your life. Know what kind of people and situations you want to avoid, as well as those you want to cultivate.

As you think through your list of what to avoid, remember what David said in Psalm 101. He said that he would have nothing to do with people who exhibited the following:

- *Vileness*—someone who is worthless or destructive
- *Faithlessness*—a derelict, or one who turns away from faith
- *Perversity*—someone whose views are distorted and false
- *Slander*—someone who speaks evil of others
- *Evil*—someone who causes calamity and distress, someone who is wretched
- *Pride*—someone who is arrogant and holds him- or herself above others
- *Deceit*—someone full of betrayal and treachery
- *Lying*—one who is untrue and a sham

What kinds of things would you put on your list?

It would seem that these character flaws would be obvious, but people can be pretty subtle about their dark sides. So have a set of values that inform your dating decisions. Those values should act as an alarm system when someone you are dating violates them. If that happens, say, "One of my values is honesty. What happened the other day was not honest, and I cannot go forward until we resolve this issue." Then make sure to follow through. If the person's values don't align with yours, then get out of Dodge.

Aside from the character flaws you want to avoid, think about what you want and which values you want to cultivate. Think about the things that are important to you—your spiritual growth, health, growth as a person, sexual purity, independence, ownership, and so on.

You get to choose who you date. Your participation in a dating relationship is 100 percent voluntary. No one can choose this person for you. You can't pick your family or determine many of the other things that happen in life, but you can choose the person you date. You alone are responsible. So, if you are in charge, exercise that right and *be in charge* of the things that are important to you.

5. Expand your tastes. I've talked with singles who tell me they rarely date or that they never meet anyone they would like to date. I often find that these people have an excessively long list of requirements for someone who would interest them. I spoke with one woman whose list even contained things that could not exist in the same person! For instance, she wanted someone who was extremely well organized and creative. I told her that I had never met a creative person who was extremely organized. These are somewhat contradictory traits, and it would be highly unusual to find them in the same person. Yet her list went on from there. Though she was creative and attractive, she had not had a date in more than a year.

I suggested that, for a while, she should go out with anyone who was not dangerous. Of course, she was to use all of the normal precautions, such as meeting in public places until she knew someone better and could check him out. Yet the idea was for her to be open to finding out who someone really was, *apart from her list of requirements*. This was a specific assignment for a woman who had been much too limiting in her tastes.

When I told her what I wanted her to do, she looked at me as if I were kidding. I assured her that I was not kidding and that I wanted her to go out with men that were nowhere near her little "box." She balked at first but agreed to try.

As she began to go out with men she never would have dated

before, she found that a lot of the things she had deemed "important" were not important at all. Furthermore, she found out that there were great qualities she had never thought to put on her list. What she needed in a man was character strength, spiritual strength, and emotional depth, not big biceps. In meeting and dating men who were not her "type," she broadened herself in many ways, both personally and interpersonally. A few years later this young woman married a man from a profession that never would have been on her "list," yet she is very happy.

Be open to going out with people whom you would normally not have on your list. Date to learn. Date to have fun. Date to have meaningful interactions with human beings. Look at each situation as a chance to get to know a person and find out something about yourself.

6. *Be yourself, from the beginning.* In the beginning, dating is a lot about looking good, trying to impress someone, and putting forth your best foot. There is nothing wrong with that, as after you know someone better, you are more comfortable allowing yourself to be seen for who you are.

It's another thing, however, to put forward a foot that is not yours. Not being yourself can be dangerous, yet many people do this when they date. For example, some women who are bored by sports act as if they love them because the men they are dating are avid sports fans.

Be yourself instead of adapting to what you think the other person will like. If you don't like a certain kind of music, say so. If you disagree with a person's views on something, give your own. If you have certain feelings about an area of life, express them. You don't have to be obnoxious, give your views on everything, or have your way all the time. Just be true to who you are. Otherwise, you are asking for problems. It's okay to do things that the other person enjoys that you don't; this is essential to compromise and sacrifice. We are not talking about being selfish. Yet you shouldn't lie about how you feel or act like someone you aren't.

For one thing, what if it worked? What if the person got serious about you—or the person he or she *thought* was you? You would begin to realize that this person didn't know you or how to meet your needs, and you would begin to feel dissatisfied. You would likely voice some of those things, and then the other person would find out that you were not the person that he or she thought and that the relationship was built on quicksand. The best-case scenario would be difficult conflict, especially if you began to be honest only after engagement or marriage. The worst-case scenario would be a nasty breakup—or divorce—and heartache.

Furthermore, you might attract someone who is a control freak. Controlling people are often drawn to people they can dominate and turn into what they want. Control freaks cannot appreciate or accept others' wishes or likes if they are different from their own.

In addition, pretending to be someone you aren't rules out the possibility of real intimacy. Differences are exciting and part of what a real relationship is about. Sparks and chemistry come not only from where you are alike and already connect but also from where you are different. Differences create space between people where longing and desire can develop. There is a desire to join and enjoy what you do not possess. You are enlarged by the other.

So when you date, be yourself. Be who you are and give the other person the freedom to do the same.

7. *Don't put up with bad behavior, and set good boundaries.* Many people put up with a lot of disrespect in dating and then wonder why they are in a problem relationship. Remember, *you will get what you tolerate.* You are always training someone how to treat you. You are telling someone what will work with you and what will not. We are not suggesting that you be the kind of person who is inflexible and cannot let some things slide. The Bible says that it is a glory to you to be able to overlook an offense (Proverbs 19:11). So don't get all bent out of shape over little things or if someone is late once. However, if someone has a *pattern* of not being respectful, then don't put up with it.

If you see patterns that you do not want to be there, deal with them early. If the person you are dating stops the negative behavior, you come out ahead. If he or she dislikes being confronted and goes away, you still come out ahead. Both results are good for you. You cannot lose.

8. *Take your time.* You would not allow a stranger into your house without proper identification, but many people allow virtual strangers into their hearts, minds, souls, and bodies. Take the time to make sure you know someone well before getting into a serious or exclusive dating relationship. If the other person has a problem with this, see that as a warning sign. What's the rush? Why can't he or she enjoy just getting to know you as a friend first? If this is a problem, it may point to a need to control or be dependent. Get to know this person in different situations; get to know his or her friends, values, family, faith—everything you can know about someone. You have to make sure that you are not just indulging your hormones or fantasies when you open the door of your heart and get serious with someone.

Besides, if you move into a serious relationship too quickly, you may be tempted to drop out of your own life. Sometimes people quit doing all the things that were important to them before the relationship. They give up their interests, hobbies, and life for the other person. If you are doing that, it means that you have some dependencies of your own and that you are losing yourself in this relationship. Take your time, and keep your life in the process. You will need it later.

9. *Stay connected.* We talked earlier about making sure your relational needs are met before you enter the dating scene. This advice is just as important after you are dating someone as it was before. The sheep that wanders away from the herd is the one that gets eaten by the wolves.

Your support system, your friends, and sometimes your family are the people who love you the most and know you the best. They are also are the ones who are most objective about the people whom you are dating. Sometimes someone can be smitten with a person and bring that person to meet his or her friends, only to have the friends say, "What on earth are you thinking?" Your friends can see things that you can't, because they are not emotionally involved.

I once knew a woman who thought she had found "the one," until she told her support group that he wanted her to have plastic surgery before he would get more serious with her. They screamed in protest—and they helped her see that this man was not someone who would ever be happy. Because she had been so charmed by him, she was unable to see this on her own. Thank God for the community.

Don't date in isolation. Integrate the person you are dating into your community of friends. Allow your friends to be your spiritual family and depend on them for input. By staying connected to a community, you will ensure that your deepest needs will be met, you will get support and accountability, and from that strong base you will make better decisions.

10. *Get active.* I talk with a lot of singles who have inactive dating lives. Men ask me, "Where are the good women?" and women ask, "Where are the good men?" It seems as if I am talking to both of them, but they are not talking to each other! Why is that?

One reason is that in our highly urbanized, noncommunity-based world, some of the old, tried-and-true methods of meeting people no longer exist. People are on the run and have little sense of community. Also, singles often frequent places—like their church—where they meet the same people over and over again.

For example, many women tell me they are disillusioned about their dating lives. When I ask them how many new men they meet every week, they look at me like I am nuts. "Tell me about your traffic pattern," I will say.

"Well, I go to work and work with the same people pretty much every day. Then, I get off and go home or have dinner with my roommate or a friend. Then, I go to bed and do the same thing the next day. On the weekend, I go to my church."

"How many new men do you meet every week who have enough of an interaction with you to be interested in asking you out and enough information about you to make that happen?" I ask.

The disheartening answer I get often is, "None, really."

So how can these people expect to meet anyone different? Men or women, it does not matter.

Would you take this same approach if you were looking for a job? I don't think so. You would get active about solving the problem. You would read the ads, hire a headhunter, attend a job fair, go on interviews, and the like. You would go out in the real world and get active about seeking what you want.

Some teach that when it comes to dating you should just wait on God to bring the person to you. We began this chapter by quoting Matthew 6, which says that God will provide as you seek him, just as he takes care of the birds and feeds them each and every day. We believe that.

It's true that God provides for the birds to eat. *Yet the birds get out of the nest each and every day and fly around looking for food!* In other words, God provides, but he also wants us to be doing our part of getting out into life and being in the real world. Just as a bird flies around looking for food, enjoying the scenery, and meeting other birds, we have to be "out there" in all areas of life if we want to date. Whether you are looking for a job, a church, or a dating life, take some action.

Here are a few ways that you could begin to meet more people:

♦ *Network with friends and family.* Let your friends and other people who are in the position of meeting eligible singles know that you want them to look out for you. Friends have been matchmaking for friends for a long time, and it still works. Yet, often they have to know that you need them to do this.

♦ *Pursue the things you enjoy.* Take a class to learn that sport that you always wanted to learn or that skill you have been dreaming about. Chances are better that you will meet new people by being active in life than by sitting at home watching television. This will also make you more well-rounded and fulfilled. Do things that are of interest to you, and you will be more likely to meet people who share your interests.

♦ ***Join others who have the same need.*** Maybe you know other frustrated singles who would like to do something about it. Two women I know organized a singles social group with two churches that held a gathering each month. People brought friends to meet other friends, and lots of good things happened as a result. Don't be a victim; do something about your situation.

♦ ***Use your gift of hospitality.*** If you are good at entertaining, throw some gatherings yourself. It will be fun, and if your friends invite other friends, all of you will meet new people.

♦ ***Do something structured.*** It is a curious thing to me that some people would never think of joining a dating service. With adults having the kinds of schedules they have now, sometimes it is very difficult to meet people to date. Their work lives almost prohibit it from happening. So a dating service that has a good screening process and asks questions about faith and values can be an excellent resource.

Become active about seeking what you want, and ask God to help you. Sow some seeds and you might find a harvest.

11. *Look in the mirror.* If you are taking steps to meet new people and no one is showing any interest in you, ask yourself why. Maybe there is something about your personality, or behavior, or the way you come across to others that you are not aware of that is getting in the way.

I remember talking with one woman who wondered why no one ever asked her out. I knew the answer—she in no way seemed open to people. Even though she wanted to date, no man would have approached her. She gave off vibes of being very closed. When I told her this, she was completely surprised, but she felt like she had something to work on.

So ask yourself, "What am I doing to make myself someone to whom others would be attracted? What do I need to learn about myself that might be keeping me stuck?" Find some friends who will be honest with you and ask for their feedback. Maybe there is a real problem that you can work on, and you may find some good things happening.

12. *Keep yourself pure.* In our culture, the idea of remaining sexually pure in dating seems an outdated value. Many singles think it's fine to have sex if both people want it, particularly in an exclusive relationship. Yet sex outside of marriage can set you up for a lot of misery and can cause you to lose out on a lot of good things.

First of all, if you are having sex, you can't know the true reason that the person you are dating is with you—or vice versa. The sex can be gratifying enough, especially without commitment, that neither of you knows if you really would like to be with the other person long-term. Furthermore, you do not want to be used, even if you feel like you care for the person you are dating.

Second, if you are having sex, you are robbing yourself of the chance to find out who the person would be if he or she had to delay gratification and actually build a relationship. Sex can get in the way of people having to learn how to relate at a significant level—the level that is going to make a relationship last.

Third, your sexual relationship may be keeping you or your partner apart. If your heart is not 100 percent committed, yet your body is, then you have split your heart, soul, and body. When that happens, you can find later that your heart cannot be brought back into sex, or vice versa. People who have done that kind of splitting often have difficulty making sex and love work out together. Also, you could be masking some other issues inside yourself that sex is medicating.

Do not set yourself up in dating by being promiscuous, even in a more serious relationship. You will have no idea what is truly going on and will not know what part sex is playing in making it all work. Then, later, when there is all the pressure of commitment, conflict, children, and the like, you might find that there was a shaky foundation from the beginning.

For all these reasons and more, God has told us to honor sex as something holy and keep it confined to the marriage relationship.

This will serve to make it better then, as well as help to make sure that you end up in a real relationship with a person who is there for more than just your body. Treat each other with respect and it will give you great returns (1 Thessalonians 4:3–8).

◆ ABIDE IN GOD—AND HAVE FUN!

God is the one who will make a way. So walk with him daily. Pray about your dating life and ask him what he wants you to do. Most of all, have a vibrant spiritual life. If you are fulfilled spiritually, then you will not determine your worth or feelings based on your dating life. Instead, you will determine your worth from your spiritual connection with God and the community of people who love you and care about you.

When you abide in God, you'll be far less likely to fall for someone who does not share your faith, which is just asking for trouble. If you end up getting serious, you will forever be going in two different directions. Be wise and date only those people who are going for God—and be one yourself.

While dating is serious business, it's supposed to be fun. Don't forget that. Use dating to find out more about who you are and who you want to become. Learn from your experiences. Abide in God, and enjoy him and the life he has given you. If you do, you won't be worried about not dating; you'll be having too good a time living!

Start dating with God, with faith, in community, and with wisdom—and have a good time!

MARRIAGE AND RELATIONSHIPS

M arriage is the most significant relationship any of us could ever have. It is a symbol of the relationship God has with his people (Ephesians 5:25–33) and is as close as we can get to being "one" with another person. Because of this, good marriages can be heaven on earth.

So what's the key to having a good marriage?

I (John) often ask couples who have good and longstanding marriages, "Okay, so how do you do it?" They will turn to each other a little sheepishly and then tell me about a thousand things, such as love, respect, God, time together, or shared interests. Marital experts weigh in, claiming the key to a good marriage is anything from childhood development to intimacy to commitment.

Let me make my own contribution to the list. I think the key to a good marriage is this: being *in the marriage*—being totally invested, with all the parts of yourself, in building and sustaining the union. A married couple should love each other the same way that we are to love God: with all our heart, soul, mind, and strength (Mark 12:30). People who are truly in the marriage, people who are connecting every part possible to their mates—their good parts, bad parts, angry parts, loving parts, weak parts, and strong parts—have the best foundation for a lifetime of relationship.

I'm not talking about being committed to marriage. Being in the marriage is more than being committed. Commitment has to do with agreeing to and fulfilling a covenant to one's spouse, and that is a good and necessary part of marriage. Some marriages, however, have high commitment but low connection. The covenant stands, but the hearts are not truly attached at the deepest levels. These couples will often have a stable and long-lasting relationship, but sometimes one or both individuals feel empty inside. The opposite problem also exists. Some have hearts that are genuinely bonded, but their commitment is weak. These couples do very well in good times but fare poorly when things get rocky. Being in the marriage means being deeply committed and deeply connected at every juncture of one's self and one's life.

All of us long for a good marriage, yet for many people this is not to be. Their marriage is a struggle and a profound disappointment. The hopes and dreams they have cherished for years may be in jeopardy, or lying dormant, with little hope of restoration. This is a very painful place to be.

If this is your situation, my heart goes out to you. However—and this is not to minimize the difficulty—*your struggling marriage may be bringing you closer to the path that God has for your life.* As you seek God, his way may heal not only your marriage but also your very soul.

Many times marriage difficulties have pushed people, for the first time in their lives, to look beyond themselves and their own answers because they have encountered a problem that is larger than themselves. Because they have had nowhere else to go, they have sought Someone with broader shoulders than theirs—and they have not been disappointed.

In marriage, as in every area of life, God will make a way, especially helping you know what to do *when you don't know what to do.* God has put his personal seal on your marriage. He has placed you two together. He is, in a mighty and supernatural way, also *in* your marriage. Let him work his way and will in something about which he cares deeply: "Therefore what God has joined together, let man not separate" (Mark 10:9).

With that in mind, let's take a closer look at what a good marriage is like.

◆ Have a Framework That Reflects God's Purposes

Most people, relationships, and organizations have an underlying structure of values or important beliefs that influences how they order their actions. For instance, a gang may value loyalty above all else, or a business may say that the customer is always right. Every marriage operates on a set of values as well, and good marriages have values that reflect God's purposes and design.

We'd like to encourage you to sit down with your spouse and discuss the kinds of values on which you want to build your marriage. Think them through, and even write them down so that you can return to them for clarity and grounding when you need it.

Here are some of the values that we believe reflect God's purposes for marriage.

1. *Our marriage has God at its center.* Some people think that making God the center means making God happy. While it is a good thing to please him, that is not all that we mean here. Making God the center of your marriage means inviting him into your relationship and going to him for guidance and direction about your marriage. After all, God is the Author of the institution of marriage and the Creator of your souls. He knows you better than you know yourselves. He knows what is best for you as individuals and as a married couple. He has made a way for you. Commit your marriage and your lives to his care and guidance: "The Lord commanded us to obey all these decrees and to fear the Lord our God, so that we might always prosper and be kept alive, as is the case today" (Deuteronomy 6:24).

2. *Our marriage is our most important relationship.* Hold your union in the highest esteem and make your spouse your top priority. Good marriages are costly. In little ways and big ways they require dying to yourself for the person you love the most. Invest your time and energy in your mate, and work even harder on the relationship when things are difficult. Remember that what you invest in the most tends to grow the most: "For where your treasure is, there your heart will be also" (Matthew 6:21).

3. *We are committed to truth without compromise in our marriage.* A marriage is only as strong as the honesty that the partners bring to it. Truth brings the person to the relationship, for better or for worse, but dishonesty and deception remove the person from the relationship. Insist on, and require, the truth from each other: "Do not lie to each other, since you have taken off your old self with its practices" (Colossians 3:9).

4. *We will grow personally in our marriage.* According to God's design, marriage provides us with a context in which to mature and grow. It exposes our selfishness, immaturity, and brokenness, and it holds us accountable for dealing with these things. Actively pursue your own spiritual and personal growth, and continually work on your relationship with your mate.

Keep in mind that your spouse does not exist to make you happy. This is an immature idea, and it's ruinous. If your mate is going to help you grow, he or she will sometimes make you unhappy, such as pointing out when you are irresponsible or hurtful. People who commit to growth are more likely to receive happiness as a by-product. Jesus spoke about the blessed (literally, "happy") state of those who seek God's righteousness: "Blessed are those who hunger and thirst for righteousness, for they will be filled" (Matthew 5:6).

5. *Our marriage will be lived in community.* A marriage that is thriving and isolated is an oxymoron. Decide to live your marriage in the grace and scrutiny of healthy community. Marriage was never designed to be a self-sufficient organism, in which each spouse meets all the needs of the other. Nor is this what the Bible teaches. Instead, it instructs us to be connected to God and to the body, the church, a group that encompasses marriage and supplements it. Couples who are in a good marriage will seek out and find people who can love them, show them compassion, be direct and honest with them, and also be vulnerable with them about their own lives. "This is the message you heard from the beginning: We should love one another" (1 John 3:11).

Yet having a strong framework is only part of what it takes to build a good marriage. In addition, those who want healthy marriages also need to know which character in the marriage should be center stage.

♦ RESPECT I, YOU, AND WE

Every couple has encountered the three principal characters in the play of marriage: I, you, and we. Couples in good marriages are aware of the importance of all three and know when each one needs to be at the forefront of the marriage.

Your marriage created one flesh, not one soul (Genesis 2:24), and couples in good marriages have a healthy respect for "I" and "you." They value each person's individual perspectives and distinctions and understand that each person brings gifts, talents, strengths, and weaknesses to the union. There is a legitimate place in the marriage for the differing needs and interests of each partner, and the relationship validates the needs and interests of both. Neither person's identity swallows up the other.

It is a beautiful part of a good marriage when one spouse can give up something simply for the well-being of the other. This sort of love is a very high love. The "I" submits to the "you" out of deep caring. For example, a husband may work to communicate and listen better, simply because his wife needs that from him: "Husbands, love your wives, just as Christ loved the church and gave himself up for her" (Ephesians 5:25).

At the same time, couples in good marriages are also able to give up "I" for "we." That is simply the price tag for one of God's greatest gifts to us. Each person sets aside his or her desires, dreams, goals, and conveniences for the good of the relationship. For example, a wife might put off career goals until the kids are older, or a husband might decline a promotion in another state for the sake of the marriage and the family.

Giving up "I" for "you" or "we" does not, however, mean being compliant or going along with everything the other person wants. It is a very active and deliberate stance. Sometimes you will find yourself asserting your "I" in the service of the "we." You may be very direct and honest in how you feel about a problem in the marriage, not for selfish reasons but because you love your spouse and want him or her to grow. For example, a wife may need to confront her husband's emotional unavailability and distance. While it may seem to him that it is "all about her," she may actually be alerting him to a marriage-killer that they need to address and work through. At heart, this wife is concerned about "we."

Another quality of a good marriage is closeness.

◆ DEVELOP CLOSENESS

Marriage brings two people together in a mysterious and wonderful fashion. Good marriages draw those people even closer together, in ever-deepening ways that they never dreamed about at the beginning, so that both people's core experience is this: *My favorite place on earth is in the presence of my spouse.* As the years go by, and as they come to know more and more about each other, the closer and more attached they become. This is the nature of closeness.

Closeness in marriage has to do with a couple's ability to bring all of themselves to each other. They expose themselves to each other, naked and unashamed (Genesis 2:25). This kind of vulnerability is one of the greatest risks you can take. When you allow your mate to experience your neediness and incompleteness, you are giving him or her the freedom to reject those parts of you. Yet in good marriages, the more vulnerable parts often become the most cherished parts, and also the most private. Each partner understands and protects the fragility of the other's heart.

Closeness in marriage also requires dependency. Each person must be willing to need and be needed by the other. Both must be dependent on the presence, compassion, and care of the other to give them the strength to follow God's course. This deep level of intimacy comes from both partners' acknowledging their incompleteness and bringing it to the other for love and comfort.

Another mark of closeness is empathy. Empathy requires the ability to put your own perspective and viewpoint aside for a time in order to take on your spouse's. That means that a husband will put himself into the emotional shoes of his wife and feel what it must be like to be her. In turn, she will put herself into her husband's emotional shoes and feel what it is like to be him. Without empathy, none of us will grow, for no one can grow without feeling understood. This is one of the reasons that Jesus took on human form—to experience the trials of the human experience. "Because he himself suffered when he was tempted, he is able to help those who are being tempted" (Hebrews 2:18).

Sometimes people resist feeling empathy for their mate because they fear that empathizing means approving of something their spouse is doing with which they don't agree. Yet approval and empathy are not the same. You can be understanding and compassionate with your spouse, while clearly not seeing things the same way.

However, closeness is not enough to make a marriage work well. Responsibility provides the protection and structure necessary for closeness to thrive.

◆ BE RESPONSIBLE

The word *responsible* doesn't sound very romantic, does it? It certainly isn't the first word a woman uses to tell her roommate about a guy she likes. Yet in the passage of a lifetime, a sense of responsibility is critical to a healthy marriage. Unless both people are responsible, a couple can't grow in closeness.

When we say that in close marriages both people are responsible, we mean that both partners have a high sense of ownership for themselves and for the marriage. They take on the roles and burdens of the relationship as well as of their individual lives. Each one does what he or she should do, and neither blames the other for things that don't get done. In fact, each person takes on more than what he or she needs to.

It always makes me sad to see a couple try to make a marriage work on a fifty-fifty basis, because it's inevitable that there will be days when one person puts out only 40 percent of the effort. Then, because one person didn't hold up his or her end of the bargain, bills don't get paid, problems aren't confessed or reconciled, a task goes undone, and tempers flare. It doesn't have to be this way—and it won't be if law does not rule the relationship (Matthew 5:41). In good marriages both people are willing to go the extra mile in love, so that the other person is served.

It's not that these couples are codependent or enabling. They aren't. While they are sacrificially caring for the marriage and their spouse, responsible husbands and wives know when their own resources are depleted, when to let their spouse take ownership of some problem, or when to confront. They keep love and limits separate. Each person can say "no" to the other without disconnecting their love and attachment: "And let us consider how we may spur one another on toward love and good deeds" (Hebrews 10:24).

Healthy couples embrace each other's freedom, *even the freedom to be selfish or hurtful.* They understand that you cannot take charge of a life that is not yours, for that is the essence of slavery. While they may not always agree with the other's behavior, and may even take a stance against its destructiveness, they refuse to limit each other's freedom. These wise couples understand that if they do not have the freedom to do the wrong thing, they cannot wholeheartedly do the right thing. This is one of the lessons from the story of the prodigal son (Luke 15:11–32). Healthy couples allow for differences, and *they do not make the other person the bad guy for having freedom.* They protect that freedom, in the name of love.

Finally, couples in good marriages make friends with reality.

◆ MAKE FRIENDS WITH REALITY

Spouses in strong marriages do not have a tendency to try to be some-one they are not. There is no pretense. Each spouse knows the faults and failings of the other, and offers the other acceptance and forgive-ness. Love and the marriage can grow when each spouse has made friends with the reality of who the other truly is.

The very nature of marriage forces this reality. When a husband and wife merge two lives into one, they can no longer hide from each other. The truth emerges as time passes. I remember one day when my wife, Barbi, was talking to me about a school event she had been to with our kids while I was away on a trip. I was really tired from the traveling and was not in the most receptive mood for new informa-tion. I did manage an occasional "uh-huh" so that she would think I was engaged. Yet I wasn't paying attention to what she was telling me, and a couple of hours later, I asked her, "So how did the school thing go?" So much for my being a psychologist who knows how to listen and attend to others!

The person you love the most is the one you can hurt the most. In marriage our imperfections become quickly apparent, but in a healthy marriage both spouses can safely "let their hair down." As a couple they know how to resolve problems, let go of what is not real, forgive, accept, and remain loving and caring toward each other. This last part is important, for it has to do with genuine forgiveness and acceptance. When spouses forgive and accept things, it's not out of some sort of a depressed resignation that says, "That's the way she is. She'll never change, so I guess I'll just have to live with it." It is far more than that—it is accepting reality. When this happens, life often truly begins in a marriage.

When you accept and forgive, it releases you from a dependency on your spouse to make you happy and content. You are free to love your spouse without demanding that he or she be a certain way in order for you to be fulfilled. Love is not self-seeking (1 Corinthians 13:5). When you can accept each other's faults, you can take the time to understand each other's roots, hurts, and sins without reacting. You are also more likely to see your own need for acceptance and the deep need both of you have for the grace and help of God. "Be kind and compassionate to one another, forgiving each other, just as in Christ God forgave you" (Ephesians 4:32). When you can accept and forgive, you allow your spouse to avoid experiencing the wrath of the law (Romans 4:15), offering instead an opening to experience grace, which supports growth.

One of the hallmarks of a good marriage is that each spouse has made friends with reality. Embrace it, and you will find the path to growth.

♦ SEEK GOD'S PATH OF HEALING

Perhaps as you've been reading this chapter, you've been thinking, *My marriage is nothing like that! It has been the greatest disappointment of my life.* Perhaps you've longed for a marriage based on mutual love, values, and purposes, but so far that has eluded you. Or maybe your struggle is internal, say an emotional disconnect between you and your spouse. Perhaps it involves a crisis, such as an affair or abuse.

Part of what makes marital difficulties different from other issues, such as fear, weight, addiction, or depression, is that a good marriage requires two people. If both are truly willing to be *in* the marriage with all of themselves, a disappointing marriage can become a good marriage, even a great one. Yet oftentimes one person has disconnected from the relationship in some way. This can be disheartening, and it poses a genuine obstacle to the marriage's healing in the way God intends.

Whatever your situation, God has not left you alone; he has made a way for you. If you are seeking healing for your marriage, make your prayer to God and your covenant to him the following passage: "Teach me your way, O LORD, and I will walk in your truth" (Psalm 86:11).

God's path of healing for marriage includes the following steps:

1. *Begin with God.* If your spouse has chosen to disconnect from your marriage, either emotionally, physically, or simply from the growth process, understand that God's way does not include changing your spouse unless your spouse invites him to do so. Yet neither will God remove his hand from your life. Your spouse's freedom does not dilute God's power and willingness to help you. Follow him and his ways, no matter what your spouse chooses to do. God's way for you is always that you become the most healthy, loving, holy, and righteous person you can be. That is your part. This choice allows God to use you in redemptive ways: "But seek first his kingdom and his righteousness, and all these things will be given to you as well" (Matthew 6:33).

2. *Identify the underlying problem.* Whatever your marriage struggle, be it emptiness, a parent-child dynamic, or horrible fights, take the time and energy to look below the surface at what is truly going on. While external events should be addressed, especially if they are dangerous (financial ruin, infidelity, physical harm, and the like), at some point you need to get to what is driving the issues in order to deal with the source. Some marital problems have to do with control, some with irresponsibility, some with hurt and weakness that may be *no one's fault*. Some problems are due to a lack of trust, and there are many more. Refer to the chapters in this book on wisdom (chapter 3) and embracing problems (chapter 6) as a guide. Consult with experienced people who can help you see the issues more objectively. Avoid dealing with only the symptom, because the problem will simply reemerge in some other form down the line. For example, if your husband is into Internet pornography, the solution isn't to install blocking software on the computer. Your husband needs to have someone inside his head and heart, helping him face himself, his sins, his injuries, who he is now, and what kind of man he wants to be. Such intervention will provide help and hope of real change—the software will not.

I often hear couples in struggling marriages play the "differences" card. They think that they are so unlike each other that there could be no love or compatibility. In reality, nothing could be further from the truth. In fact, differences add depth, interest, spice, and growth to a marriage. Couples who are clones do not generally have exciting and satisfying marriages.

My parents are a great example of how differences can add to a marriage. They are unlike each other in so many ways. He likes being alone, while she is the social animal of all time. He is casual and she is intense. He is into jazz and she likes opera. The list goes on and on. Yet after fifty-two years, they are still crazy about each other, and a lot of that has to do with the fact that they get joy and pleasure from the quirks and different perceptions of the other. He gets a kick out of seeing how she socializes. She enjoys his depth and perceptiveness about life.

The only type of difference to be concerned about is one in basic values: God, love, honesty, and growth, for example. These values will dictate the path of your life. When people don't agree on these, they need to treat those differences as a problem. As for things like styles, interests, and perceptions, however, differences can add much to the years together.

3. Remove the log from your own eye. Virtually every marital battle involves contributions from both parties. While the contributions may not be equal, each spouse shares part of the burden. So search your own heart, or, as Jesus taught, remove the log from your own eye first (Matthew 7:1–5, NASB), and investigate what you may be bringing to the problem.

In a struggling marriage it is easy for one spouse to feel judged, condemned, or treated as a child by the other. Yet if you come to your mate humbly and gently, having taken ownership of your own part in the problem, your attitude will bring mutuality and grace into the situation. Be diligent to make sure you have, from the heart, dealt with your part.

This is often difficult to do when your mate is out of control or resistant in some area, and you are trying to hold things together. Remember, however, that even the "good" spouse is often guilty of some important problems. You might be avoiding speaking up and confronting an issue that needs to be addressed (Ezekiel 3:18–21).

Or you may have difficulty following up on the consequences you are setting. You may even possess a spiritually superior attitude, the "saint married to a sinner" problem, which can destroy love quickly. Do not be afraid to look into the mirror. God's grace is abundant toward both of you (1 John 3:19–20).

4. Speak the truth lovingly. Marital wounds heal to the extent that truth can be safely spoken, internalized, and obeyed. The truth is the reality of the issue between you. There can be no resolution without a transfer of, and agreement with, the truth. Be direct, but speak with a mind toward healing the problem so that love and growth can increase between the two of you. Show your value of and love for your partner's feelings and situation. At the same time, ensure that the issue is clearly brought out, along with your own feelings about it. Bring out what you desire to happen, now and in the future.

Your task is to deliver the truth while, as far as it depends on you, living at peace with your spouse (Romans 12:18). Beyond that, you cannot control what your mate does. That is between your spouse and God. Your spouse may be grateful to you, hate you (Proverbs 9:8), want to understand the problems from all angles, or be pierced to the heart. Whatever the response, work toward both of you responding to the truth that is there.

5. Use God's resources. When a couple faces a problem together, that alliance of heart goes a long way toward solving it. Yet even if you are alone in your stance, the reality that you are being honest about it and desire God's healing is a major step toward resolution. In either case, an awareness of the problem is generally a beginning, not an end. Most of the time, if a couple could have solved a problem by trying harder or starting over, they would have by now. What is needed is God's grace, people, resources, wisdom, and time to bring the fruit you desire in your life.

Check your sick marriage into the hospital. Get involved with people and places that deal with the kinds of things with which you struggle. If you or your spouse is an addict, go to your pastor, a counselor, Narcotics Anonymous, or somewhere that has people who have experience with these matters. If you and your spouse have found that you are growing apart and are not able to reverse the direction of the marriage, seek help from people experienced with helping couples uncover the causes for the distance and with expertise on how to reconnect. There are well-traveled steps to follow.

Whatever you do, don't fall into the trap of thinking that you and your spouse can solve your marital problems without reaching out. One of the functions of the church is to nurture and mature its people (Ephesians 4:16). Let others into your marriage, heart, and hurts, for that is where restoration lies.

You have many, many resources available to help you. There has been a great deal of marriage research conducted, so people know a good amount now. You will find that the work is not quick, however, so be patient. God brings fruit when we sow deeply, not in shallow soil (Matthew 13:1–23). Give yourself and your spouse time and grace to change patterns that may have been in place since childhood. Live on the balance beam of protecting your hearts from injury (Proverbs 4:23), while at the same time giving love, support, and encouragement to each other (1 Peter 1:22). You and your spouse need forgiveness, love, and hope from each other, as well as honesty, holiness, and good limits.

◆ Go to Him Now

God is true to himself. He reconciled the world to himself (2 Corinthians 5:19). That reconciliation encompasses the difficulties in your marriage. Seek him and the path that he will show you. It may be a difficult one. Yet he walks it with you—and with your spouse. I have seen many couples take the steps we have outlined and find healing for their marriages. I've seen God and his process breathe new life into problematic or even failing marriages, and people's lives have been changed forever. Go to him now, and turn your face the way he leads. He wants your path to lead to his face and the face of your spouse.

11

INTIMACY AND SEX

Sometimes when I (John) am speaking to a group about marriage, I will reverse a stereotype to see if everyone is awake. I'll say something like, "You women just don't get it. All you have on your mind is sex, and we guys just want to be held. Can you imagine what it's like for us to feel like such an object?" Most of the time, people will look at each other with amusement, as if to say, "Yeah, right."

Sex is a significant and important part of being involved in the life of God. We are sexual beings, and God authored and designed sexuality for our good. Sex can result in the creation of children, it brings closeness to a marriage, and it symbolizes God's love for us. God is clearly in the bedroom, and he wants to make that room a place where love, relationship, and his presence belong and are integrated together. He can make a way for you and your spouse so that you can develop a healthy sexual relationship in your marriage.

◆ A GOD THING

Sexuality reflects the nature and heart of God. It is truly a God thing. Sex is deeply rooted in relationship, as God is. A satisfying, intimate sexual life is always built on a foundation of emotional connectedness and love between a wife and a husband. The better the relationship between a husband and wife, the greater the likelihood of great sex. When a husband's eyes meet his wife's during the intimacy of those moments, they are looking into each other's souls. They are reaping the harvest of all the years they have spent in getting to know each other, and celebrating the love that has blossomed, grown, and deepened. They are promising and anticipating a future of even more love, surprises, and new horizons in their union. Sex both reflects and develops love. The two belong, not to themselves, but to each other: "My lover is mine and I am his" (Song of Songs 2:16).

Sex, like God, has a mystery to it that we cannot fully understand. Though we know a great deal about the mechanics of sex, we cannot fathom every aspect of the depth of the attraction between the sexes. So much is involved—from the subtle eye contact that can convey worlds, to the gradual progression of increasing involvement, to the sexual act itself, with all its tenderness, passion, and energy. Its shape and form at any particular time cannot be predicted: romantic and sweet, aggressive and powerful, recreational and athletic, quietly or outrageously humorous, or so deep and vulnerable that it can bring a couple to tears.

That two become one is a mystery. The sexual union symbolizes the fact that two people, though still distinct individuals and souls, have merged their lives to create a new and unique entity in marriage. Scripture states it this way: "For this reason a man will leave his father and mother and be united to his wife, and they will become one flesh" (Genesis 2:24). The sexual act itself portrays this oneness. The sexual climax, one of the greatest and most intense physical sensations we can experience, involves a temporary loss of separate identities, and an emotional merger into the other person. Sexual union also symbolizes, at the highest level, Christ's union with his bride, the church (Ephesians 5:32).

Sex also has a timeless quality. Research tells us that people can be sexually active much later in life than we once thought. While some couples who have been married a short time have a sad, dying sex life, others who have been together for many years still enjoy sexual intimacy as an important and regular part of the marriage. Long past the childbearing years, they connect at the sexual level for closeness, recreation, and a celebration of God's care for them. The difference between these couples has more to do with the character and qualities of the people and the relationship than with their age.

Sex brings together the "sacred" and the "secular." Henry and I always feel very sad when we hear of couples or individuals who have felt forced to bring their sexual concerns to someone outside of the church because their own Christian community's attitude about sex was that it was something dirty. The view of the Church Lady on *Saturday Night Live,* with her crusade against sexuality, does not represent what the Bible teaches about the topic. God, the Author of sex, talks about it in positive and graphic terms: "May your fountain be blessed, and may you rejoice in the wife of your youth. A loving doe, a graceful deer—may her breasts satisfy you always, may you ever be captivated by her love" (Proverbs 5:18–19).

Throughout the ages other religions have included sex with their worship. Though they did not understand what God's full design was, they seemed to have some sense that there is a quality to sex that brings us out of our routine existence. Sex makes us feel and experience something larger than ourselves, and at its best, in a deeply rooted and connected marriage, it gives us a sliver, for a few moments, of a glimpse of the face of God.

◆ BODY AND SOUL

Sex cannot be cleanly parsed into either physical or emotional terms. It is sensual. It is anatomical. It is spiritual. It brings all parts of life together, and is described by experts as being *psychophysiological*— that is, both psychological and physiological in nature. Sex involves our brain and neurological functions as much as it does our emotions and passions. Sexuality gives us a wonderful image of how God integrates body and soul, physical and emotional. Both the physical and nonphysical aspects of our being long to be connected to God (Psalm 63:1); he is involved with all of our being. We have truly been "fearfully and wonderfully made" (Psalm 139:14).

Sex researchers and clinicians have brought home this spiritual reality in the past few decades. They have found that sexual problems are rarely isolated only to one part of a person's life; they often have a physiological, emotional, or relational component. For instance, impotency can be caused by diabetes or atherosclerosis, and premature ejaculation is sometimes helped by antidepressants. It's also true that if a wife feels like her husband is attracted to her only sexually, she may lose interest in sex because she feels like an object. Couples can be quite physically healthy and active, but if they have severe discord in the relationship, their sex life may be nonexistent.

In other words, it is often what is underlying the sexual relationship—the heart of the person or the fabric of the marriage—that is the real issue. You can have a clean bill of health from your physician and know all the sexual techniques you should know, and still have sexual problems. Sex can't be disconnected from our souls. If there are hurts or problems in the soul, they will often manifest themselves in the sexual area.

In addition, God made us sexual beings, apart from the act itself. Being sexual has much more to it than the act of sex. The arena of sexuality is one of the many ways we experience ourselves and others. Just as we notice other people's personalities, styles, career paths, and family situations, we also notice them sexually: how attractive or unattractive they are, whether they are covert or overt, and other areas of sexuality. We need to keep the sexual part of ourselves connected to God, our values, and our support community in order to receive guidance in dealing with the realities of sexual temptation and desire, for when "desire has conceived, it gives birth to sin" (James 1:15). However, whether our sexuality is integrated into our soul or out of control, it is still a part of us.

This spiritual connection of body and soul forms the context of the sexual act. Orgasm, technically the end result of the act of sex, is best viewed as part of a whole, including tenderness, communication, nonsexual body pleasuring, and closeness. Because of this, some sexual experiences will not end in orgasm but simply in arousal and intimacy. (Husbands, pay attention here!) In and of itself, an orgasm is somewhat of a nonevent. Orgasm without relationship, closeness, communication, and love is not truly a meaningful experience between a husband and a wife. Sex is not about orgasm; it is about two becoming one. It's God's desire that you experience the joy that surrounds this mystery.

◆ What Can Go Wrong?

As we've been saying throughout this book, God can make a way for you, even in this area. This is probably a good place to present the categories of sexual problems and dysfunctions that couples can experience.

First, there are problems with *desire,* meaning that a person has little appetite for a sexual relationship. For example, a woman may believe that sex is a good thing, and even perform sexually, but not experience an internal desire for it. This problem can occur at different degrees of severity and for varying lengths of time. Some people have never felt any desire for sex. Others will experience diminished libido after a loss, a life problem, or a medical issue. Still others, while able to have sexual appetites in general, have no desire for their spouse for some reason.

The second category of difficulties concerns *arousal.* God made our bodies to prepare themselves for sex in physiological ways. A woman's vagina begins to lubricate, and her genitals begin swelling. A man's penis becomes erect. When there are arousal dysfunctions, these elements of sexual functioning do not occur as they should. The woman's lack of lubrication can make intercourse very painful for her. The man's lack of an adequate erection, also called impotence, makes penetration impossible.

Third, there are problems with *orgasm.* A woman is either unable to experience an orgasm or finds that it takes a very long time to climax. A man may have the same problem, or the reverse, which is *premature ejaculation,* a condition in which he climaxes too quickly.

These terms are not precise. There is a range of what is normal, healthy, and satisfying to a person and a couple in terms of how frequently they desire sex and can be aroused, and how long it takes to reach orgasm. A lot has to do with finding what makes the couple happy or unhappy, and why.

We have good news for couples who are willing to work on the issues and address all aspects of their relationship—physiological, emotional, relational, and sexual. You can get help for improving your relationship from a competent professional.

Sexual addictions are an increasingly visible sign of a marriage in trouble. (Technically, this is not a true addiction, but more of a dependency.) In these situations, the spouse (more often it is the husband) is spending time on pornography, telephone hot lines with sexual content, strip clubs, or prostitution. This is a heartbreaking situation, as the wife must bear the pain of being betrayed, as well as being deceived by the one with whom she has covenanted her life. This is not a small problem, and most of the time the couple will require help from people experienced in these matters.

The man may attempt to justify his indiscretions by blaming his wife's lack of sexual attractiveness or responsiveness. In reality, the difficulty is not with her, nor is it really with sex either. It generally has to do with some part of him that is disconnected from relationship and life. Sometimes it is a sexualized wish for comfort and validation. In other cases, it is a desire for power, control, or choices. In still others, the man has a conflict between his real self and his ideal self that he cannot reconcile. Or he may be angry and rebellious against the perceived controlling nature of the women in his life.

In these cases, not only does the wife need to realize that it is her husband's issue, not hers, but she also needs to seek outside help and insist that he get help. Such assistance is available, and it works, but the husband must become involved. She needs to use every resource and person available to influence him to get help.

In addition, there are other sexual problems that a spouse might have that can greatly disturb the marital connection, such as gender issues. While we will not deal with these in this book, people facing these problems can find a great deal of hope and help, both personally and as a couple, with trained professionals who have expertise in these areas.

Now that we've dealt with the spiritual core of sexuality and summarized some of the sexual problems in marriage, let's turn our focus to what it takes to have a healthy sex life, and how couples who are struggling sexually can rekindle sexual passion.

◆ Love: The Foundation

A healthy sex life begins with love. Love brings a couple together and allows sex to flourish. Love encompasses sex; it's larger than sex. Love can create the desire for sex, but when the passion of sex is over, love remains. It continues and is present with the couple, holding them close to each other and to the Author of love himself.

A large part of sexual love is *knowing*. The Bible refers to Adam and Eve's sexual relationship with a Hebrew word that means "to know" (Genesis 4:1, KJV), and it indicates a personal understanding and knowledge of the other person. Sexual love is about knowing your spouse, personally and intimately. That means you should know your partner's feelings, fears, secrets, hurts, and dreams, and care about them—and likewise, your partner should know and care about yours.

The vulnerability of sex increases that base of knowing, as husband and wife reveal their innermost souls to each other through sexual love. By its unveiling and exposed nature, sex demands that sort of openness. In sexual intimacy two people show each other the privacy of their bodies as well as the privacy of their hearts and feelings.

Love involves the whole person: heart, soul, mind, and strength

(Mark 12:30–31). Love and sex both require an emotional connection between two people; both should be emotionally present and available. When two people can attach to each other in their hearts, a healthy sex life will emerge and develop. Yet when a couple lacks this kind of intimacy, their sex life will become atrophied because it cannot feed off the emotional connection. This can happen in several ways. Sometimes one mate will withdraw love out of anger, hurt, or a desire to punish the other. Other times one will be unable to take in or receive the other's love. Still other times one mate has an inability to live emotionally in the world. Both people's hearts must be available in order to connect emotionally. If this is not the case, while sex can occur, it more often than not does not have enough fuel to be enflamed.

It's also true that love, and healthy sexuality, cannot exist without trust. Because sex is such a symbol of personal exposure and vulnerability, a healthy sex life requires that couples develop a great deal of trust in each other, trust that the other person will not use what he or she knows to hurt the other person. When people trust each other, they feel free to continue their explorations of one another at deeper and deeper levels. In fact, one of the Hebrew words for trust also means "careless." In other words, when you trust someone, you are careless with him or her. You are not anxious and fearful, editing what you say and feel. You are free to be yourself with the other person, because you can trust that he or she will not do wrong by you.

On the other hand, broken trust will often create sexual problems. This breach of trust doesn't even have to be in the sexual arena, such as an affair or emotional unfaithfulness, though these can certainly be devastating to a relationship. A breach of trust can have to do with a financial matter, such as not being dependable with money, or it may be a commitment matter, such as promising something and not following through with it. Broken trust can greatly diminish a person's desire for sex with a spouse. The deficit in emotional safety translates into a deficit in sexual safety. Broken trust can also affect a woman's ability to achieve orgasm, for a sexual climax requires a great deal of willingness to lose control. If a wife is afraid she can't be "careless" with her husband in some area, she may be unable to let go of her own controls because of her fear. All of the techniques in the world will not cure this. Only God's solution of repentance, ownership, and rebuilding trustworthiness can accomplish it.

Love also changes our focus. It shifts our perspective from an emphasis on "I" to a focus on "we." That is, in love, the whole is truly greater than the sum of its parts. It is not self-seeking (1 Corinthians 13:5); it is relationship-seeking. That's why couples don't talk about building their lives together. They discuss and dream about building a *life* together. There is a continual emphasis on how "we" are and on caring for the other person's welfare. Love is the ultimate cure for self-centeredness and narcissism.

This identification as "we" means a great deal sexually. It means that your spouse desires you, pursues you, and wants to be closer to you. In other words, when you identify yourself as "we" rather than "I," you will see yourself as better off, the more you have of your spouse. It also means that you want to know your partner better, more deeply, and to invest your life in knowing who the two of you are as a couple. This is fertile soil, from which a great sex life sprouts.

I have a friend who has discovered that when he talks with his wife about "our life together" and "what we want," it is a great aphrodisiac. He's not being manipulative—he means what he is saying to her—and his wife is aware that he uses phrases like this instead of "you" and "me" when discussing their goals, desires, and team efforts. Of course, when they discuss themselves as separate people, he doesn't blur their identities either. At any rate, his wife is a very "we" person and derives a great deal of value from being part of a team with him as they explore their lives and make their way in the world. As a result, it turns her on sexually. My friend finds that when he talks in terms of "you" and "I," he just doesn't get the same results—so he is a real "we" person now!

Couples who don't see themselves as "we" can have sexual difficulties. When one person feels that his or her own interests and needs are dismissed, or that the other person has little investment in the union and inordinate interest in living as two singles under the same roof, it can impair both desire and arousal. This can cause impotence in some men. When couples renew their emotional partnership, these problems can start to resolve themselves.

◆ OWNERSHIP: SHARING THE SEXUAL PARTNERSHIP

In healthy marriages, both people wholeheartedly take ownership of whatever they are supposed to do. Both take responsibility for themselves as individuals and as part of the marriage. Jesus said something similar about the way we are to live: "If anyone would come after me, he must deny himself and take up his cross daily and follow me. For whoever wants to save his life will lose it, but whoever loses his life for me will save it" (Luke 9:23–24). In other words, all of us need to take up our own burden in life in order to preserve our lives. Furthermore, as we will see, when both people take ownership in the marriage, it creates a context for healthy sex. Ownership involves shared responsibility, separateness, and self-control.

1. *Ownership means shared responsibility.* Responsibility is an aphrodisiac to a healthy person. For example, when a wife experiences that her husband is who he says he is, is dependable, and shoulders the burdens of his life, she experiences freedom. It frees her from the job of being alone with all the weights of the world on her, because she has someone with whom to share the load. Also, she doesn't have to take responsibility for her partner's life and problems, because he is doing that job for himself. She doesn't have to worry that he won't keep up his end; nor does she worry that she will have to constantly nag him about duties.

She is also free to be more sexual, as part of good sex is the ability to abandon oneself. Because she's free, she feels lighter and younger, and has more emotional energy for sexual connection. Sex has room to exist in her mind and imagination.

When a wife doesn't feel free, however, when she has to bear her husband's burdens as well as her own, it can impair her ability to experience desire, arousal, and orgasm. Without freedom from extra responsibility, sex is too costly a luxury.

In addition, when a wife has to shoulder her husband's load, she will begin to feel like she is married to a child—to someone she must take care of and solve problems for, someone who requires her to put out the fires he sets in life. In turn, he will begin to feel he is married to a parent. He will feel controlled and put down. One of the basic requirements God set down for marriage, and sex in marriage, is that it is *for adults only.* Children are not to marry or to have sex. They are developmentally unequipped for either. So when this parent-child dynamic occurs in a marriage, sexual desire and arousal often begin to decrease. This dynamic can also cause a man to struggle with premature ejaculation, a symbol of his sense that he is being treated as an inexperienced, young child.

I have seen and treated many marriages afflicted with this dynamic, and it can be changed, especially when appropriate boundaries are set. Sometimes the change seems magical, as in the case of Sandra and Jim. They came to see me because he did not take sexual initiative with her. She had to do all the pursuing, and even then he was often uninterested. This was a source of great frustration and pain for Sandra. As we talked, we found out that in the rest of their marriage, Jim never disagreed with Sandra on anything. Whether or not he agreed with her opinions on money, the kids, or work, he would comply quietly, even when he had a different viewpoint or was angry with her. We found that Jim was very afraid of losing Sandra's love, and so he would not jeopardize that by standing against her, as a spouse should. In other words, Jim was fearful of taking responsibility for his adult feelings and differences with Sandra. He was treating her as if she were a mom who he could not disappoint. This childlike attitude toward her resulted in a diminishing of his sexual desire for her. Remember, kids don't have sex with their parents.

In addition, there was a second dynamic in their marriage. Not being sexually interested was also a way for Jim to have a little power; if he couldn't say "no" in life, he could in bed. As Sandra understood these issues, she told Jim, "It's okay for you to disagree and get mad at me. I want to be your wife, not your mom." Jim began taking risks with Sandra, and they began to negotiate differences as a couple should, in love, honesty, and respect. Jim began to feel strong sexual feelings for Sandra, and things began to heat up between them. Later, she reported with a shy smile that their love life had improved dramatically.

Healthy marriages are a mutual covenant of two people, gladly giving up certain liberties and conveniences in order to serve the bond. So when a couple doesn't have a shared sense of responsibility, the relationship is out of balance and often brings dissatisfaction and sexual problems. Not only can we see this in marriages that have a parent-child dynamic but also in marriages where one person tries to control the other. A controlling mate resists the other mate's freedom, choices, preferences, and opinions, and when the other person says "no," a controlling spouse will become angry or withdrawn.

This too can cause sexual dysfunction. There is a large power differential between the two people, and they are not equal in choices and decisions. The controlled spouse does not experience freedom, and as a result love cannot flourish because love grows out of freedom. This lack of freedom produces fear: fear of loss of love, fear of retribution, fear of the other person's anger. The Bible teaches that love and fear cannot coexist: "There is no fear in love. But perfect love drives out fear, because fear has to do with punishment. The one who fears is not made perfect in love" (1 John 4:18). When you are not made perfect in love, the sexual expression of your love is also bound up in fear. You often withdraw inside of yourself sexually, with diminished desire, little arousal, or an inability to achieve orgasm. Sexuality begins to reemerge only when you and your mate reestablish a more mutual power relationship, where neither controls the other.

2. *Ownership means separateness.* Ownership, by definition, creates space between two people—separateness. When two people take responsibility for their lives, they are defining themselves as individuals.

They are saying, in effect, "I love you, but I am not you. You have your feelings, values, and opinions, and I have mine. Let's put them together and make something better as they interact." Separateness is simply realizing that while the two in marriage are one flesh, they are still two souls, each of whom must give an account of him- or herself before God one day (2 Corinthians 5:10).

Separateness helps each person to assist the other's growth. One has a strength from which the other can learn. One has feedback and perspective that the other one needs to hear. This can certainly cause conflict, but not all conflict is bad (Proverbs 27:17). As the saying goes, "If you never disagree, one of you is not necessary." More than this, however, *separateness creates the longing that is required for sexuality.* For good sex to develop, there need to be two clear, distinct, well-defined people in the equation. There is space between these two people. Desire and longing have room to grow, and each wants the other person. When, however, there is little separateness, or when one of the spouses is undefined or highly dependent, it is much more difficult to feel longing. The experience is more that of being smothered by someone's presence or needs. Sexual desire requires someone "over there" whom you can move away from, or closer to. There is freedom, not clinginess. Like the country song title says, "How can I miss you when you won't go away?"

This does not mean that separateness is isolation, detachment, and abandonment. While two spouses are separate, they still share their hearts, lives, and loves. However, while they deeply *love* each other, they *are not each other.* There is a big difference.

3. Ownership means self-control. Self-control, a fruit of the Spirit's work in our lives (Galatians 5:23), has to do with things like having our values dictate our behavior and attitudes, as opposed to allowing our impulses, instincts, and appetites to control them. People without self-control tend to be out of control or are controlled by something else. People who are self-controlled make their decisions based on their heart, soul, and mind all coming to a conclusion about something.

Self-control has a great deal to do with sexuality, as sexual impulses are, at their core, oriented to *now*. Like a small child, they demand instant gratification and release. Sexual impulses have nothing to do with the feelings, timing, or desires of the other person. However, mature lovers are able to tame their sexual impulses so that they serve the relationship, not just themselves. So if you have self-control, you allow your love and value for your spouse (not your passions) to control your sexual urges, "that each of you should learn to control his own body in a way that is holy and honorable" (1 Thessalonians 4:4). For example, women need time to move from their arousal to orgasm. A husband without self-control can have his orgasm too quickly to allow her to also climax. In other situations, a lack of self-control can influence a man to masturbate instead of having intercourse with his wife, as it requires less effort and no consideration of her feelings and situation. In both cases, neither his wife nor the marriage has been served.

◆ ACCEPTANCE: EMBRACING REALITY

Acceptance has to do with being able to relate lovingly and without judgment to everything about your mate. It is embracing the reality of his or her strengths and weaknesses, gifts, and imperfections. It does not mean that you approve of everything about your spouse, but it means you are willing to relate to all of him or her without condemnation, even those parts with which you don't agree or of which you don't approve. God in Christ offers us this kind of acceptance (Romans 15:7).

Sexuality requires you to be open and exposed, with all your blemishes and scars. Acceptance creates an environment in which you and your spouse are aware of what the other lacks, but you don't allow those imperfections to stop the flow of love and gratitude for each other. You are so much in love with the character and soul of your beloved that accepting the body is a small thing. However, if you don't convey acceptance, or your partner does not feel acceptable regardless of what you say and do, then your spouse will tend to hide, emotionally and sometimes physically. For example, a lack of acceptance can cause a wife not to feel comfortable wearing sexy clothing or to want to make love in total darkness. Lack of acceptance can also diminish desire, arousal, and fulfillment. Acceptance opens us up. The lack of it shuts down our hearts.

Husbands who don't feel accepted by their wives may have performance anxiety about being sexually competent. It can drive problems such as impotence and premature ejaculation. However, when spouses work to accept each other without judgment, they can begin to resolve these kinds of problems in their relationship.

Here's an example of what can happen. I know a couple in which the wife, after having two kids, had gotten out of shape. She was not obese, but she did not look or feel the way she wanted to. She felt very physically unattractive, and she was one of those people who tend to be self-critical. Her husband didn't help matters when he nagged her to get back in shape. His pestering joined with her self-condemnation, and she began to feel conditionally loved and under the law of perfection and guilt. As a result, she began to lose her sexual desire.

When they discovered what was going on, her husband rallied to her side. He let her know, "I am really sorry I've made you feel worse about your body. I want you to know that no matter what happens, I love you and I desire only you. Let me know if I put you under the law again, because I don't want you to feel that." His acceptance and grace helped her to feel more loved, and, in time, more sexual. In fact, she began to get back into a good diet and workout program too. Things went well for them after that, but it is important to note that these events happened only after she experienced acceptance from him.

One of the greatest gifts of marriage is that of sex. If you are experiencing difficulties in this wonderful area of life, do not resign yourself to the problem. God has a way, through your growth in him, your marriage, and his resources. Ask him for the next step.

TOXIC PEOPLE AND CONFLICT

I (Henry) was giving a seminar once when a woman asked me, "How do you deal with critical people?" Her question caught me a bit off-guard, and as I was going through all the possible things I could say, a question came to mind. So in response I asked, "Why would you want to do that?"

"Do what?" she said.

"Why would you want to deal with critical people?"

"What do you mean 'why'? Because you have to!"

"Why do you have to?" I asked further.

Obviously, I knew that we all run into difficult people and that sometimes we have to deal with them. Yet the way that she asked the question made me think that she was looking for a strategy that she was planning to use a lot.

She looked at me and said ominously, "Because they're *everywhere!*"

I could not help but laugh. It sounded like she was talking about the birds in the Alfred Hitchcock movie by that name or the corpses in *Night of the Living Dead.* Critical people are not *everywhere*—and if she truly were encountering them everywhere, her experience wasn't normal. I was thinking she might have a hand in why critical people kept appearing in her life.

As I quizzed her, she told me about critical people at her work, at her church, in her family, and within her circle of friends. From the sound of it, she was right. She found them just about everywhere she went. Clearly, something was going on. As we talked, I could see a pattern. It seemed that no matter what situation she found herself in, this woman would somehow find one of the most difficult-to-please people in the group and end up being close to that person. She attracted critical people like a magnet. She drew them to her and then spent her time trying to live up to their expectations.

I explained to her the simplest way that I knew of dealing with hurtful or toxic people. "Be honest with them," I said. "You might never hear from them again."

Okay, let's talk. Do you feel like this woman did—that there is absolutely no escaping difficult people? Do you feel like they are "everywhere"? Do you feel that my overly simplistic answer is true? That all you have to do is be honest, and they will leave you alone?

Most of the time, the truth is somewhere in-between.

We have all found ourselves in situations with difficult people. To some degree, we know that we are not helpless in dealing with them; we can play a part in attracting and encouraging the conflict. We could all use some help from God in making a way for us to respond to people who are hurtful or abusive, influence toxic people to change, and be forgiving and yet take firm stands.

There are many situations in life in which we need God to make a way, but few can be as troublesome as those that involve difficult people. Have you ever wondered why that is true? There is a deep spiritual reason for it, and one that can also unlock the door to understanding why it is so important to deal with and avoid the toxic people in your life.

◆ A SPIRITUAL ISSUE

Over the years I have talked to many people who were dealing with difficult individuals. To a person, they were struggling with an internal dilemma. They wanted to take a stand and address the problem, but a part of them was saying, "If you were doing what God wanted you to do, you would be more forgiving and less judgmental. You would be patient and love the person unconditionally." These beliefs put them in great turmoil. They wanted to be loving people, but at the same time, they did not want to put up with the pain or abuse that they were encountering. Could they be spiritual, loving, and forgiving people and yet not be a doormat? Was that even okay?

If these thoughts reflect your own, please listen to the truth: God never wants anyone to be oppressed by another person. In fact, he always sides with the one who is oppressed. That does not mean that he does not want us to forgive hurtful people, for he certainly does, as many times as is necessary (Matthew 18:21–22). Yet forgiveness and love have nothing to do with whether you are to *deal with* and stop the hurtful things that people are doing to you. You can forgive what has already happened and still say "no" to further pain.

In fact, *the degree to which God can make a way for you often depends on how strong a stance you take against the things that destroy the way that he is making.* Taking a stand against hurtful things that people do and against the things that are opposed to the life that God wants you to create is one of the most positive spiritual things that you can do. God's way is to stand up against bad things. That is what he does, and it is what he tells us to do as well.

God gave his life to us and then created a way for us to give that same life to others. We are to pass his life and his ways of love, responsibility, freedom, creativity, and redemption on to other people. That has been his plan from the beginning, for one life to beget another life. "Life to life" is the theme of the Bible. When God gifts someone with the ability to love or help another person, he says that his love and grace is being passed on. As Peter tells us, "Each one should use whatever gift he has received to serve others, faithfully administering God's grace in its various forms. If anyone speaks, he should do it as one speaking the very words of God" (1 Peter 4:10–11).

One of the primary ways that God gives us what we need in life is through other people, as we said in chapter 2. We repeat it here to remind you of the *power of relationship.* Remember, *a relationship has the power to build you up and be a channel of good things from God to you, and it also has the power to tear you down and keep you from experiencing the life that God wants for you.* That is the deeply spiritual reason that relationships can be so difficult.

◆ DEALING WITH TOXIC RELATIONSHIPS

Therefore, the Bible often warns us to avoid toxic people or at least their toxic behavior. God wants us to be very careful to stay clear of people who can destroy the life that he desires to create for us. Listen to the way that King David put it:

> The deeds of faithless men I hate; they will not cling to me. Men of perverse heart shall be far from me; I will have nothing to do with evil. Whoever slanders his neighbor in secret, him will I put to silence; whoever has haughty eyes and a proud heart, him will I not endure. My eyes will be on the faithful in the land, that they may dwell with me; he whose walk is blameless will minister to me. No one who practices deceit will dwell in my house; no one who speaks falsely will stand in my presence.
>
> —PSALM 101:3–7

David loved God and others with all his heart, and God made a way for him many times. Yet this faithful and loving servant avoided certain kinds of people or dynamics so that they would not "cling to" him (v. 3). The apostle Paul said the same thing when he urged us to avoid certain kinds of people because they could corrupt us (1 Corinthians 15:33). His warning was so strong that he told us not even to eat with people who are hypocritical, saying they are spiritual but denying their behavior (1 Corinthians 5:11). Jesus told us not to give what is holy to dogs or to cast our pearls before swine (Matthew 7:6). The Bible clearly sees relationships as capable not only of doing great good but also of doing great harm if entered into unwisely. The overriding message of Scripture is this: *Love deeply—and be careful.*

Solomon put it this way: "A righteous man is cautious in friendship, but the way of the wicked leads them astray" (Proverbs 12:26). He also said, "He who walks with the wise grows wise, but a companion of fools suffers harm" (Proverbs 13:20).

Most people would be further down the road of growth if they had done one of the following key things:

◆ Avoided toxic people altogether
◆ Taken a strong stand against the hurtful things in a toxic relationship, and meant it
◆ Separated themselves from people who had destructive patterns and yet were unwilling to change despite many loving efforts
◆ Sought out people who could give them good things and the strength to do the three things above

Relationships carry power, power to do good or power to do evil. *One of the most spiritual things that anyone can do is to combat toxicity by avoiding it or by confronting it.* God has spent a few thousand years doing this very thing! The story of Scripture is the story of God dealing with toxic people who hurt him and others. He confronts toxicity and works with it, but ultimately he draws the boundary and puts an end to it. He does so by letting toxic people be themselves—just not with him. He separates himself and allows them to go their own way. He does not control them or force them to change. He just refuses to take part in their darkness.

When you think about it, this is pretty much what I said to the woman who asked about how to deal with critical people. I did not tell her to try to win them over or to change them in some way. I just told her to do what God does, what Jesus did, and what we are to do as well. When I said, "Just be honest with them. You might never hear from them again," I was describing the process of living out your values and then letting the person deal with you and the light that you emit. Your best defense against the harm of toxic people is to be like David and have a clear set of values that you live out with all people. One of three things will happen:

1. The people who are good for you will respect your values, and you will enjoy good relationships with them.
2. As you take a loving stand against toxicity, you will influence some toxic people to change their behavior, and then you will enjoy good relationships with those people.
3. Some toxic people will remain in denial and move away from the light that you are living out despite your loving confrontation of their behavior. Your relationship with those people might even end, in extreme cases.

This is the way that God has made for all of us when we encounter toxic people. When we follow his path, we will not only enjoy many good relationships, but we will also deal with the difficult ones. This means not simply walking away from those who are difficult or harmful. Instead, you must first lovingly work with them to change. Don't nag them or ignore or attempt to control their toxic behavior; simply refuse to participate in their darkness. As an honest and loving person of light, live out that light by living out good values and kindly taking a stand against darkness. Face the problem, and require that the toxic person do the same. If that person is wise, he or she will repent and change, and the relationship will be good again. You can offer forgiveness, and then the two of you can go forward.

Jesus gave us this same model for dealing with relationship problems, and he also gave us the key for determining what kind of person we are dealing with when he said: "If your brother sins, rebuke him, and if he repents, forgive him. If he sins against you seven times in a day, and seven times comes back to you and says, 'I repent,' forgive him" (Luke 17:3–4). When someone hurts us, we are to deal with the problem. If that person repents, even time after time, we are to forgive him or her. Yet this verse also gives us an important principle for determining whether we are dealing with a person who can change his or her toxic behavior. Safe people have *the ability to see where they are wrong, apologize, and change direction.* To repent means to have a change of mind, to see the harmfulness of the behavior and make an effort to change. Even if that effort is not perfect or perfectly sustained (for whose is?), if the person truly sees the harm the behavior is inflicting and makes a visible effort to change, the relationship can go forward with positive results.

Repentance and forgiveness are essential to any good relationship. We all need to forgive and be forgiven in order to have relationships at all. Yet forgiveness moves forward to reconciliation only when the one being forgiven admits that he or she was wrong and then makes a change of direction. So be willing to forgive, but do not give forgiveness and reconciliation to someone who is not willing to change destructive behavior. If you are being seriously hurt, take a stand. If the person sees the problem and repents, then you have solved the problem. How? *You did it by living out your values.* As Proverbs 11:6 says, "The righteousness of the upright delivers them." *By doing right, you have delivered yourself.*

◆ THE SIMPLE PATH (NO ARGUMENTS)

When you are dealing with difficult people, be prepared to encounter a lot of resistance, arguments, justifications, excuses, attacks, and the like. Just learn to accept that as part of the territory and do not try to fix it. That is not your job, and the less you get caught up in rabbit trails, the clearer things will be for you. Here is what confrontation should look like:

◆ The other person makes an offense.
◆ You go to that person and tell him or her how the behavior hurt you, using statements that are nonjudgmental, factual, and stating your feelings, values, and wishes. For example:
   "Joe, yesterday you told me that you were coming by for

dinner at 7:00. I prepared it and was looking forward to it. When you didn't show and then called at 9:00 to say you weren't going to make it, I was hurt. I value having my time respected. So please do not leave me in the lurch again."

"But, Susie, the guys came by and we went out for a few drinks, and I just didn't know what time it was. Don't be so critical. It's not that big a deal."

"Right now, Joe, we are not talking about the reasons for your behavior. I am interested in knowing that you hear me. Do you understand that it was hurtful to leave me hanging and that I do not want to be treated that way again?"

◆ If the person owns up to his or her hurtful or disrespectful behavior and apologizes, you may offer forgiveness and go on. You have solved the problem. However, if the person gets defensive or angry, do not get into an argument. Kindly let the person know that you will talk about it further when he or she has had some time to think about it and see how important it is to you. Keep your stand. If a person fails to take ownership for destructive behavior, he or she will repeat the behavior.

◆ SOMETIMES NOT SO GREAT AN ENDING

Wouldn't it be nice if confrontation ended positively every time? Wouldn't it be nice if every time you confronted a hurtful person, he or she repented and you could go on? Of course it would. In fact, God would like for that to be true also. Yet that is not the case. What then?

If the person doesn't respond to the initial confrontation, we need to take a stronger stand by giving him or her some consequences. Consequences work at times when talking does not. For example, if your spouse gets argumentative when you bring up an issue, and continues to do so despite your requests otherwise, you can tell your spouse, "I would love to talk about this. But as I have told you, I don't like the angry attacks. So I will talk to you about this issue only when a counselor is there. I will make an appointment, and if you want to talk to me about it, I will talk there." Consequences should not be punitive, just something that naturally follows the behavior.

Here are some other examples of natural consequences:

- "I value talking to people, not being yelled at. I will be in the other room when you stop yelling and want to talk."
- "I have asked you to limit your drinking. When you don't, I will ride home with someone else."
- "I do not associate with drugs. As long as you are not dealing with your problem, I won't be seeing you."
- "I will not sleep with you as long as you are into pornography. I will not share myself with others, even in your mind."
- "Honesty is one of the most important things in any relationship. What happened the other day was not honest. I cannot go forward until we solve that."
- "Kindness is an important value to me. What you did was mean, and it hurt. I do not allow myself to be treated like that. When you can see that what you did was wrong, let me know."
- "I desire feedback, not condemnation. What you gave me is not helpful. They were only put-downs. If you can be constructive in your criticism, I will be glad to listen. Do you understand?" If the person says "yes," great; but if the person says "no," say, "Then until you can say it nicely, please keep your thoughts to yourself."
- "Faithfulness is one of the most important things in a relationship. I will not tolerate being cheated on. You can leave until you figure out what you are going to do about making this right."

In addition, you might need to bring other people into the conflict, as in an intervention. (See Matthew 18:15–17 for a gradual progression from talking to intervention to separation.) We bring in others who have some leverage in the person's life in order to turn up the heat and to get the person to see the problem. It's critical to remember that we cannot control another person's response to confrontation and the truth. That is between the other person and God. All we can do is confront in love and offer consequences. If that person does not respond to the light, and the issue is serious, the blueprint still applies: *Stand on your values. Do not go forward to participate in evil.* You remain in the light. If the person wants to remain in the darkness, so be it, but you are not to participate. You may need to separate yourself from this person until he or she faces the issue and is willing to change the harmful behavior.

For example, let's say you are in a marriage or a significant relationship with a person who is engaged in substance abuse. You have tried to get your partner to see the light. Having said and done it all, you finally say, "I cannot get you to change. You will have to make that choice for yourself. Yet I cannot be around this kind of behavior any longer. I cannot be with you until you see this."

When we don't follow God's blueprint for dealing with difficult people, we complicate the situation. We usually go off of God's path in one of two ways. Either we put off dealing with the problem or deal with it unhelpful ways, like nagging or being judgmental, or we just leave and avoid the person without lovingly confronting him or her. Remember, God's way is to bring light and life. Relationships are sacred, and we are not to separate ourselves from them easily. Separation is never meant to be the first thing we do, unless there is danger or destruction, as with child abuse or other very destructive things. First, we should confront the person. Talk about the hurtful behavior and try to help the person to see what is going on. Be patient and loving in that process (Galatians 6:1). We are trying to give the person a chance to change. We should separate ourselves from someone only after we have confronted him or her many times, enforced consequences, and even brought in others to help.

God's way for you always resides in your being a person of light instead of darkness. Do the tough work of trying to resolve problems.

Set your values as David did, and then take a stand on those. When you do, you will be naturally avoiding destructive patterns and ensuring a path for your future that avoids many pitfalls.

We need to take a stand against bad things.

◆ IMPERFECTION OR TOXICITY?

A decade ago, John and I wrote a book called *Boundaries* (Zondervan, 1992). It's about setting limits in relationships in order to end destructive patterns and bring about healing and reconciliation. In talking with some people who have read the book, we've realized that a few have selfishly misused the point, which is to make relationships better. Instead, these people have tried to use boundaries to control other people or to make a big deal out of very small issues. So understand what we mean when we say that you are to avoid toxic people: *Imperfect behavior is not the same as toxic behavior.* It's important to learn the difference between problems that we should expect in relationships because people are imperfect, and problems that are toxic and need to be worked through or else avoided.

The Bible teaches us that not all things or people are toxic. There is no reason to start a war over someone's immaturity or imperfections that rub us the wrong way. That is the time for us to grow in patience and longsuffering, the ability to wait on people as they grow and mature. Listen to the advice of Proverbs: "A man's wisdom gives him patience; it is to his glory to overlook an offense" (19:11).

Wisdom tells us that not every battle or imperfection is the place to take a stand. Sometimes it is not the right time or season to worry about a certain problem or issue. Other times, the issue is not worth worrying about at all. It says more about our own perfectionistic demands than it does about the other person. We all have to learn to be patient with one another's imperfections and flaws, and to give each other time to grow.

The key tends to be the degree to which someone is not being the person we want him or her to be, versus the degree to which that person is destructive to us or to him- or herself. Avoiding toxic people will keep you on the path that God has set. *Yet if you avoid imperfect people and refuse to love them, you will get off the path that God is making for you.* Your path will always include imperfect people, just like you and me. Don't be too demanding or judgmental. Love others, and be patient. It is the only way to build long-term relationships. However, if a person's behavior toward you is truly destructive, and that person refuses to repent and change, then that is the time for stronger limits. You are to avoid things that destroy at all costs.

◆ IN THE WORKPLACE

There are some scenarios in life where it is not prudent to have the kinds of confrontations we've been talking about, like prisoner of war camps or some work situations! Whenever I teach on this, I get a question about the workplace, because people often do not feel free to say anything, out of fear of losing their jobs.

I appreciate that, as there is a hierarchy of needs in life. It's more critical that you have food and clothing than a boss who is kind to you. However, that does not do away with the need to be treated in humane ways either. If you are in a toxic work environment, here are some thoughts to consider.

First, people are usually more able to hear feedback than we give them credit for. You may be able to let someone know how his or her comments or behavior affect you. Look past your fear to see if he or she takes feedback from others, for example. If so, then you might just need courage.

If you do think you can talk to the person, then ask if he or she would like some feedback about how to improve your working relationship. If the answer is "yes," then tell the person that certain remarks or actions have hurt you and made it difficult for you to do your work and that you would like for him or her to not do that anymore. That is pretty simple.

Second, make sure that you are not looking for validation from your boss. You have to give up that wish and find your compliments somewhere else, or get another job. If your workplace is toxic, you have to leave your needs for affirmation at the door and allow your friends to meet that need. Do not try to get something from the person that he or she can't provide. If you need the job, do your work and get your pay.

If the situation is really bad, and talking does not work, then you still have some options. Get together with a few others in your office who have the same problem and request a meeting with the boss. It is more difficult to stay in denial with three people talking to you than it is with just one. Or tell your boss that you do not feel like you are getting resolution on the issue and that you would like another manager to meet with you. Different companies have different policies for handling grievances, but your company likely has one. Talk to someone in HR about the policy. If your company doesn't have such a policy, you will have to ask yourself some tough questions.

Are you ready to take the risk of dealing with the problem? People do get punished for trying to solve problems. It is not the norm, but it does happen. You have to deal from a position of strength, not need. If you need a job, you have to take care of your need first. That means either knowing that you have another job in place or doing something to up your skills and "hire-ability." If you are going to make waves, do not do it from a position of need. Get to a position of strength first. Have other options, just in case.

If a person is really abusive or you are wrongfully terminated for trying to solve a problem, then you may have to talk with a lawyer. God instituted the law to protect societies from destructive people. Labor law protects you from discrimination, harassment, abuse, unsafe workplace issues, and other things. If toxic people have hurt you, you can always talk to a good attorney. However, stay away from the ones who are looking for any reason to sue employers. They usually have bad reputations in the city, and you do not want to be led astray. You simply want just and fair treatment, so make sure that if you have to go that route, you pick honest counsel.

Let's go back to Susie, the client I mentioned in chapter 2. If you remember, she was growing and doing well. God was making a way for her. Yet when she reconnected with some toxic people in her life, she began to go backward. At that point, we had some new work to do, and it was not the work that she expected. My hunch is that the same might be true for you as well, if you struggle with toxic people.

One approach I could have taken was to tell her that these interactions had put her behind and that we needed to turn around and regroup. "Put them and their negativity behind you and let's go forward." That sounds like good advice, but it would have violated many of the life principles we read about earlier in the book. If Susie had continued forward, trying to forget these people and their influence and failing to look at the role that *she* played in allowing them to have that influence, then she would only have failed further down the line.

Susie needed to recognize some things that allowed her to get caught in the snare of toxic people in the first place. Remember the proverb about guarding your heart? "Keep your heart with all diligence, for out of it spring the issues of life" (Proverbs 4:23, NKJV).

Susie had something to do with the fact that these people could ensnare her. If I had not told her that, I would have rendered her a hopeless victim to other toxic people as well. I wanted to empower her so that she would no longer allow toxic people to get her off the path that God was making for her.

So I went to work with her on the principles we have discussed here. Susie had to use many of them in overcoming her tendency to fall prey to toxic people:

- ◆ She began with God by asking him to show her where she needed to grow and to empower her to do it.
- ◆ She chose some wise, supportive people to help her get back on track and work through the issues regarding her desire for her family's approval and her lack of assertiveness.

- She learned the principles discussed in this chapter about taking a stand against relationships with hurtful dynamics.
- She learned to be assertive and how to confront kindly and directly.
- She dealt with some old hurts and dynamics with her family that made her still seek their approval and desire their validation. She learned not to be so passive with them.
- She connected with some external structure to keep her on the path, including a twice-a-week support group meeting.
- She stayed in counseling.
- She looked at herself and the part that she played in getting sucked in by toxic people.
- She saw it as an opportunity to learn how to avoid relapse.
- She gave herself the season to grow.
- She took all the parts of herself to God that needed to change and do things his way, even when it was hard.

As Susie continued down her path, she had found the courage to say "no" to the old boyfriend with the help of her support system. A new one came along who seemed "wonderful" and was very charming, and she quickly fell for him. Yet soon, he too began to be controlling. This time, however, it didn't take long for Susie to recognize her patterns of passivity and allowing him to dominate her. She used her new skills in confronting destructive behaviors. Her boyfriend put up a fight and got defensive, but Susie held her ground. Before long, he was gone. "How appropriate," I told her.

At first Susie did not understand. She was sad over the loss. Yet soon she began to see what Jesus taught. She did not have to judge this guy at all or try to figure out how to deal with him. All she had to do was to live out the light, and he answered the question for her. Her boyfriend had "judged himself" to be unworthy of the light of the new life that God was making for her. As Jesus put it, "This is the verdict: Light has come into the world, but men loved darkness instead of light because their deeds were evil. Everyone who does evil hates the light, and will not come into the light for fear that his deeds will be exposed" (John 3:19–20).

When Susie lived out the light that Jesus lived out, she got the same result that he sometimes gets. She was rejected, but for good reason. She was too healthy to date a toxic person. I rejoiced with her.

Susie had passed a test. She was growing, and as she did, she slowly began to "draw" good people to herself, including good men. I am not altogether sure how that happens. I know that something spiritual is at work, that God made this world so that "light attracts light." I have seen this over and over. Healthy people attract healthy people, and our unhealthy parts attract toxic people.

Susie would never have been able to move forward on the path that God wanted to make for her, had she been stuck in her pattern of putting up with toxic people. She had to learn to take a stand, to change that dynamic, and when she did, she discovered the truth of what I'd said to the woman in the seminar. Just be someone of the light, and chances are you will never hear from the toxic people in your life again.

CHILDREN AND PARENTING

Parenting can literally force us to reach out to God and his ways. Good parents give a great deal of themselves in order to rear their children to become loving, responsible adults. We give our heart, soul, mind, and strength. Yet parenting constantly brings us face to face with our own inadequacies, making us aware of our dependence upon God for help, guidance, and the resources to do our job well.

I (John) will never forget the night our older son, Ricky, had a severe asthma attack and was having difficulty breathing. My wife, Barbi, and I knew we had to get him to an emergency room immediately. Barbi stayed with Benny, our other son, and I hurriedly secured three-year-old Ricky into his car seat in back of the car and took off for the hospital.

Every second of that twelve-minute trip was a nightmare, because I couldn't see my son's face to see if he was still breathing. So I would say to him, every few seconds, "Ricky, if you're okay, say, 'I'm okay, Dad.'" And he would say, "I'm okay, Dad."

Remembering that eternally long drive still brings tears to my eyes, as I can distinctly recall how terrified I was that I might lose my son. I can also remember just as distinctly how desperately I prayed to God to preserve Ricky's health and very life. That night, I truly understood what it meant to depend on God for help.

As we look at how God makes a way through the joys and fears of parenting, we'll focus on three things: the origin and purpose of parenting, the key things you need to teach your kids, and some universal principles for handling difficulties. We'll start where everything good begins.

◆ THE FIRST AND LAST PARENT

Parenting begins with God, the Parent of all of us. He is the Author and Finisher of the parenting process, the first and last Parent. He created and birthed the human race. He breathes his life into us, calls us his sons and daughters, protects us and nurtures us, and disciplines and trains us. He designed things so that he would always be our Father, and we his children. "Have we not all one Father? Did not one God create us?" (Malachi 2:10).

All of this has a purpose: God parents us so that we will be transformed from kids to adults. He wants us to grow up. In the spiritual and personal world, the theological term describing this process is "sanctification," by which we become no longer children but adults. We are to grow up in our salvation (1 Peter 2:2).

All of this is deeply related to human parents and their kids, because God not only raises us himself but he also uses us to help accomplish his purposes. He delegates a great deal of the work to parents. We parents take on the burden of representing God and his ways to our children. Yet God doesn't expect us to do this task alone, without guidance or help from him. His design is that we come to him for the resources needed to do the tasks of parenting. So if you are a parent, you are standing in God's stead for your child and also depending on him to give you the guidance to do the job.

All this is to say that parenting uniquely brings together the spiritual and the personal. The psalmist says, "Yet you brought me out of the womb; you made me trust in you even at my mother's breast"

(22:9). What a tender picture of spiritual and personal worlds coming together! As newborns nurse, they are learning to trust their mother's care and safety. On another level, they are learning to trust the Eternal Parent also, in preparation for a relationship with his care and safety. Every time you, as a parent, help your children grow in some way, you are preparing and helping them for an eternal walk with God himself.

That's a tall order, but God makes a way for parents to do their job well.

◆ From Here to There

As we mentioned, God's purpose is to grow up his kids, and that is the parents' goal as well. Good parents provide an environment that, over time, prepares their children to enter the adult world and flourish in it. Simply stated, our goal is to create *independently functioning adults* who can accomplish the tasks, duties, and responsibilities of life on their own, without being dependent on the resources of parents.

Children by their very nature are *dependent;* they cannot function or survive on their own. If they could, they wouldn't be children. Kids don't possess the abilities to manage life's demands, requirements, and problems. The job of the parent is to provide love, truth, experiences, and other things that help the child develop the abilities he or she will need to become independent of the parent. The Bible describes the process this way: "For this reason a man will leave his father and mother and be united to his wife, and they will become one flesh" (Genesis 2:24). That is God's ultimate design for parenting: giving children all the necessary ingredients they need to leave their first home and establish a home of their own.

No one ever said this would be easy. One of the most difficult aspects of parenting is that the job ends. *Parenting is successful when it has ceased being parenting.* So when your kids no longer need you and are functioning on their own, you hang up your parenting cleats and change roles. Instead of being the repository of resources your children need to survive, you hopefully become good, close friends with them. In other words, God's design for you as a parent is to be constantly *working yourself out of a job*. When your kids leave your home, they should no longer be dependent on you emotionally or financially.

As parents we need to let our kids go—and therein lies the challenge. You see, parenting is at heart a relationship; we have deep and loving feelings toward our children. The more time and emotion we invest in others, the closer we become to them, the more we care about them, and the more we want their presence and love in return. All other types of relationships, such as marriage and friendships, are designed to grow and increase in depth and love, with no end in sight.

However, parenting is different. Since its goal is separation and leaving, it is the one exception to the Grand Design of relationship. In fact, *parenting is the only relationship God designed with the goal being that it ends.* That is why, in a sense, if you are a good parent, you are headed for a heartbreak. You spend years loving, training, denying yourself, and sacrificing for your children, and in return they move away from you! The Bible reflects this reality in the passage just quoted from Genesis. The Hebrew meaning for the word translated "leave" actually includes the idea of "to abandon or forsake."

That is the costliness of parenting. We embrace that heartbreak and sadness, knowing that it is our very heart that our children have internalized over the years. It is our very heart that has given them their own hearts, so that they have the strength to leave and follow their true Father in the ways he has prepared for them.

Some parents have a hard time with this, because they do not want to experience the pain of their child's leaving them, and they unknowingly resist helping their kids grow up so that they will always be dependent and nearby. Some parents blame their child, causing him or her to feel guilty and conflicted about leaving the nest. Others withdraw emotionally, so as not to feel the pain, which then communicates to the child that he or she is hurting them by following God's path. We hope that you can accept the reality of your children's goals and destiny, feel all the love and sadness you have for each one, and help each one leave successfully and well, with all your support and help.

◆ What Your Child Needs to Learn

Now that you understand the big picture of parenting, let's focus on some of the lessons your child needs to learn in order to mature in life. Keep in mind that your child needs help in learning each of these throughout childhood, from infancy to the teen years. Parenting involves a fluid and constant ability to be dealing with all of these areas at all times. To accomplish this, you'll need wisdom, observation, prayer, and the support of others who will help you.

1. *Love and connect with others.* The most important and fundamental ability that your child needs your help in learning is how to *connect in relationship.* God designed us for emotional connection, or bonding, with himself and with others, as we saw in Psalm 22:9. This connection happens in three different ways. It is first the task of reaching outside of ourselves for what we need. This means taking the initiative to respond to our isolation, pain, or hurt and asking another for something. Second, connection requires that we learn to receive, accept, and take inside us what we need from others, such as love, comfort, soothing, grace, or encouragement. Third, it involves learning to use what we have received in ways that help us survive and grow.

To put all three together, let's look at how connection happens with babies and then how it happens as the child matures and becomes a teen. For the sake of this example, let's say the baby is a girl. When the baby feels lonely, she cries or fusses as a way to signal to her mom that she needs love and attention. Mom responds by picking up and holding her daughter, and the baby becomes less agitated, calmer. Sometimes her eyes even "drink in" her mom. The baby has received what her mother has offered. After a while, the baby will wiggle and become restless again, signaling that she has used the "fuel" of love that Mom has provided and is tanked up and ready to start crawling around. Or she may simply go to sleep, having used the love to calm down inside enough to rest. Either way, the baby has utilized the relationship with her mother to get what she needs.

When the baby girl becomes a teenager, she goes through the same process, but it looks different. For example, let's say she has a problem with a boyfriend. If things are going well, she goes to lots of people for love and relationship, including her parents, peers, and other safe adults, such as youth workers and the like. She telephones, asks, and talks. Then she receives the comfort and advice of others to help her. After that, buoyed by the love and help, she hopefully solves the issue with her boyfriend.

We teach our children how to connect emotionally by helping them experience that if they reach out for love, good things happen. Children need to learn that whatever is going on with them, "home base" for them is relationship. So much of helping kids with this is simply "being there." God designed your kids to need you. Not only do they need you to provide them with food, clothing, and protection, but they also need you to fill up the relational void in their hearts. So when you are present and responsive to them emotionally, you are helping them develop their ability to connect or bond with others in relationship. Your baby boy reaches his arms out and you are there. Your school-age daughter carries on endlessly about her day in school, and you listen and respond. Your teenage son is struggling with his self-image, and you empathize.

In order for your children to learn how to reach out to others for the rest of their lives, they need many, many experiences in receiving your love and support, so that they can internalize these positive experiences and use them for survival and growth. Numerous studies show that people who have received steady doses of healthy love live longer and better lives than those who have been deprived of it. They have internalized healthy love, made it a part of their soul, and turned it into something they can draw on through life, whether to self-soothe or to gain courage in times of aloneness, stress, or conflict.

Yet if your children are going to connect with others throughout life, they need more than your internalized love. They also need your help in becoming proficient at the task of finding, connecting with, receiving, and giving emotionally to others. In other words, don't allow them to depend on only you; expand their world to include nurturing relationships with others who are safe. Some friends of mine did this. Their grown kids can now make friends with just about anyone, and everyone loves them. While they love their parents, they are also out in the world, meeting people and going places. When I asked the mom how this had happened, she said, "I took them everywhere and forced them to meet people of all kinds." From the time they were young she had exposed her kids to others, enabling them to experience that people besides Mom could be fun, loving, and helpful.

Finally, as your children mature, they need to learn that it is more blessed to give than to receive (Acts 20:35). Altruistic, selfless love— the highest form of emotional connection—gives back what it has received. God loves us with this kind of love. When we help our kids to be grateful for the love they have received, to take responsibility for it, and to learn to give to others out of that bounty, they will be much more likely to love God and others in selfless ways. It is the best road to follow.

2. *Shoulder the burdens of life.* I have a friend whose teenage sons are very relational, caring, and fun to be around. At the same time, they don't know where the dishwasher is or how meals end up on the table, because my friend does it for them and doesn't require them to learn those sorts of tasks. So while they are loving people, these kids' lives are marred by a lack of self-control and responsibility.

Love needs structure and form. Just as the heart needs a skeleton, love requires another ingredient; it needs *ownership,* the ability to take upon one's own shoulders the responsibilities, burdens, and problems of life. "For each one should carry his own load" (Galatians 6:5).

It may seem odd to think of a child, especially a young one, learning ownership. Children certainly are too young, inexperienced, and frail to take full responsibility for their lives. Yet they can learn to do so gradually. Little by little, as your children mature, you can ask them to carry more and more responsibility, so that by the time they are ready to leave home, *they, not you, are taking ownership of their own behavior, life, goals, and problems.* The young adult who has learned how to shoulder the burdens of life is ready for the responsibilities that come with marriage and career.

Children begin to take ownership even as infants. Babies learn how to signal their mom when they are lonely, an experience that forms the intersection of bonding and ownership. Moms need those signals of crying, whimpering, or squirming in order to know how to meet their babies' needs. Mothers learn which cries are about hunger or holding or changing. In a sort of learning feedback loop, infants learn to signal their mothers for what they need, and as good things result, they experience that as they "own" their signals, they can be in some sort of control of how their needs are met. Through trial and error, toddlers can learn how to treat their friends and to take some responsibility for their behavior and attitudes. School-age boys can be responsible for getting their homework done, doing chores, and deepening their friendships. Teens can begin to own their outside interests, spiritual values, sexuality, and career dreams.

Parents need to be intentional about transferring ownership. While your kids will reach out to you for connection, they are quite content to let you take on the burdens of caring for them, solving their problems, and dealing with the consequences of their actions. A child separated from his mom in the supermarket will search for her frantically, but how many teens offer to pay the bill when they go out for a meal with Mom or Dad? Who am I kidding, right? Yet you can teach your kids to take ownership for their lives. The Bible refers to this as a training process: "Train a child in the way he should go, and when he is old he will not turn from it" (Proverbs 22:6).

To successfully train your kids to take ownership, you need to give them four things: *love, rules, choices, and consequences.* They need your love and care to be able to tolerate the pain of learning responsibility. They need rules—house rules, conduct rules, and social rules—so that they know what is right and wrong. They need the freedom to make choices to keep or disobey your rules. And they need consequences to learn that their choices have an effect on their lives.

This is a little story about a little thing, but it serves the purpose of illustrating this point. My wife and I think that people should say "please" when they ask for something, and we trained our kids to do this. First, we made sure they knew we loved them and were on their side. Then, we told them that we wanted them to say "please," because it shows care and respect for the other person. We also said that if they didn't say it, whatever they were asking for would not be available for a period of time, a minute or a few minutes. That might be a hamburger or it might be the telephone. Third, we gave them the freedom not to say "please"; we didn't nag them about it. Fourth, when they forgot the word, they didn't get what they wanted until the time period was up, even if they said "please" twenty times. We've done our best to be consistent, and now our kids rarely forget to say "please."

Remember that in helping kids learn ownership, what is important is not just them *hearing* our instructions but also *experiencing* the consequences of not responding to us.

3. *Adapt to reality.* The third important ability to develop in your child is how to live in a place called reality. Reality is the world as it really is. It is what exists, what is here and real. The better your children learn this, the more equipped they will be to deal with life in adulthood.

In the beginning, before Adam and Eve's fall, reality had no blemishes or marks. Everything was perfect. There were no sins, hurts, or wounds. Clearly, things have changed. We live in a world where people hurt each other, fail, and suffer imperfections and losses, and this world is the reality into which your children have been born.

Children can't handle the demands of reality—they are natural perfectionists and idealists. Many kids expect to be perfect, and unless their parents teach them by example that it's okay to fail and that everyone makes mistakes, they punish themselves harshly when they fail, or they simply give up, unwilling to risk failure again. Kids may also expect perfection from you, their friends, God, or the world. When others fail them, let them down, or hurt them, they may get angry or argumentative, protesting that things aren't fair. Some kids will learn to externalize, or blame all bad things on those around them, so as not to deal with the reality of their own limitations.

I'm willing to bet that you know some adults who respond to failure and disappointment like this. Not only are they miserable, they make everyone around them miserable too. As a parent, you play a key role in making sure your child doesn't become one of those unhappy adults.

God has made a way for us to resolve the struggle of living in a fallen world. His solution is: *grief, forgiveness,* and *acceptance.* If you can help your children learn to grieve, forgive, and accept, they will be able to adapt to whatever comes their way in life. In a nutshell, here's what each of these means:

- *Grief* is an emotion of sadness. If children learn to feel the loss and value of something they want but cannot have, they eventually resolve their feelings and move on.
- *Forgiveness* is a legal term that means canceling a debt that is owed. It means letting go of our right to punish another. When we receive forgiveness, we are receiving freedom from our own debts. When children experience forgiveness, they learn freedom from condemnation, and they also learn to give up revenge for love.
- *Acceptance* is the ability to deal with reality, in both heart and mind. When we accept the way things are, we stop fighting for what cannot be and become content with what is. Children who learn to accept life learn to live within its parameters,

instead of struggling to be someone they are not or demanding that someone else be who they are not.

Recently my wife and I decided to have a large tree in our backyard cut down. It was too big, and the root system was ruining the yard. The morning the crew came to do the work, we woke up our kids early to watch the guys with the chain saws. To our surprise, one of our kids was horrified. He loved that tree. It had been there all his life, and it reminded him of many happy memories. He became angry, hurt, and upset about losing it. To him, Mom and Dad were bad for having the tree cut down. He said, "You never even asked me what I thought about cutting down the tree." He thought he would never get over it. We talked about it with him several times over the next few days. Each time we talked, elements of empathy, understanding, and reality came in. We would ask him, "How are you doing with the tree thing?" He would say, "I'm still mad at you guys." We would say, "We understand. It must be really tough to have a great tree and then have it gone so suddenly like that. You must be really angry about that, and you probably miss the tree a lot." Gradually, he became sad instead of mad. He figured out that Mom and Dad didn't need forgiveness (at least on this issue), and he accepted the loss of the tree. Finally, he began to have fun with the extra space in the backyard.

Make reality a part of your parenting. As you do, you'll enable your kids to deal with the realities of today, in order to be free to become better people tomorrow.

◆ What Do I Do If . . .

As every parent knows, at times problems can be synonymous with parenting. Even if you are applying the principles in this chapter, your children can have difficulties—or may cause some difficulty—that you aren't sure how to address.

Be thankful that you are there to help your children through this.

It is far better for kids to experience these challenges with you than by themselves or with people who don't have their best interest at heart. What better place to display rebellion, mistakes, selfishness, and impulsiveness than the home? In situations like these, kids need a lot of love, safety, structure, wisdom, and patience. God has given you the authority and resources to help your children grow and resolve problems.

From the day a child is born to the day he or she leaves home, a number of different problems may come up: disobedience, out-of-control behavior, bad attitudes, friendship struggles, school problems, underachievement, laziness, low motivation, depression, sexual activity, and substance abuse, to name a few. Even if we had room in this chapter to deal with all of these, we still would be omitting many more. It's wise to learn all you can about your child's particular struggle, but we have found that there are several universal principles that can help you deal with most of the problems that kids face. In fact, as you understand and apply these principles, you may resolve several specific problems at the same time. For instance, consider a boy who can't sit still, is too talkative in school, and is aggressive. In many cases, all three of these problems will be resolved if he begins experiencing appropriate consequences. Experiencing consequences will motivate him to gradually develop self-control and self-containment.

Here are some principles that will help you be the parent your child needs you to be.

1. *Stay future-oriented.* When your child disobeys or struggles in some area, it can become a crisis, large or small, that disrupts your home and your family and takes up all of your waking moments. When that happens, it is easy to slip into the mentality that everything is about solving the crisis.

While resolution is certainly important, and doubly so in dangerous or life-threatening situations, it is not the entire picture. How you deal with the issue bears great weight on your ultimate goal of parenting, which is, as we established at the beginning of the chapter, to produce an independently functioning adult. So keep the future in mind. Ask yourself, *What can I do about this that will help create a grownup in a few years?* This perspective also helps you get out of the futility of solving only symptoms and not the real problem. When we simply solve the external symptom, we can be assured that the underlying problem will manifest itself again, in the same form or some other form.

For example, some friends of mine had a teenage daughter who was reserved and liked to stay at home. While she loved her friends when she was with them at school, she would not take initiative to call or visit them. She would stay home, read, or talk to Mom and Dad. She was a great kid in a lot of other respects: friendly, obedient, responsible, and had a healthy spiritual life. Her parents loved that she was with them so much, and they were tempted not to push her to go out with her friends more. When they finally did, she got upset and spent several days being sullen and resentful. Yet they believed, and I agreed, that if she didn't learn how to reach out while she was at home, she would lag in her ability to relate to the outside world later. So they insisted that she regularly call and join up with friends. This was anything but fun for the parents, as every time they made her reach out, their loving, pleasant daughter would become angry and withdrawn from them. Yet with a mind to her future, they kept it up. Eventually, their daughter began getting interested in her own friends and started taking initiative completely on her own. She is doing well today. However, had her mom and dad given up the future for a more peaceful present, I doubt that would be the case.

2. *Distinguish between can't and won't.* If your child is experiencing difficulty with something, it helps to distinguish whether it's because your child *can't* or *won't*. Let's say your freshman son is performing poorly in school. Is it because he lacks the ability, or because he doesn't pay attention or do any homework, or is something else going on? Sometimes we are weak and need support (Hebrews 12:12), and sometimes we are willful and foolish (Proverbs 22:15). As a parent, you need to know the difference.

When children are unable to do something, all the encouragement and discipline in the world won't bring results. Instead they need you to work with them in developing the skills that they are lacking. For instance, perhaps you realize that your son is struggling at school because he's depressed. He needs to see a child specialist or someone who is well-trained to treat depression in adolescents. Until his depression is resolved, it's unlikely his grades will improve—in fact, other things may be negatively affected as well.

However, willfulness and foolishness also run in a child's heart. We are all born with a desire to be God. As a parent you want to help your child get off the throne and take his or her place with the rest of humanity, where we were designed to be. Let's go back to our example. Let's say you talk to your son's teachers and find out that he rarely turns in his homework and has failed to make up a test that he missed because of a sick day. You realize that your son resists the self-control and diligence he needs in order to perform. He needs you to approach him with love, confrontation, instruction, and consequences. You might say, "Bobby, I need to talk to you about your homework problems. I am on your side, and I don't want to punish you about this. Yet I am concerned, and we need to do something about getting things done. So Mom and I are setting up a deal for you in which there are certain times after school when you cannot play with friends, watch TV, use the computer, or do anything but study. Once you've shown your completed work to us, then you can have free time. Also, we will need to see better grades from you, nothing less than an A or B on your report cards [if that is the caliber student he is]. If you don't do the work or get the grades, we will take you off the baseball team until the next report card comes in. I hope this works for you, and we will help you in any way we can."

To apply this principle, you have to know your child. One way to determine the difference is to look at patterns. Does your child have a history of good-hearted attempts to obey and take responsibility, and is the problem behavior an exception to this? Or does your child demonstrate resistance and willfulness in lots of areas of life? Use wisdom, God's guidance, and the input of others to help in this situation.

3. *Keep love and limits together.* A major factor in solving problems with kids has to do with your own influence as a parent. Remember that you are God's representative to your kid, not to be perfect but to do a good enough job of giving your child what he or she needs to grow. One of the best things you as a parent can do for your child is to keep love and limits together, what we would call *integration.* Just as God is both compassionate and holy (Psalm 86:15), parents need to be emotionally connected and strict at the same time. This kind of home environment helps kids feel safe enough to experience their emotions, look at their weaknesses, confess their faults, tell the truth, receive consequences and love, and grow.

It may help you to look at your own balance in this area. You may be deeply connected to your child but have problems with boundaries and limits. Or you may struggle with being able to tolerate your child's hatred and rage toward the rules. If so, you may want to look at your lack of structure or at your fear of dealing with negative emotions. If you discover either of those, it is a signal that you need to grow and get help in those areas, perhaps through a healthy study or growth group at church. Other parents may do a good job of providing limits and structure but have a harder time being loving and compassionate. They may need to see if they are anxious about emotional connections or dependencies, and then deal with that. For example, I have a friend who, while he was responsible and disciplined, had difficulty being emotionally close to others. He didn't really see the issue clearly until he noticed that his kids were going toward Mom and not him, because they didn't feel any warmth from him. That reality got to him, and he got into a spiritual growth group at church. He began to look at his fears of closeness and worked on opening up his heart and vulnerabilities with others. He began growing in this area, and his kids began gravitating toward him also.

Sometimes parents are divided between themselves. One is the "loving" one, and the other is the "strict" one. This can cause problems for their relationship and for their children. The children will experience two worlds: the world of license, and the world of condemnation. Neither world produces a healthy adult. However, if both parents bend their knees to God and his ways, and submit to each other's strengths, they both become loving and holy, and the child reaps the benefits.

◆ You Are Not Alone

In conclusion, know that you don't have to do all this alone, because you aren't alone. God is always present with you. He has given you his Spirit and his Word. He always directs parents who are at the end of themselves not only to himself but to his people. Look to him and his resources. Let him parent you as you parent your kids.

14

FEAR AND ANXIETY

Don't worry about it; you'll be fine. There is nothing to be afraid of. Just go for it! You already know what to do," my instructor said with loads of confidence.

For some reason, his reassurance did not help me much. I (Henry) had a sick feeling in my stomach, and it was moving quickly throughout the rest of my body. I remember thinking I was glad that he was a skydiving instructor and not a psychologist specializing in fear. His prescription was not very helpful. He would have had his license revoked.

I was about to get on an airplane headed for 12,500 feet, where I would do a solo, pull-your-own-ripcord jump with a free fall of 7,500 feet. When the instructor said that I already knew what to do, he was referring to the short morning course that I had taken at the facility. It consisted of showing you how to count, how to pull the cord, and then how to jettison your chute if it got tangled, torn, or did not open for some reason. We had also studied an hourlong video of an attorney citing case law and contractual reasons that the company was not liable for our deaths since we (the people in the class) had voluntarily signed up to die. What I did know how to do was be prepared to expect bad things to happen when I jumped out of the plane.

As we ascended to our jump altitude, I was amazed at how high we were. At 2,500 feet, one-fifth of where we were headed, the instructor told us to look out the window and see what the landing area looked like. When I did, whatever part of me that was not afraid caught up with the rest of me. We were so high already that I could not believe there was more air above us. The land was becoming patchwork. What was I doing?

We got to 12,500 feet. I looked out and could no longer recognize anything on the ground. It just looked like an ocean of color. I said a prayer, put myself in God's hands, thought for sure that I was going to die anyway, and walked over to the door. Before I knew it, another instructor went to the door and dived out. Gone. Disappeared. Vanished. I could not believe that I was about to do the same thing.

I looked out and just made a decision to go. Locking eyes with my instructor, I forgot all that could go wrong, counted to three, and jumped.

The first thing I was aware of was the force of the wind. At a fall rate of 120 miles per hour, the wind is so strong and loud that it gets your attention. I did not even feel a falling sensation; I was just trying to fly. The instructors had taught me that if you lose one of your angles with your arms, legs, torso, or head, you could go into a spin and totally lose control, finding yourself wrapped up in a bunch of lines and cords with a chute that has become a lettuce wrap. So I just tried to fly. Then, after falling 7,500 feet, I pulled the ripcord.

I felt some movement and then there was a jolt. I looked up to see what a tangled mess of a chute looked like, ready to jettison it and try to open the spare. Yet a miracle had occurred. My chute looked picture perfect. I could not believe it. I was probably going to live.

I adjusted the chute, retrieved the guidelines, and began to look around. I was floating in the most amazing quiet I had ever experienced. I could see mountains, lakes, and sky. Outside of a spiritual experience I have never felt the combination of freedom, surrender, and serenity that I had at that moment. I didn't want it to end. I felt like a bird must feel, just soaring with the wind, enjoying God's creation, not a care in the world. I was not even afraid of the landing, the power lines, trees, breaking a leg, or any of the other things about which they'd warned us. I knew that all was well with the world. I just floated down, thanked God for his creation, and enjoyed every minute of it. The ride down lasted about seven or eight minutes, and I was ready to do it again!

If I had not faced my fear, I would not have had that incredible experience. It taught me that I could do something that I was afraid of doing; I learned that we can get through fear to the other side, and find more of life. This experience also reminded me that *just telling people, "Don't be afraid, you'll do fine," does not make the fear go away.* Until the reasons for the fear are addressed, it will remain.

Unfortunately, fear is unavoidable. We will all have to deal with it, but thankfully, God knows more than my instructor did. He created your mind, spirit, and soul. He knows why you fear, and how to get rid of it. Better yet, he knows the future as well. When he says, "Let not your heart be troubled" (John 14:1, NKJV) or "Do not fear" (Matthew 10:31, NKJV), he really knows that the chute is going to open and that he will bring you through. You can trust him.

Let's take a look at some of the causes of fear, and the resources that God has given us to make a way through it. Believe it or not, no matter how fearful you are now, you might find yourself floating above it all, enjoying the view from a new place after God makes a way.

◆ SOUNDING AN ALARM

Fear is our emotional response to danger; it warns us that something dangerous is either happening or about to happen, and when that signal goes off, our entire system calls out the resources. Our blood pressure goes up, we may sweat, or we may even go numb in some way. Our heart may begin to palpitate, our stomach may start to churn, and our muscles may flinch or get tight.

Our mind and emotions will follow suit. Sometimes we may begin to think in irrational ways. We may think up all the bad outcomes and then begin to experience them as if they had already happened. We may obsess and worry, and yet find that we can't think our way out of the fear. In fact, if the fear is strong enough, our very ability to think may be hampered. We may have a feeling of dread, apprehension, or anxiety. The thought "what if" may create waves of terror that go through us like a tornado:

> Listen to my prayer, O God, do not ignore my plea; hear me and answer me. My thoughts trouble me and I am distraught at the voice of the enemy, at the stares of the wicked; for they bring down suffering upon me and revile me in their anger. My heart is in anguish within me; the terrors of death assail me. Fear and trembling have beset me; horror has overwhelmed me. I said, "Oh, that I had the wings of a dove! I would fly away and be at rest—I would flee far away and stay in the desert."
>
> —PSALM 55:1–7

Sound familiar? If so, then it means you are human. God created you in a way that enables you to respond to danger when it arises. Of course, when it gets debilitating, fear can get in the way of helping you. Yet it's not supposed to be that way. God created fear to be a good thing. *Fear is good when it motivates you to move away from the danger or to resolve the source of the fear.* For example, if you are in the Midwest, and you look out the window and see a funnel cloud coming your way, you don't say, "Oh, isn't that interesting?" That is not a sane response. A sane response is to fear that if you do not get to the cellar very soon, you are going to die. Fear motivates you to get away from the danger.

In and of itself, fear is good. It is there for a reason: to alert us to danger. Yet fear can also be a problem.

◆ WHEN FEAR IS BAD

Although fear can save our lives and even enhance performance in the right doses, it also can do exactly the opposite of what it is designed to do. Instead of making us perform better, it can keep us from performing well or at all. It can cost us our lives if in a dangerous situation we panic and cannot think or make choices. *Fear can keep us bound so that we live less and less of life. The cost is the life that we did not live because of fear.* A man who is afraid of rejection, for example, loses a life of love because he cannot risk relationship. A woman who is afraid of failure loses a life of accomplishment because she will not put a skill or talent into practice.

Fear can become a problem as well as a solution. The key for all of us is to figure out the difference between our healthy fears, which keep us from harm, and our unhealthy fears, which hold us back from experiencing many of the good things God has for us.

Let's take a look at some situations when fear is hindering us.

1. *Bad things truly are happening, but your fear is overwhelming.* You could be in the midst of something that is truly frightening. Your internal resources may be overtaxed, putting you into a constant state of fear. The best recent example of this is September 11, 2001. When terrorists successfully attacked the World Trade Center and the Pentagon, everyone felt fear. For the first time in our history, Americans were not safe within our own land. People did not know whether it was safe to get on an airplane or to open a letter. Life itself had become something of a risk.

If you found yourself feeling so afraid that it was difficult for you to function, then you were not alone. Many people had problems going about their daily lives. They were unable to function because their resources, both internal and external, were being overtaxed by the number of bad things happening. We all differ in our ability to transcend bad experiences. People with a lot of care and connection to others, a very structured life, a support system, and good internal coping skills are able to adapt better than those who don't have these things.

If real-life events seem to get to you more than they get to others, the principles in this book may help you learn how to bolster your internal and external resources. At the end of this chapter we'll offer some suggestions for how you can do that.

2. *You feel alone in the universe, without God.* We were designed to be on this earth with a heavenly Father who is concerned about us, loves us, and promises to guide us, be with us, and show us what we need to know. Some people either do not know their heavenly Father, or they have not learned that he is available to them each and every day, and that their very lives are in his hands.

If you feel alone—without God—in the universe, life and the future can seem overwhelming. You are not meant to live life by yourself. It is too big. You were not designed to be here without help, guidance, and provision. God longs to bring those things to you.

3. *You feel alone inside, cut off from people.* Love and connection make us feel secure. God has made us so that we actually take other people into our hearts and allow them to "live inside" us. When we know that others love us and we feel deeply connected with them inside our souls, we feel secure. All of the events of life, all the things that we experience, are filtered through a matrix of love inside of us that says, "Don't worry, it will be okay."

If you feel all alone in the world, whether or not you have people in your life, then life is going to be terrorizing to some degree. You will feel like a little child feels: alone and helpless. This aloneness is frightening, always looming and ready to be felt. If you are in this situation, nothing very bad has to happen in order for you to be filled with fear. You walk around with it very close to the surface. Many things in life are frightening if you are going through them alone.

4. *You have experienced a lack of acceptance.* All of us have failure, sins, and negative emotions. If we have known a lot of acceptance and have had our imperfections loved, forgiven, and accepted by God and others, then we do not fear failure, imperfection, or other "bad things" about ourselves. Forgiveness and acceptance make it possible for us to live within our own skin and be unafraid of being "found out." We aren't afraid of what we don't know because we feel secure enough to learn, and even if we fail, we put it in perspective and move on without beating ourselves up.

However, if we have not known acceptance and forgiveness, then we may feel that we have to be perfect in order to be loved or even to be safe. People who feel that their failures, sins, or negative emotions make them unacceptable live with a lot of fear—either of failure or of being "found out."

I remember a friend who had panic attacks every time she entertained houseguests. She would obsessively clean for hours before they arrived, so that they would not find one imperfection in her house. The thought of something being "out of order" terrified her. She had experienced a lot of criticism, rejection, and judgment in life, and she lived in fear. However, when she began connecting with some good, accepting people who modeled God's love to her, accepting her as she really was, good and bad alike, she began to give herself grace. As the apostle John says, "There is no fear in love. But perfect love drives out fear, because fear has to do with punishment. The one who fears is not made perfect in love" (1 John 4:18).

Much fear comes from not being "made perfect in love," which actually means being made complete. If you have no "completing experience" of love, then you will be fearful of being judged. Love and acceptance cure fear.

5. *You have some old baggage.* A number of years ago, I developed a hernia that required surgery. I knew the procedure was routine, but as I thought about going to the hospital, I started having strong fear reactions. I told myself that my fear didn't make sense, but it didn't help. The fear remained. As the time for the surgery approached, I began to recall memories of the time when I was in the hospital as a small child (see Prologue). Then I understood my reaction: My body was "remembering" things that had scared me as a child that I had not finished processing. I was feeling all the fear of an overwhelmed little kid, not an adult going in for a routine surgery. As I talked it out, felt some strong emotions, and received support, my fear of being hospitalized went away. I've been in the hospital since and have not felt that fear again.

Why was I feeling fear about things that had happened years before? Our spirits and minds record everything that ever happens to us, so our entire life is accessible at some level. What happens with fear is very specific. *If a person goes through more fear and trauma than he or she has the resources to process at that time, the fear is stored in the brain in an unprocessed state.* It is stored in a place that is different from the parts of our brains that process time sequencing and understanding. The part of the brain that feels the fear is not the part of the brain that knows what day it is. So you can be afraid as an adult to the same degree that you were as a child.

This is why people who were abused as children, for example, often "relive" those feelings. Current events activate feelings from the past. If you are feeling a lot of fear, it may be because of a former trauma, event, or relationship that is in need of attention.

6. *You have a sense of powerlessness.* We were not created to be omnipotent or to have power over other people, circumstances, and life. In fact, people who want to control everything have lots of problems, and we refer to them as "control freaks." They are forever upset because of their inability to get everything to go their way.

On the other end of the spectrum are those who feel like they do not have the control that God intended each of us to have; they have little or no sense of personal power. Consequently, *they allow people and circumstances to control them.* They feel like they have very little choice, and allow others to make choices for them.

What a frightening way to live! In order to feel secure, we need to be able to stand up and say what we want, what we do not want, what we will do, and what we won't do. We need to be able to say what we agree with and what we don't, what we will participate in and what we won't. We need to be able to say what we will allow to happen to us and what we won't. If we don't feel or have the freedom to say these things, then life can be a frightful enterprise.

7. *You have critical voices inside your head.* Many people go through life with an internal critic, a "voice" inside their head that's always telling them fearful, negative, or critical things that make them afraid.

People who suffer from panic attacks often have an internal voice that interprets events or feelings in catastrophic ways. At first they may feel a normal amount of anxiety over something, perhaps even a real event. But then they think, *Oh no, I am feeling out of control. I am going to have a heart attack. I am going to lose my mind. I am going to act like an idiot.* This interpretation makes them more afraid, and they interpret that fear as horrible, and the cycle continues.

Part of the initial treatment for panic attacks is to get people to accept the fear that they have and not interpret it in negative, catastrophic ways. Part of the treatment for anxiety in general is to get people to monitor their internal voices and the ways that they interpret events, feelings, thoughts, and the like. What they find is usually amazing to them. When they really start listening, they hear things such as:

- *See, you are a loser. No one is going to like you if you screw this up.*
- *If that deal does not go through, your career is over and you will never get another job.*
- *You'll never be forgiven for that.*
- *Did you feel that? You are losing it. You'll go crazy. They will have to lock you up and everyone will know. You are out of control.*
- *That is the worst thing that you could ever do. You are such scum.*
- *If this happens, it will be terrible, awful, horrible, and your life will be over.*
- *If this person rejects you, it proves you are worthless and that no one will ever want you.*

If you are constantly hearing these kinds of critical messages in your head, it's likely that you internalized the meanness of someone who said these kinds of things to you in the past, and perhaps is still saying them. We can internalize meanness just as we can internalize love.

8. *You avoid doing what you fear.* If I am afraid of flying and avoid flying because of it, I may feel better initially, but I've also made it harder to overcome my fear. The very act of avoidance does something very tricky in the mind. Because we do not have to face whatever it is we fear, we feel more secure. We reward the act of avoidance, and in the process feed our fear. Yet when we face our fear, even in small increments, the fear decreases. Exposure decreases the power of the fear.

9. *You have learned to fear something in particular.* If you are hurt or terrorized in some specific way, you will fear that activity in the future. Not long ago I treated a man who had been in a car accident and had developed a fear of driving. In his mind the trauma was associated with getting in a car, and he became very fearful.

Sexual abuse victims have learned that sex is dangerous as a result of being overpowered and abused. They associate sex with violation, loss of control, hurt, and a lot of other fearful realities. As a result, they often have strong fear reactions to sex or sexual contact. People can also learn to be afraid of intimacy if they have been hurt, betrayed, abandoned, or rejected by people whom they trusted.

Usually such fears are resolved by talking out the trauma, gaining a sense of control, and gradually getting back into the feared activity. The mind has to gradually learn that the activity that has been dangerous can be safe again. Sometimes this takes an enormous amount of work, and people have to be patient with themselves, especially if the trauma has been severe. They should also avoid retraumatizing themselves by taking on too much before they are ready.

10. *You lack certain abilities.* We are afraid when we do not know what to do.

I was once on a boat with a group of people who were enjoying the water. They were having the time of their lives. Yet I noticed that one woman in the group was not taking part. I thought I would encourage her. "Why don't you go for it? They are having a blast," I said.

"I don't want to, thanks," she said.

"Oh, come on. It's not that cold. You'll get used to it in no time. They are having so much fun. Come on, I'll go with you," I encouraged her. I was certain that the Pacific temperatures were discouraging to her, but I knew that the cold went away quickly (as the numbness set in!).

"No, really," she said. "I don't want to." I could tell that she was a little agitated.

"Are you sure?" I asked again. "It really is not that cold."

She looked at me with an icy glare that was a lot colder than the water could have been. "I can't swim," she said. "Now do you get it?"

That is a big difference. I was mistaken, badly.

You may find yourself in situations in which you are asked or required to do things that you have never learned how to do. For instance, if you have to make it on your own for the first time financially and have never acquired the skills needed to make it, it is a frightening prospect. Even making friends can be a fearsome task if you have not been taught how.

If you are afraid because of an inability, then you are very normal. See your task as not only to gain courage but also to apply yourself diligently to gaining the skills that are needed to face your task with confidence. Remember, there are very few "naturals" in life. We all have to learn how to do what we need to do.

◆ RELATING THE ANSWERS TO THE CAUSES

One of my favorite proverbs is Proverbs 18:13, which says, "He who answers before listening—that is his folly and his shame." There are not many places where this proverb rings more true than in dealing with people's fears. We need to understand the cause before we can prescribe the cure. If you can identify what specifically is causing your fear, then you can go a long way toward finding the cure for that issue. In this way, fear can be conquered.

Here are some prescriptions, based on the things that cause fear:

1. *Fear God and stop the insanity.* The deeper your relationship with God, the more you will know and understand life from his perspective. You will fear him more, and fear people and circumstances less.

However, just like any other relationship, your relationship with God takes time and work. Study the Bible. Learn what it says about fear and everything else. As David said, knowing and following God's Word makes us strong in standing up to all that life can bring us. It brings us salvation, courage, hope, freedom, strength, and delight:

> May your unfailing love come to me, O LORD, your salvation according to your promise; then I will answer the one who taunts me, for I trust in your word. Do not snatch the word of truth from my mouth, for I have put my hope in your laws. I will always obey your law, for ever and ever. I will walk about in freedom, for I have sought out your precepts. I will speak of your statutes before kings and will not be put to shame, for I delight in your commands because I love them. I lift up my hands to your commands, which I love, and I meditate on your decrees.
>
> —PSALM 119:41–48

Grounding your life in God and his Word helps you know that nothing can come to you that he cannot see, understand, and bring you through. All of life belongs to God, and he is always in control. Remember the stories with which we began the book, and the terrible situations that people discovered that God could make a way through. As you understand God and the life that you can have with him, your fear will lessen. Make a commitment to spend a certain amount of time each day praying through your concerns, praying for other people, and just talking to God.

Then go further than that. Talk to him throughout the day, every moment. Talk to him in tough situations. Learn that every moment of life is a moment that you can be united with him, and you will get stronger and stronger. Then when bad things happen, you will know that he is already with you. You will think like a man I had lunch with today who just had a big business deal that he was really counting on fall through. He said, "Oh, well. Obviously God has something else in mind." This man understood that he was not alone in the universe, and through his relationship with God and all that he had learned, he did not fear bad news.

He was living out this verse: "He will have no fear of bad news; his heart is steadfast, trusting in the LORD. His heart is secure, he will have no fear; in the end he will look in triumph on his foes" (Psalm 112:7–8). You too can have this confidence—by being grounded in a relationship with God.

2. *Get deeply connected.* Remember, you were made for relationship. If you are dealing with fears, you need other people. Support and love drive fear away. Even your stress hormones will respond to the presence of a safe person who is with you as you face the fear. If you are dealing with deep fears, you will need specific support as well. Don't just depend on your friends or the relationships in your church or community. Find a specific support group, therapy group, or counselor to help you deal with your fears.

3. *Up the resources to weather the bad things.* If you are going through difficult times, you may be feeling overwhelmed by fear because your resources are overloaded. If so, up your supplies! This means finding regular support and structured time to process things—not just haphazard times when you run into people you know. Also, up the resources by finding out the information that you need to deal with your crisis. Read, listen to tapes, and go to classes. Attend midweek worship services. Join a Bible study. If you are overwhelmed, then you need more than you are getting, whatever that means. Some people even need to take time off and go into a clinic. Just remember that until you are getting enough, the formula is "just a little more until it is enough."

4. *Overcome alienation.* If feeling alone has caused you to be fearful, and you have a hard time getting close to people, you will need to face your fear of opening up. Begin to allow others to know you. Risk—rather than avoid—trusting others with your heart. You need their love inside you, not just their external presence. Gatherings and support groups will not help you if you are not being touched in your heart, where you are afraid. Refer to the previous chapters where we have discussed this and begin to learn how to trust and to allow others to get inside your heart.

5. *Create structure in your life.* Structure and fear can't coexist in the same space. The more structure you have in your life, the more your fears will subside. I know a woman going through a transition time right now who has a thirty-minute phone call scheduled every morning at 7:30 with two other women who struggle in the same area. They have been doing this for a few months now, and the results have been powerful.

Here are some ways to create structure:

◆ Schedule regular meeting times for support.
◆ Schedule regular support calls at certain times.
◆ Keep regular spiritual activities.
◆ Keep regular work hours.
◆ Learn principles and insights that add meaning to what you are going through.
◆ Journal.
◆ Balance your schedule with active problem-solving time as well as self-care time and support time.
◆ Memorize Bible verses on fear, faith, hope, and God's faithfulness.
◆ Structure a time for risktaking at regular intervals during which you have assignments to conquer your fears.

6. *Get accepted.* The only way you will begin to find grace and acceptance on the inside is to begin to be known in all that you are, both good and bad. As you "confess your faults to one another" and find forgiveness and acceptance, you will be healed (James 5:16, KJV). Find a place where imperfect people are known and accepted by other imperfect people. Recovery groups are good places to begin. This is so powerful for overcoming lots of kinds of fears.

7. *Deal with old baggage.* If you are reexperiencing old hurts and are in a support group or in counseling, then you are in a safe place in which to deal with your baggage. As you learn how to open up about your pain, discuss the experience you went through, and share your feelings and fears, your brain will begin to put the experience in the past, where it belongs.

If you are reexperiencing a specific trauma, then we suggest that you find a professional who knows how to deal with it, along with a good support group for people who have been through what you have. You will find a lot of healing in just being around others who understand what you have gone through, and that will help the fear as well.

8. *Ask God to help you gain a sense of personal power.* God wants each of us to have self-control, or power over self. Put becoming honest and direct as a primary goal. Learn to set good boundaries. Learn to say "no" and to stand up for yourself. Stop allowing others to control you. This is probably playing a big part in your fear. If you cannot do this on your own, join a group that can help you.

Since we wrote *Boundaries* (Zondervan, 1992), scores of people have told us how developing boundaries has cured their fears. Sometimes the task of learning and implementing new boundaries of self-control can be daunting. Yet we *know* it can be done, for it is being done each and every day by people just like you.

As you deal with your fears of rejection, abandonment, or whatever else is driving your lack of boundaries, you can develop a better sense of self-control, and the effect on fear can be life-changing. Developing boundaries is one of the strongest things that you can do to treat your fear. So take that first step, even if it requires a counselor or a group. It may very well be the way out of a lot of your fears.

Learn

- to say "no" when you need to;
- to make your own choices instead of always adapting to other people's choices for you;
- not to be controlled or manipulated by others;
- to assert your own opinions and values;
- to be more honest in your relationships about what you like and don't like; and
- whatever other personal boundaries you need.

9. *Find models.* Spend time with people who are doing what you are afraid to do and learn from them. If you are afraid to confront, then ask someone who is good at it to show you how. If you are afraid to make sales calls, then get a coach to show you how. A lot of fear comes from thinking that what you are afraid of is really impossible. When you see others successfully face what you fear, it can help diminish your fear, especially if they share your fear and are willing to talk with you about their own process of dealing with fear.

10. *Make some fear normal.* One of the biggest causes of escalating fear is the "fear of fear." Fear increases when we say things like, "I should not feel afraid," or "This fear is awful. I can't stand it." Everyone has some fear, and that is normal. Make some space for it in your head. Remember, courage is not the absence of fear. Courage is moving forward in the face of fear. I have a friend in business who says, "If there is not some moment in every day that I am totally afraid of what I am trying to make happen, then I know that I am not stretching myself." Learn to think that way. Feelings will not hurt you, but seeing them as more powerful than they are can hurt you.

This may sound like we're simply saying, "Don't be afraid." Actually, we are saying the opposite. We are saying that one of the best things you can do is allow yourself to be afraid and not fight it. We are saying that you should accept your fear and allow it to be there. Learn that it is not going to destroy you, and you can just let it be. That process in and of itself is very powerful, as you will find that you are not fighting the fear as much. When you fight fear, it increases. Accept it, and let it be there. Treat it as normal.

11. *Evict negative voices and find new ones from God and others.* As we have said, some fear comes from your internal dialogue. Listen to those voices, and tell them to be quiet. As Paul says, learn to "take captive every thought to make it obedient to Christ" (2 Corinthians 10:5). Do what Jesus did, and quote Scripture back to the voices. When they say, "You will blow it," say, "So what? Even if I do, God will help me. Nothing can separate me from his love and I will still be a conqueror. No failure can do me in" (Romans 8:37–39)! When you

feel like the future scares you and the voices predict it will be terrible, say, "I have nothing to fear." Remember this promise from God: "Trust in the LORD with all your heart and lean not on your own understanding; in all your ways acknowledge him, and he will make your paths straight" (Proverbs 3:5–6).

When David was afraid, he reminded himself of God's provision and protection. Do a Bible study on fear and find your favorite verses to quote to yourself when you are full of fear. Then do three things. First, memorize the verses that speak to your fear by reminding you of God's protection, guidance, strength, provision, or whatever it is you need. Second, write them down and carry them with you. Third, read them every time you are afraid. Quote them to yourself.

Find out where those negative voices came from and renounce them. They are trespassing on holy ground. Evict them! Remember, something must take up that space, so be sure that you are in good, supportive relationships and that you are internalizing their affirming voices so that they can take the place of your mean critics. How can you be sure to internalize the new voices? What control do you have over this? This requires work from you. You can do it as you become more vulnerable with safe people and develop trust with them. As you let down your guard with people who are good for you and believe in you, your trust in them will give their voices more power than the negative voices in your head.

Then, work on grieving and letting go of the old ties to the critical voices in your head. Let them go.

12. *Get back on the horse, gradually.* We overcome fear by facing it gradually. As you take small steps and expose yourself to what you are afraid of, your confidence will grow because your mind will learn that there is nothing to be afraid of. However, the key is taking very small steps. If something feels overwhelming, back up to the last place that it was not and stay there for a little while; then take a smaller step forward.

As you do this, monitor the voices and thoughts in your head. Combat those thoughts with prayers, scriptures, and new thoughts. Your thought life is very important in dealing with fear.

If you have learned that some things are dangerous, approach them in small steps so that you have more self-control. Some victims of sexual abuse, for example, begin to overcome their fear of sexual intimacy by staying in control with their spouse. If this is a fear from which you suffer, for example, you might agree to a partial body massage as long as you can direct what will happen. Make a rule against going too far. Then make sure that you are in control so that nothing goes further than you want or against your will. That way, you will begin to learn that touch can be pleasurable and not dangerous. Small steps and remaining in control are keys to unlearning fear.

13. *Gain new skills.* If you are afraid of some area of life because you lack the necessary skills, apply yourself to learning them. For instance, if you are afraid to take a job promotion because you lack skills, find out exactly which skills you need and then look for a way to learn them—take a class or approach someone with those skills about possibly mentoring you. If you have trouble in relationships because you don't know how to speak your mind when you disagree, take an assertiveness course. The more you develop competence and control, the more your fear will diminish. Knowledge and skill are parts of the kind of power that God designed you to have. Apply yourself to becoming a "complete person" with personal integrity, and as the Bible says, then you will walk securely (Psalm 25:21; Proverbs 10:9).

14. *Discover that you can learn by learning.* Knowledge that you can learn to do whatever you need to do is one of the best ways to defeat fear. If you are not a seasoned "learner," then do something about it. Take a course just to learn that you can learn how to do something. Yet, as we said earlier, if there is something specific that is related to your fear, then begin there and learn whatever you need to learn. Let that become a rule in your head: "I don't know how to do that . . . *but I can learn.*" Remember, God created you to be a learner. You are wired with that equipment.

15. *Depend on the Holy Spirit through faith.* Moment by moment, ask the Holy Spirit to empower you to do what you are afraid of

doing. Remember, the God who created the universe says that if you put your faith in Jesus, he will come to live inside you. His power is available to help you do things that you are afraid to do. Step out in faith and take those small steps, but take them in faith that he will do his part. You might have to say, "I am afraid, God, but I am going to step out and depend on you to make it okay and empower me." Then ask him to do just that.

Here are a few verses that describe the power and help available to you:

- ◆ "I pray also that the eyes of your heart may be enlightened in order that you may know the hope to which he has called you, the riches of his glorious inheritance in the saints, and his incomparably great power for us who believe" (Ephesians 1:18–19).
- ◆ "And we pray this in order that you may live a life worthy of the Lord and may please him in every way: bearing fruit in every good work, growing in the knowledge of God, being strengthened with all power according to his glorious might so that you may have great endurance and patience, and joyfully giving thanks to the Father" (Colossians 1:10–12).
- ◆ "With this in mind, we constantly pray for you, that our God may count you worthy of his calling, and that by his power he may fulfill every good purpose of yours and every act prompted by your faith" (2 Thessalonians 1:11).
- ◆ "His divine power has given us everything we need for life and godliness through our knowledge of him who called us by his own glory and goodness" (2 Peter 1:3).

16. *Seek professional help.* All of these principles are tried and true, and have been shown to be very powerful in dealing with fear. We believe that if you practice them, they will prove helpful. Some of them are things that you can begin to put into practice by yourself and with others who are good, safe people. Yet that might not be

enough. You may need some good, professional or otherwise "structured" help.

If your own attempts to rid yourself of fear are not working, by all means find a good referral to a professional, such as a psychologist or other counselor who has experience treating fear and anxiety. Don't fear getting help with fear. That is why the pros are there. Ask someone for a referral who has had good experience referring people in your area. Usually, pastors and physicians know professionals to whom they refer those in need. They might be a good resource, as well as any in your circle of friends who have seen good counselors. However, if you need help, make sure you get it.

◆ FAN THE FLAME!

The apostle Paul wrote this note of encouragement to Timothy: "For this reason I remind you to fan into flame the gift of God, which is in you through the laying on of my hands. For God did not give us a spirit of timidity, but a spirit of power, of love and of self-discipline" (2 Timothy 1:6–7).

I don't know what Timothy was afraid of, but Paul was clear that God wanted more for him than fear or timidity. We know that he wants the same for you. So reach out to him and to the encouraging "Pauls" in your life. Find the gifts inside you, and "fan them into a flame"! Take hold of the Spirit, and develop the kind of power, love, and discipline that we have talked about here. As you do, you will find that God is a God who has been making a way through fear since his people were fearful in Egypt. He can do it for you too.

DIVORCE AND LOST LOVE

I f you are reading this chapter because you have experienced divorce or the loss of a love, my (John's) heart goes out to you. This experience can be unbelievably brutal.

Randy, a pastor friend of mine, began having marital struggles with Marcie, his wife. At first they seemed like the kind of problems that lots of couples have during the five- to ten-year period of marriage: disconnection, lack of communication, and so on. Then it got worse. Over time it became clear that Marcie didn't want to resolve the issues. She just wanted out. She told Randy that one of them had to move out. Whoever went wherever, she clearly wanted no part of the marriage.

Randy was by no means a perfect guy, but he loved Marcie, was faithful to her, and was willing to change anything he could to keep her in the relationship. He would call me, and we would talk about his options. For his part, Randy diligently did everything he could to help put things back together. He asked Marcie to tell him all the ways she was unhappy with him. He listened to her complaints about him without defensiveness. He took ownership of his failings with her and worked hard to make real and deep changes. He submitted himself to God, the process of growth, and the safe people in his life. He even offered to leave the ministry if that would bring her back.

All to no avail. Marcie left and filed for divorce, and, in time, the marriage ended. Randy was devastated. His world, his hopes, and his dreams had all been turned upside down. He still loved and missed Marcie, and yet the marriage was truly over.

This ordeal was difficult enough for Randy to bear. Yet something else made matters even worse. Several of his friends were building up Randy's hopes by telling him that Marcie would return. They would tell him, "Just trust God and obey, and Marcie will turn around." "Humble yourself and her eyes will be opened to your love." "God hates divorce, and he will fix this." When Randy felt discouraged by his situation, his friends' assurances would lift his spirits. Then things would get worse, Randy would get down, and his friends would assure him again.

These friends meant well, but the final reality was very different from their assurances. Marcie never came back. She began a new life elsewhere. Sadly, the fact that Randy was not prepared for this possibility hampered his recovery from the loss. God has, since that time, done a lot of healing in Randy; he too has a new life and is doing well. At the same time, the false hope unwittingly planted by his friends kept him from believing that she might leave, and therefore the shock when she did go was worse for him.

Randy's experience points out several realities that anyone who is touched by divorce will come across at some point or another: *Divorce is not a good thing. Divorce is a real thing. And most of us do not know what to do with it.* We are not ready for it. We want to think God will prevent it. We want to believe that something can be done to turn things around. There is a little of Randy's friends in all of us. At some level, we all protest against the reality of divorce, as it takes so much from us. Yet it is a reality. It is fact. And if you have been through divorce, are now going through it, or have lost the love of someone to whom you were close, you also need to know that God makes a way for you out of the depths into which relational loss can plunge you.

For the purposes of simplicity, we will deal exclusively with divorce in this chapter; however, the principles and ideas presented here will also apply to lost love, such as the breakup of a significant dating relationship. Though there are real differences between the two, the similarities are close enough for our goals here.

◆ ASSESSING THE DAMAGE

It's impossible to overstate the damage done by divorce. More than just about any of the other losses a person can experience, it permeates through every part of your life. It changes your identity from being part of a couple to being a single person. If you have kids, divorce turns their world upside down. Your friends take sides or get weird. You undergo massive lifestyle and geographical changes. The financial implications can be devastating.

Divorce means you have to learn the rules of life all over again. Gone is the safety of knowing you *belong* to someone who will care about you and always be there. You no longer have the blessing of a soul mate with whom you can walk through the joys and tears of life, each feeling what the other feels. Divorce rips away your hopes and dreams of building and growing in love and intimacy. The deepest parts of your soul, where reside the most precious, fragile, and vulnerable parts of your heart, are shattered and torn apart. Divorce breaks your heart. No wonder God thunders that he hates divorce (Malachi 2:16). It breaks the lives and hearts of those he loves.

◆ MARRING THE IDEAL

What is it about divorce that makes it so hard to accept? People can change jobs, roommates, and homes and feel fine. Not so with divorce. As we've shown, it wreaks havoc. We believe the answer to this question is found in the depth and importance of the marriage covenant. If marriage were not so profound, divorce would not be so devastating.

When God created Adam, he designed him for relationship. Every part of Adam was to be emotionally and intimately connected to someone outside of himself. God created Adam with a need that only God could fill. Yet God also created within Adam a similar, but different, horizontal need for connectedness. That need was so great that God said it was not good that Adam was alone (that is, in the human-to-human sense; Genesis 2:18). So God created Eve, and she and Adam met that need for each other in the marriage bond. They were one flesh and designed to experience life together, being intimate, caring for each other, and sharing the wonders of the world God had given them to care for. Two separate people, with their own personalities and thoughts, kept together by oneness of spirit.

Of course, marriage is not the only way that people can meet that deep relational need. Single people can find fulfilling, abiding, deep connectedness in the right sorts of people also. Yet, more than any other type of relationship designed by God, marriage reflects the way that God wants to relate to us. That is why he refers to his people as his bride, in metaphors that instruct us about his love (Isaiah 54:6; Ephesians 5:25–33). Marriage was designed to knit lives and hearts together for life, deepening and strengthening the connection over the years.

So it makes sense that when a marriage is severed, much becomes disconnected. On one day, God made two to become one. On another day, the one became two again. And they became separated, torn asunder from each other. That is why in many wedding sermons you hear Jesus' warning: "So they are no longer two, but one. Therefore what God has joined together, let man not separate" (Matthew 19:6). God not only designed marriage to be complete and lifelong, he literally knit the two souls together into a relationship called a marriage. Divorce tears apart what God has sewn for two people.

If you are not recovering from your divorce as quickly as you would like, it may simply be an indication that you loved deeply. You likely experienced your marriage as God experienced it. You were deeply committed; you cast your lot in life with a partner and gave unreservedly, you gave up individual conveniences and freedoms for the greater good of the covenant, and you literally gave your life for something larger than the two of you individually. Is it any wonder that it sometimes takes a long time to move on? The only way you would be able to "get over it and put it behind you" quickly would be if there had not been that much there in the first place. *The depth that you have loved another is the depth to which that person can hurt you.* It is as simple as that.

God knows the pain of divorce. He can identify with how you feel. He lost his own "wife," Israel. His people's unfaithfulness wounded him. He said, "I have been grieved by their adulterous hearts" (Ezekiel 6:9). The Hebrew word translated "grieved" here also means "to break or shatter." God knows what it is like to have a broken heart. He has truly "been there."

God is with you—and he makes a way for his own. You are not left to grieve and be stuck in the pain of your divorce forever. We do not believe that dealing with divorce is simply a matter of coping with it, accepting it, hanging on in faith, and then one day going to heaven. God has something much, much better for you than that. Your divorce may not have been intended or designed by God, but he will find a way that is good for you through this.

◆ Working through the Pain

What follows are some of the issues that occur in divorce. Your ability to work through these will be critical to your recovery from divorce's effects. With God's help you can work through the pain and come out on the other end a better, more mature, and more complete person.

◆ Becoming the Person God Wants You to Be

What once was a "we" has now become an "I." In marriage, God brings two people together to form a union for life. The two think of life in terms of a pairing: where we want to go on vacation, what we want to do about having children, who our friends are, and so forth. Marriage means letting go of individual conveniences and interpreting personal desires in terms of the greater good of the marriage. If I am weak, we can be strong together. We bear the load, the responsibilities, and the burdens of life together. We think in terms of "we." "We" shapes our identity, the way we see ourselves in the world, and how we belong.

Divorce ends the "we" and brings you back to "I." You no longer have a soul mate to count on, dream with, and go to for help with life's constant problems. The divorced person is alone again, but in a different way than that of a single, never-married person. It is not simply a matter of resetting the switch to "single." The divorced person *has known and experienced* marriage. You lost something that you valued: "we-ness." For many divorced people, the state of being an "I" is almost intolerable. So intolerable, in fact, that these people often rebound into a relationship that is not right for them, simply to get out of the pain of their isolation and loneliness.

However, God has made a way for you to bring good out of this bad situation.

First, *you can develop and grow into the individual God created you to be.* God meant marriage to be a union of two distinct people, with distinct opinions, viewpoints, and values, who each contribute to the other's growth and path. As the old saying goes, "If you never disagree, then one of you is not necessary." Ideally, we are to experience our existence both as an individual and as a couple. Yet when one spouse lacks individuality, it can cause major disruptions in the marriage. Sometimes the reason for divorce is that one spouse did not develop his or her soul or have a strong sense of self. The undeveloped spouse may bore or smother the other spouse. Sometimes one spouse will control or dominate the other to the degree that the less dominant one loses his or her sense of self. Sometimes a spouse neglects his or her inner growth and development, believing it more important to make a good marriage, never realizing that a marriage is only as good as the two souls that comprise it.

Does any of this ring true for you? Divorce can be a wake-up call to own and be aware of the many treasures and talents that God has uniquely given you. If you realize that you have lost your true self—or never even found it—you can view the new world created by divorce as an opportunity to grow individually and personally. This is both good news and bad news. The bad news is that you must now make your own decisions. The good news is that now you *can* make your own decisions. Rather than hiding behind marriage in order to avoid dealing with choices, freedom, opportunities, and problems, begin to use this as a season of finding what you love, hate, are talented in, desire, and have a vision for. Make your new single state a time of exploration and seeking God's ways for your life. As Jesus said, "But seek first his kingdom and his righteousness, and all these things will be given to you as well" (Matthew 6:33).

That's what my friend Ruth did. When she was married, Ruth was like the "we" person I described earlier. She had no life of her own and was dependent on whatever her husband said or thought. After they divorced, she went on a search for the person God had wanted her to be all along. In time, this homemaker mom found she had a real knack for business and making money. She learned all she could, took courses, got mentoring, and began making some forays into the business world. She is now a successful businesswoman, has found that her life is quite meaningful and interesting, and feels that she has a lot to contribute.

Second, *you have the opportunity to discover the richness of life apart from marriage.* Life is more than marriage. God intended us to find a relationship with him, a community of safe people, some meaningful tasks, and a mission and purpose in order to have a good life on this earth. Marriage is one of the best experiences in this life. However marriage is not life. It is part of life. And for many, life does not ever include marriage.

Yet many divorced people conceptualize life in terms of marriage. They feel incomplete and lost without a spouse and look for a new mate far too quickly. This is not a desire for marriage; it is a fear-based reaction to the unknown. If you find yourself in this situation, look at building a life for yourself rather than making marriage an equivalent to life. As they say, "Get a life." Let go of the demand that you need to be married to be complete. This will allow you to find and experience all the other aspects of life that are available in a well-rounded and balanced existence. Many people who have done this have later on met someone else who has a life; then they have built a new marriage together that is far stronger and closer then either one of them had dreamed.

◆ EMBRACING GRIEF AND LOSS

A divorce is, by definition, a loss. In fact, one of the Hebrew words for divorce speaks of "cutting or severing a bond." Something has been lost. The loss is real, genuine, and deep, and it must be grieved.

Grief is accepting the reality of what is. It is internalizing the reality of the severing of the marriage bond on both the intellectual and emotional levels of the heart. That is grief's job and purpose—to allow us to come to terms with the way things really are, so that we can move on. Grief is a gift of God. Without it, we would all be condemned to a life of continually denying reality, arguing or protesting against reality, and never growing from the realities we experience.

When you allow yourself to embrace the sadness and shed the tears for what you have truly lost through divorce, then you can move on to a new phase of life when grief tells you it is time. It is important to note that *those who have not fully grieved the losses of their divorce are in jeopardy of either never getting over it or repeating it*. When I am speaking to groups of divorced people, I often talk about this in terms of dating. I'll tell them, "When someone you are seeing tells you the divorce wasn't that hard on them and they really didn't have a difficult time with it, burn rubber out of the driveway of that house." A person who hasn't grieved a significant loss has unfinished business inside and can cause others great grief as a result.

What does it mean to embrace grief in divorce? It means many things, including:

◆ Allowing painful feelings to come and go, without prohibiting them
◆ Reaching out to others to comfort and support you through this, rather than going it alone
◆ Putting an end to the protests and arguments in your head about how it shouldn't have happened, or whose fault it was or was not

Grief doesn't allow us to be right, strong, and in control. Grief basically says, "You loved and you lost. It hurts." Yet God is on the other side, waiting, with his safe people, to catch, hold, and restore us.

One of the most difficult yet important tasks of grief in divorce is that of *remembering and experiencing value for the loved one.* Let yourself feel the love you still may bear for your former spouse, the positive emotions you have, your desires for togetherness, your appreciation for that person's good traits and characteristics. Most people who are trying to get past divorce don't recognize the importance of this, thinking instead that they need to be aware of the other person's faults, sins, and mistakes. Sometimes they do this out of a desire for revenge; other times it is a reaction against the need they feel for the person, which causes them to fear getting hooked back in. Sometimes they do this as a way to complete the letting-go process.

Yet grief does not work this way. When you let go of a love, you are to let go of the whole person: good and bad, weaknesses and strengths, positives and negatives. When we allow only the negative feelings, we then let go only of the person we dislike, which is just a part of the whole individual. We won't grieve the other part, the person we still love and want, and with whom we have in our memories a repository of good experiences. That person is still in our present world, still active within our heart, and causing all sorts of difficulties. Let go of the desire to see only the bad, and allow yourself to appreciate and let go of the good person you are leaving. This is the key to freedom beyond grief in divorce.

◆ TAKING STOCK OF YOUR CONTRIBUTIONS

When I speak to divorced groups, I often ask, "Now that you are divorced, what is your single biggest problem?" Invariably, someone says, "My ex!" We all laugh, and then I get serious and say, "Well, if anyone here truly believes that, they are pretty much doomed. Because if your biggest problem is not yourself, your soul, and your areas of growth, and if you are more invested in the failings of your ex, then your ex still controls your every move." That generally makes for a lively discussion at that point.

If all you can see are the faults of your ex, you are helpless. You have nothing to work on, change, or improve. You have no way to alter the course of your life for the better. That's why one of the most helpful things you can do after a divorce is to take stock of your own contributions to the problems in your marriage, identifying and admitting where you screwed up, were unloving, or hurt your then-spouse. If you do this growth exercise, you will gain a lot. You will be able to solve whatever internal problems you had, and thus be more objective about any problems the other person has. Jesus said, "First take the plank out of your own eye, and then you will see clearly to remove the speck from your brother's eye" (Matthew 7:5).

This task has nothing to do with making you feel bad or guilty about the past. What is done is done. *It has everything to do with ensuring that you grow past the mistakes of the past and do not recreate them in your future.* Do not run the risk of making your past your future.

Though many times one spouse is very much more at fault than the other, I have never seen a divorce in which it was 100 percent one person's fault and 0 percent the other person's. Even the most loving, faithful, and righteous person can contribute to the problems in a marriage. To deny this is to prevent great growth and preservation for the future.

Here is a brief list of contributions to look at, own, change, and grow through—whether you were the "bad guy" in the marriage, the "good guy," or in-between:

- *Withdrawal of love.* You removed the very glue that the other person needed to feel secure and valued.
- *Control.* You did not allow your spouse to have his or her own feelings, opinions, and decisions separate from yours without some sort of punitive response on your part.
- *Unloving criticism.* You put down your spouse out of anger, superiority, or not being able to accept who he or she was.
- *Irresponsibility.* You did not take ownership of your part in the marriage.
- *Passivity.* You made the other person take on too much because you avoided making decisions.
- *Deception.* You were untruthful in love, time, money, or whereabouts.
- *Moral superiority.* You saw only your ex's faults and your spiritual or moral higher ground; a form of arrogance and pride.
- *Codependency.* You rescued your spouse, or enabled him or her to stay irresponsible.

Ask God to show you what things you may need to change. As you bring these issues before God and your friends, you can then safely work on them and improve yourself, and you will find that you choose better people and become a better person yourself.

◆ Knowing When to Date Again

Divorced people often ask me, "When can I start dating again?" While they don't want to make the same mistakes again, they want to go out and meet the right sorts of people. While Henry and I think personal and spiritual growth is the real work of the day, and that dating should come second, we believe that dating is a very good thing.

Here are some things to do and know before you jump into the dating scene after a divorce.

1. *Wait.* It is wise to wait until you have stabilized, grieved, and grown through the effects of your divorce. To begin dating while separated and not divorced, or immediately after a divorce is finalized, is to risk covering up or minimizing what you need to learn, feel, and experience about this major event. Give yourself time for God to help you work through the divorce.

2. *Develop a long-term and stable relationship with God.* Work on getting to know him and his ways. Seek him and his life and guidance. He will help you know when you are ready. Often, as people develop their spiritual lives, they find fullness in knowing that God takes the edge off any desire to be in the dating world.

3. *Get connected to a community of healthy, stable, loving, and honest people.* Make them your "family," where you bring your life, your needs, and your struggles. People who have supportive communities often find that they are not as desperate to be married, because their community is meeting some of the needs that drive their urge to marry. This frees them to date and marry according to their values, their freedom, and their choice, rather than their fears and needs. You need to be deeply emotionally invested in nondating relationships, which then help healthy dating relationships spring forth.

◆ GOD IS THE GOD OF FRESH STARTS

If you are divorced or have lost love, you may be thinking of yourself as damaged goods. This is not at all how God sees you. He knows our frailties and empathizes with them. He desires more than anything to restore and redeem his people to himself. You may be damaged, but God can repair the damage. No damage is beyond his repair. You may feel you are of second-class status, but God is the God of fresh starts and renewal. Go to him with your past and your present, and ask him to show you the way to a life of renewal: "And the God of all grace, who called you to his eternal glory in Christ, after you have suffered a little while, will himself restore you and make you strong, firm and steadfast" (1 Peter 5:10–11).

BAD HABITS AND ADDICTIONS

W hat does the word *addiction* mean to you? My (Henry's) hunch is that there are almost as many answers to that question as there are people who answer it. For instance, people have said:

- ◆ "There is no such thing as an 'addiction.' People who engage in addictive behaviors don't have a disease; they simply refuse to exercise control over their actions."
- ◆ "Only substances can be addicting."
- ◆ "Only behaviors like drinking or gambling can be addicting."
- ◆ "I believe that almost any kind of activity, such as shopping or exercise, can be addicting."

The more we talk about addiction, the more the term seems to lose its meaning. It becomes difficult to know if we are even talking about the same thing.

So in this chapter we are going to make some assumptions about addiction and then speak to those assumptions. *If you have picked up this book because there is something in your life that you can't stop, and you think you have an addiction, then you should look to this chapter for answers.* We want to help you.

For that reason, we have chosen to talk about addictions in the broadest use of the word. Although there are some technical inaccuracies with this approach, it allows all of us to identify with the problem, to some degree—and all of us can benefit from living our lives in a way that enables us to be connected to God and to others.

In light of that, here is the definition we will use: *Addiction is an inability to stop a repeated and compulsive use of an activity, behavior, or substance in spite of negative consequences.*

With that definition, a lot of us are in trouble! It does not include the things that we normally associate with being an addict—being out on the street, penniless, and friendless. Most of our culture's disturbing pictures of addicts are built around the devastating final stages of severe substance abuse, such as the abuse of alcohol or heroin. When those addictions go untreated over a long period, people can lose their very lives. Many of us think of an addict as someone who is down and out and has lost everything—job, home, and family.

As a result, many people who struggle in this area find it easy to lie to themselves. Even though they are unable to give up a substance or behavior despite its negative consequences, they think that since they function well in their jobs, they don't have an addiction. Yet they are wrong. It's very possible to be a high performer and still be out of control with how you use money, food, sex, alcohol, exercise, or many other things.

I talked to a woman just today who is in recovery for what she terms "romance addiction." She was addicted to romantic relationships despite their negative consequences for her. As we talked, she told me about her father. She said that he was an alcoholic, "but no one would ever know." When I asked her what she meant, she said that her dad did well in his job, but every day he came home and had several martinis to medicate his stress and his loneliness. When his wife confronted him about his drinking, he denied that he had a problem, saying that his drinking was not interfering with his life. Yet it was. He was becoming more and more detached from his family and had very little meaningful interaction with his daughter. He was just too medicated to engage with her day after day.

What was the result? She grew up totally detached from her father and began craving attention from men as a way to validate her as a person and as a woman. She found herself in relationships with men who did not value her other than for sex. Even though she realized this, she found herself unable to stop it. She became pregnant by a man who would not commit to a relationship with her, and she had an abortion. In the midst of trying to win the love of these men, she was losing more and more of herself and all that mattered to her.

Fortunately, God is making a way for this woman to break that cycle and find a deeply satisfying life, and that same God can make a way for you as well.

◆ The Picture of Addiction

What do most addictions look like? In general, most addicts follow this two-step path:

1. *They begin with a behavior that brings them pleasure.* This can be pleasure in and of itself, like what happens when people use drugs for the first time. Or the pleasure may be relief from a bad state of mind or emotional distress. For instance, a woman on the way home from a stressful job may find that when she stops off at the mall and spends a lot of money, or stops at the local bar and has a few drinks, her stress diminishes. The pleasure that she finds is the pleasure of relief from some sort of pain, anxiety, or other distress. However, after the effects have worn away, her body and mind will come back to the state in which they were without the behavior and its effects, and she will likely desire to go back to that state of pleasure. In other words, the substance or behavior has become reinforcing.

2. *They become psychologically or physically dependent on the behavior or substance.* They begin to "need" the substance or behavior, often in ever-increasing amounts to get the same effect, pleasure,

or relief. I know a man who occasionally smokes cigars. I asked him once if he had ever had any problem with smoking, if it had ever gotten out of control. He told me that early on in his business career, he would sometimes bum a cigarette from a coworker on his way out the door at the end of the day. He liked it and thought it was just an occasional pleasure. Then he noticed something happening. On the days when he was particularly stressed, he found himself wanting to go find the person and get a cigarette. He found that he desired to smoke as a tension reliever. When he saw that beginning to happen, he quit. His occasional use of a highly addicting drug had become self-reinforcing as a stress reliever.

However, most people fail to recognize that this is happening, and they continue to do what makes them feel better. In fact, in a lot of circles, their behavior is even normalized. Many people feel it's normal and acceptable to seek sexual release or to drink alcohol to blow off some steam. They do not recognize the warning signs, and so they continue the behavior. It takes over more of their soul, and they don't even know it.

Then something negative happens, some sort of negative consequence of the behavior. It could be guilt, shame, or someone's getting upset with them. *Addiction becomes apparent when a person doesn't acknowledge the negative consequence, explains it away, or acknowledges it and yet is unable to stop.* In other words, the person continues the behavior in spite of the negative consequences. Many addicts make many promises, either to themselves or to others, that they will not do the addictive behavior anymore, and yet they can't keep those promises. They have lost self-control and have become "enslaved" to the behavior. They no longer have a choice.

It is downhill from there, as the negative consequences usually increase. Addicts often have relational difficulties, such as tension in a marriage or with friends or family. They have performance difficulties, such as the inability to do their job or other tasks well. They often experience financial consequences, as addictions sometimes become expensive or can erode a person's financial well-being. As the cycle of addiction becomes more and more pervasive, many addicts suffer internal consequences, such as mood disturbances, depression, guilt, anxiety, or shame.

Yet despite all of these consequences, the addict can't seem to stop the behavior. Sex addicts lose marriages and catch diseases but are unable to stop. Gambling addicts lose their life savings yet continue to try to find more money, often in problematic ways, such as dangerous loans or going into credit-card debt. Alcoholics keep drinking even after being confronted by their families or after being told of liver problems. Food addicts may gain a lot of weight, risking their health and encountering other consequences that limit their quality of life internally, physically, relationally, and otherwise.

Of course, there are some exceptions to the general picture. Some people are able to control things for periods of time, sometimes for long periods. Yet, when they do engage in the behavior, it is out of control and destructive to themselves or others. Even though the behavior is not "continual," it results in the same kinds of negative consequences. These people are often called *binge addicts*.

The hallmark of all addictions is that the person has lost control and is experiencing negative consequences as a result.

Sadly, many of the activities that people become addicted to are things that God has designed to be a part of life, such as food, money, and sex. The problem comes when these things become consuming, so much so that the person loses control and is now a slave of the behavior or substance. As the apostle Paul says, " 'Everything is permissible for me'—but not everything is beneficial. 'Everything is permissible for me'—but I will not be mastered by anything" (1 Corinthians 6:12).

The Greek word translated "mastered" is a word that means "having power or control." In other words, the person has lost control or power of his or her own life in that area, and the addiction has taken control. Likewise, when Paul says not to be "addicted to much wine" (Titus 2:3), the Greek word translated "addicted" is a word that means to be "brought under bondage or become a servant to." God seems to recognize that people can become addicted and that a person can actually become powerless over things in life. The loss of control is ultimately the kernel of addiction. Paradoxically, the loss of control is the beginning of change—and of hope. When we admit that we are powerless to change, we can then turn to God for help.

◆ LET'S GET HONEST

Now that we've talked about addictions and how they affect a person, let's talk about you. Answer the following questions:

- ◆ Is there something in your life that has gotten control of you? Are you unwilling or unable to give up that behavior, despite its negative consequences? Do you find yourself making excuses or trying to convince yourself or someone else that the behavior is really not that big a deal? Or that others have a much greater problem than you do?
- ◆ Do you go through periods of withdrawal? Do you have cravings that can be satisfied only by the substance or the behavior? Do you find that the substance or behavior does not ultimately satisfy because you need it again or need more? (This is called "tolerance." It is the need for more in order to produce the same result.)
- ◆ Do you obsess about the behavior more and more? Do you organize more and more of your life so that you can engage in the behavior? Is it affecting the amount of time and energy you have for the things and the people that are important to you?
- ◆ Do you often feel guilty or ashamed of the behavior and yet find that you are unable to stop? Do you make promises to yourself or someone else that you will quit or cut back and yet do not? Does the behavior disagree with your value system, and yet you continue? Do you just tell yourself that you really could quit if you wanted to but just don't try?
- ◆ Have others noticed the effects of the behavior? Do they mention it or get upset by it? Do you get defensive?

♦ Do you feel better when engaged in the behavior and then find that other things in life cannot bring you the same degree of pleasure, excitement, involvement, or momentary relief that the behavior does? Do you engage in it more than you planned to? Is the behavior affecting your health or performance in life or work? Are you having emotional, mood, or thinking problems as a result of the behavior?

♦ Have you lost consciousness or memory because of a substance? Do you disappear from others and hide your behavior or use of a substance? Do you find yourself lying about what you are doing or not doing? Do you try to cover up what you do?

These questions address some of the signs of addiction. If you answered "yes" to any of these questions, then you may have a problem.

Perhaps you're wondering why some people can remain in control and still enjoy many addictive substances and behaviors, yet others can't. After all, no one goes out and says, "I want to become an alcoholic." No one chooses to become addicted to pornography, shopping, sex, gambling, cocaine, or any other substance or behavior. Why do these things sometimes take control of people's lives?

♦ WHY PEOPLE GET ADDICTED

People get addicted to things for a variety of reasons. The overarching reason is that we are human—separated from God and life—and as a result we find ourselves out of control in a lot of ways. Yet first let's summarize some of the specific forces that drive an addiction.

Some people seem to have a particular genetic makeup that is prone to addiction toward a certain substance, such as alcohol.

Environmental forces may be at work. People who are injured by significant relationships or grow up in families where certain relational and life patterns are "caught" and modeled may not develop the coping skills needed to deal with hurts and injuries. Some turn to an addiction to medicate their pain.

We live in an ongoing spiritual battle in this universe between the forces of darkness and the forces of light. There really are forces of evil, and they try to do everything possible to tempt humans to pursue darkness *instead of God and his ways.* As a result, some people make choices that take them down a road of destruction and further away from the light—a one-time experiment with drugs or a choice to turn away from God's ways and to experiment with a behavior that brings momentary pleasure. As many drug, sex, gambling, and pornography addicts will tell you, such dangerous choices can lead you into total darkness.

Some people's emotional makeup and dynamics can predispose them toward an addiction. These dynamics include

- an internal sense of relational isolation and alienation, resulting in loneliness and a hunger for love;
- a sense of powerlessness in life, and being controlled by others, circumstances, and forces bigger than themselves;
- inability to gain mastery and to cope with and thus develop a sense of personal power that is adequate to deal with other people and life;
- feelings of shame, guilt, "badness," or failure, or other ways of feeling bad about themselves;
- unresolved losses and failures and the inability to deal with them;
- unresolved trauma, hurt, abuse, and pain of all kinds;
- feelings of inferiority and inability to develop competencies in life;
- feelings of being dominated by others and not living up to their standards; and
- difficult times in life, along with the ineffectiveness of coping mechanisms and skills.

While all of these can be factors in the cause of addiction, they are all symptoms of another, deeper condition. It is the spiritual condition of being "alienated" from God and his life as he created us to live it. When we are cut off from him and his life, the Bible says that we become subject to addiction. Listen to how Paul describes it:

> So I tell you this, and insist on it in the Lord, that you must no longer live as the Gentiles do, in the futility of their thinking. They are darkened in their understanding and separated from the life of God because of the ignorance that is in them due to the hardening of their hearts. Having lost all sensitivity, they have given themselves over to sensuality so as to *indulge in every kind of impurity, with a continual lust for more.*
> —EPHESIANS 4:17–19, emphasis ours

When we become "darkened in our understanding" and "separated from the life of God," then we find ourselves in a lost state, craving things that will never satisfy. We experience a "continual lust for more." This craving drives us to want just one more drink, one more experience, one more sexual encounter, one more pizza, one more purchase. The desire is "continual," which means that it does not go away with the experience of the behavior.

This is a downward, futile, destructive cycle because it causes us to become separated from God and his life, even among people who are "spiritual." A part of the soul is disconnected from God and his life, or from the resources and healing experiences that will meet the need in ways that are truly satisfying—the things that can truly "make a way."

If separation from God and his life is the cause, then reconciliation to God and his life is the answer. That is how God makes a way for anyone with an addiction. He truly can set slaves free.

◆ THE WAY OUT

Jeri had been enslaved to binge eating for a long time. Her doctor had sent her to counseling because he feared for her health. She was very overweight and had a history of heart disease in her family, and he was very concerned about her. She had "tried" many times before to control her eating through dieting. She would initially lose some weight, but eventually she would give up and quit, only to have the weight that she had lost return, with extra pounds on top of it all. Despair had given way to detachment, and she found herself in a lonely pattern, having given up. Yet the doctor had gotten her attention, and she now feared for her very life.

When Jeri came to our clinic, the first thing we had to do was "cure" her of her commitment to dieting. She came in mistakenly believing that all she needed to do was to have more commitment and willpower. She believed that if she made a strong enough commitment, then she would be able to manage her eating. This is not how addiction works, however. Jeri had to learn that addiction was by definition *the inability to stop.* In other words, *she had to learn to admit that she was powerless over her addiction and totally helpless to stop.* You would think that after gaining a few hundred pounds and after many failed efforts at dieting, Jeri would have seen that she did not stand a chance of changing by herself. Yet that is part of addiction—the belief that one really is able to overcome the problem.

Next, Jeri had to learn that she had not truly reached out to God as the Source of power in her life of addiction. She had "prayed" about her problem before, but that is very different than leaning on God as a source of power *in the addiction itself.* She had to learn that when temptation came, she had to pray and ask God at that moment for the strength to know what to do to flee the temptation.

Then, she had to learn that God also gives us strength through other people. She began to see that part of the reason she had failed before was that she had tried to go it alone. She had thought because she had joined diet groups emphasizing group support, that she was getting that support. She discovered that in moments of weakness, when she was feeling loneliness or self-pity, she needed to be able to call a few people. She needed a "buddy system." She learned to reach out to God and to a buddy and to talk things out rather than using food to make herself feel better.

I remember the day when this insight hit her. She came to a group early that morning and said that the night before, she had been tempted to binge. "Now I get what you guys have been talking about," she said.

"What do you mean?" we asked her.

"Well, last night I found myself craving some serious food. I was just about to give in when I remembered what you had said. There were three things. First, I needed to reach out to God. So I prayed and asked him to help me get through it and to show me what was going on. Second, you said that my cravings were not really for food, but had something to do with how I was feeling inside. Third, at those times I could not just depend on myself, but had to reach out to someone else.

"So I asked God to help, and then I called Regina [another group member] and told her that I was struggling. As we talked, I began to feel really sad. The more I talked, the sadder I got. I felt this really deep aloneness that I never had felt before. She just told me to keep talking, and I did. Then, slowly, the feeling went away. And the weird thing was that after that conversation, I was not hungry anymore, but I had not eaten anything. I think I am getting it!" she exclaimed with some excitement.

As Jeri continued to work on things, she found out that there were other dynamics driving her eating. She also had a lot of fear of getting close to men because of some abuse that she had suffered. She had subconsciously gained a lot of weight as a way of keeping men safely at a distance. She gradually became aware of things that triggered her desire to eat, and she had to learn how to express that pain instead of "eating it away."

In time she came to understand that she had some character flaws as well. She was not as honest as she thought she was. She was indirect with people and then held grudges and bitterness toward them instead of talking things out directly, offering forgiveness, and resolving conflict. She had always been a "nice" person, but that niceness was covering a lot of anger and resentment, and her true feelings would come out as she would talk about people behind their backs.

GOD WILL MAKE A WAY

She had to learn to repent of that kind of indirect, hurtful behavior and to offer forgiveness and resolve conflict.

Jeri went back to school and started a new business, which became successful. She was soon hired as a consultant and was really thrilled that she was able to exercise her gifts and talents, overcoming a longstanding belief that she was "stupid" and unable to do anything significant. Now "significant" people were paying her to help them.

One more thing. Jeri lost half of her weight—and I do not mean half of her goal weight or half of the weight that she was supposed to lose. No, I mean *literally half of her body weight.* She went from 300 to 150 pounds. This was not as a result of a "diet." She lost the weight as a result of getting reconnected to God and his life.

Here are the steps Jeri took:

- She got to the end of herself, the end of her own strength. She admitted her powerlessness.
- She found strength in reaching out to God.
- She found strength in reaching out to God's people.
- She overcame the aloneness and isolation through learning how to be vulnerable and to connect with others—this healed the pain that her eating was serving to medicate.
- She grew in her character, learning how to be honest, to be responsible, and to set good boundaries with others instead of being so passive and powerless.
- She grieved a lot of hurt.
- She forgave a lot of people and gave up a lot of bitterness.
- She developed her talents, reached out, took some risks, and grew a life of work and service.
- She learned to pray at a more realistic, deeper, and more dependent level.
- She began to study the Bible in a different way, not as religious obligation but as the place to find the wisdom that was healing her.

- She learned new interpersonal skills for building better relationships.
- She worked out conflicts with people, asked for forgiveness, and made amends.
- She learned to reach out to people at the critical times when she needed help.
- She lost the weight.

These steps map the path that Jeri took and that God describes. She got to the end of herself, reached out to God, and with his help got reconnected to him and his life. He healed her, removed things from her soul and character that were hurting her, and built some new things that she did not possess before going into her recovery. Through spiritual growth, her addiction was overcome.

◆ FROM HOPE TO CERTAINTY FOR YOU TOO

If some part of your life is out of control and resulting in negative consequences, you may be struggling with an addiction. If so, you are a candidate for recovery. Here is a summary of the steps you can take to find help and healing. You will notice that many of them are the same as the twelve steps of Alcoholics Anonymous:

1. Admit to yourself, to God, and to another person that you are out of control and this addiction has gotten the best of you. Admit that you are powerless on your own to fix it.
2. Ask God for forgiveness for whatever you have done, and claim it. Receive it, and get rid of all condemnation.
3. Believe that God can help you, reach out to him, and totally submit yourself to his care, guidance, direction, and strength. Submit to total obedience to whatever he shows you to do.
4. Take an ongoing inventory of all that is wrong inside and between you and others, and all that you have done wrong. Confess it to God and to someone else.

5. Continually ask God to show you anything that you need to work on, and when he tells you, follow through.
6. Go and ask for forgiveness and make amends to all whom you have hurt, except where that might harm the person.
7. Seek God deeply, ask him what he wants you to do, ask him for the power to do it, and then follow through in obedience.
8. Reach out to others.
9. Find out the triggers that get your addictive behavior started, and then when they occur, reach out. Do not ever underestimate the need to reach out. That is why some addicts, especially in the beginning, go to multiple meetings every day and have a sponsor who they can call.
10. Discover the hurts and pains that you are trying to medicate and seek to have them healed. Find out what you are lacking inside and begin to reach out and receive the love and strengthening that you need.
11. Do not try to do all of this alone. Join a support system, maybe attending every day for a few months, and get a few buddies to call on every day.
12. Find out what relational skills you need to develop in order to make your relationships work. Work on these skills and take risks in order to relate to people better.
13. Forgive everyone who has ever hurt you.
14. Find your talents and develop them. Pursue your dreams and goals.
15. Simplify your life so that it has less stress, and make sure that you are recreating and taking care of yourself.
16. Join a structured group that is going to provide the discipline to do all of this.
17. Study God's Word and other spiritual writings that will teach you how to apply it.
18. Stay humble, be honest, and remember that spiritual growth and recovery are for a lifetime, not just for a season.
19. If you are addicted to a substance, seek medical help as well.

In the beginning it is possible that you will go through withdrawal or other serious medical conditions. Make sure that you are safe.

20. See your addiction not as the problem but as a symptom of a life that is not planted and growing in God. Get into recovery as a life overhaul, not just to fix a symptom.

It does not matter what you are addicted to—a substance, a person, a behavior, or something else. It does not matter how long you have been addicted. It does not matter how severe the consequences. If you are willing to allow God to make a way, he will. All you have to do is to stop trying to tell yourself to be strong, admit that you are weak, and get into his system of recovery. The plan works if you work the plan. The strength will not come from you but from God. Yet you have to go to him with your weakness and join his program in order to receive his strength. We encourage you to do that and to discover, like millions before you, that no matter what you have lost, God can make a way.

DISCOURAGEMENT AND DEPRESSION

I was so depressed when I didn't get the raise." "I gained ten more pounds; that was really depressing." "All this rain is making me so depressed."

Most of us have made these kinds of comments in order to describe a negative experience or a bad day or event. Though we are describing events and feelings that can be deeply sad and discouraging, *we are not describing depression*. In the last few years, the meaning of depression has changed and broadened to something different from what it really is.

Those who truly understand *depression* use the term somewhat sparingly. I (John) would not wish true depression on my worst enemy—it is one of the most painful experiences a person can undergo. There are, however, varying degrees of severity of depression. If you are depressed, you may feel

- ◆ utterly alone and utterly isolated, inside and outside of yourself;
- ◆ a deep self-hatred that constantly attacks your soul with condemnation and criticism;
- ◆ nonexistent, not really alive and real, numb and detached from life;

- lethargic and soul weary, as if trying to swim in mud;
- as if you were trapped in a "black hole."

Some people who have experienced very severe depression say it is the closest thing they can imagine to being in hell.

People also respond differently to those who are depressed, and most of us hope that we will never be in that place emotionally. Some feel confused because they can see no reason for the depressed person's feelings. They may become frustrated and angry because it can look like the depressed person isn't doing the things he or she needs to do to get better. Others have compassion, perhaps because they have experienced the listlessness of depression themselves or because they love someone who has. They can hang on to hope when the depressed person has none, offering their support through their care and prayers. Depression leaves no one unmarked or unmoved at some level.

Depression also has a life of its own, so to speak. It occurs independent of your circumstances, which is counter to what many believe. This fact is what distinguishes true depression from the feelings of discouragement or sadness that can accompany an event or experience. When you are feeling down or blue, your feelings can often be "cured" by changing your environment or setting. For example, if you have a row with your spouse you may feel distant and lonely, but you usually feel more alive inside and connected to each other after you reconcile. Or if you are stressed out and discouraged about your job, you may take a weekend off to go play somewhere and come back refreshed and invigorated. Many churches conduct weekend retreats for their members with this idea in mind, and they are very effective.

True depression doesn't go away so easily. Being depressed is similar to having a bacterial infection—all the aspirin in the world will not make it go away. When you are truly depressed, though reconciled relationships and relaxing environments can help bring some relief, they don't remove the symptoms. You then become a depressed person with reconciled relationships in a relaxing environment. It is as if depressed people have a filter in their brains that interprets any words or experiences through the depression, so they become distorted. For example, if you are depressed, a friend might tell you, "I care about what happens to you," yet you won't be able to feel any warmth or comfort from your friend's words. Instead you will likely respond with something like, "That's because you don't know me," or "I hear you, but I don't feel it."

Many people in the church do not understand this about depression, and thus they try to help the depressed person by talking about the love of God, the hope of his provision, and all the good things he has in store for us. The depressed person will try to "take it in" and experience these truths, but it won't happen. Often, well-meaning people will unknowingly sever the truth of God's Word from the experience of being present with a person. Depressed people need both God's truth and his love, in the form of his Spirit and his people. It takes more than the words themselves.

This was the case for William, a pastor who had struggled with depression most of his life. For years he was able to keep his feelings of self-condemnation and loneliness at bay, occasionally seeing a counselor until he felt a little better, but he never truly resolved the issue. When he was in his early forties, however, William took a job on the pastoral staff of a large church. Within a few months he started to lose weight and couldn't sleep more than two or three hours a night. He spiraled downward, becoming more and more listless and lethargic until it impaired his ability to do his job at the church. After about six months of this, the church had to let him go, but they did so with the promise to keep him on the payroll so that he could get the help he needed. They wanted him to see a counselor and to determine whether the cause of his condition was emotional, biological, or both.

William did seek professional help. When he told his counselor that he had lost any hope of ever feeling any differently, the counselor asked him how this felt. William told him, "I don't really feel any-

thing. I know I should feel badly about this, but I don't. Not really."
Part of the reason that he'd lost hope was his inability to feel God's
love for him—or anyone else's for that matter. He knew what God
thought about him—after all, he'd gone to seminary—but he'd never
really believed it in his heart. William's depression was severe, and it
took a long period of counseling and being on medication before he
began to experience good results and the hope that God was making
a way for him in dealing with depression.

William's depression was obvious to everyone. It was impossible to
be around him and not know that something was desperately wrong,
but many times this isn't the case. You can be depressed and not even
realize it because you don't feel sad or down or encounter hopeless
feelings. However, you may be having relationship difficulties or work
difficulties, or you may be self-medicating through substances, sex, or
food, which anesthetize you from the experience. Your involvement in
activities that are normally productive and healthy, such as work,
hobbies, sports, art, or even ministry tasks, may be so intense that
these prevent you from feeling sad or lonely. Yet if you have a hidden
depression, most of the time it will ultimately emerge. It will begin
"leaking" out; or you will become aware that you are not doing these
things out of freedom but out of fear or compulsion, and that there
you don't find true joy or satisfaction in them. You also may become
aware of being depressed when you find someone who truly loves and
cares for you. The other person's love and vulnerability may help to
melt the inaccessible parts of you inside.

◆ HOLDING ON TO GOD

God makes a way through depression—even severe depression like
William's. God is no stranger to depression; he understands it, and
his nature is such that the darker the despair, the more his love and
light grow. He heals most where we are injured the most: "You, O
LORD, keep my lamp burning; my God turns my darkness into
light" (Psalm 18:28).

If you are depressed, you are not alone. The research indicates that a significant percentage of people will become depressed at some point in their lives. Famous figures such as Abraham Lincoln and Winston Churchill have indicated depression in their writings. The apostle Paul identified with depression in his own sufferings: "But God, who comforts the depressed, comforted us by the coming of Titus" (2 Corinthians 7:6, NASB). Jesus described his experience in the Garden of Gethsemane in similar terms: "Then he said to them, 'My soul is overwhelmed with sorrow to the point of death. Stay here and keep watch with me'" (Matthew 26:38).

The suffering of Jesus also helps clarify some misunderstandings about the causes of depression. Some people believe that depression is a sign of some spiritual, moral, or ethical failure or lapse—the result of the internal conflict that comes when we are bad or miss the mark. It is true that we do experience internal conflict when we are not true to being the person God intended us to be. When we stray off God's path, he gives us signals to help correct us: "When I kept silent, my bones wasted away through my groaning all day long" (Psalm 32:3). At the same time, however, it is simply not true that sin causes all depression, just as it is not true that sin causes all the pain we endure. Suffering and depression can have very different causes.

Some years ago I went through depression. It was quite painful and disruptive for me, and it did not go away quickly. I was under a lot of stress at the time and began to withdraw from others. I lost some focus in my work, and I began having the negative and hopeless thoughts that accompany depression. I can remember being drawn to cloudy and rainy days. I felt that the weather and sky reflected my own internal darkness and sadness, and it served to comfort me somewhat. Even so, it was a period for me that many have called the "dark night of the soul."

It helped that I understood depression at a clinical level, because I was able to recognize the signs for what they were, so I knew the next step to take. I entered counseling and learned that much of my depression had to do with a lifelong tendency to disconnect from my own heart and not pay attention to my own needs for relationship. I often placed task diligence over emotional dependency. This information was very valuable to me.

The true resolution of my depression ultimately came from God and the way and path that he designed for me to follow. I can remember reading and praying through verses about God's comfort for the depressed person, holding on to him, and hoping that the process he designed would end it. I found a support system of loving, honest, and safe people whom I began to let inside. I learned to open up and be vulnerable to the love of God and others, as the Bible teaches (Psalm 119:76; Ecclesiastes 4:9–12; 2 Corinthians 6:11–13; Ephesians 3:17–19); and, in time, God proved faithful to his nature and his way. I am grateful to God, his realities, and the people he used to get me through it.

As clinical psychologists, Henry and I have dealt with many, many individuals who were depressed or discouraged, at all levels of severity. As in my case, some people suffering from depression can maintain good relationships, work successfully, and continue the basic tasks of life while going through the healing process. Those on the other end of the severity continuum, like William, need external structures that are more intensive—even to the point of hospitalization, if the person is suicidal.

Because of all the research that has been conducted on depression, we know a lot about it. The solutions and treatments are effective, not only for the short term but also in the long run. The two of us strongly believe that many, many depressions can be resolved. Even people who struggle with a chemical component to their depression can make great progress with the medication technology available today. We do not follow the notion that every person must cope with depression or accept that it is a part of them forever, or that it is something they must manage, and that is as good as it gets. We have seen God, his resources, and his answers provide, in the process of repair, healing from depression when people have entered and stayed on his path of growth.

I have noticed, however, that those who struggle with depression fall into two categories. They tend either to avoid dealing with it or they face it, deal with the pain, and bring it to God in the way that he prescribes. Those who try to deny it, rise above it, or use willpower to make it go away tend to suffer more in the long run. Those who put their faith and trust in God end up in a much better place. I have seen this time and again. That is why we want you to have the information needed to apply God's healing to depression.

◆ OUT OF LIFE

According to psychological and psychiatric researchers, depression includes these symptoms:

- ◆ A depressed mood
- ◆ Changes in appetite
- ◆ Changes in sleep patterns
- ◆ Fatigue
- ◆ Self-image distortions
- ◆ Problems in concentration
- ◆ Hopeless feelings

When you experience some of these symptoms over a period of time, you are depressed.

In addition to the emotional component, depression often has a medical component. During depression the brain chemistry is altered, and medication may be required to bring about the right balance of chemicals so that the person's brain can function correctly. When the brain needs corrective medication it signals this need by the presence of what are called *vegetative symptoms*—that is, symptoms that affect a person's ability to function, live, and carry out life's responsibilities. Problems with sleep, appetite, and fatigue are examples of these sorts of symptoms.

When these are in play, no amount of talking or support will resolve the chemical issue. In computer terms, it is not just a software issue now; it is also a hardware issue. The brain itself is not working as it should. Depression that has a medical component must be treated with medication. So if you struggle with a severe depression, we encourage you to consult with a psychiatrist in order to look at the possibility of medications that can help alleviate your symptoms while you are addressing the emotional and relational aspects of your healing.

At its heart, depression is a spiritual, emotional, and personal condition. That condition is best described as being *cut off from life*. In other words, some aspect of the person's heart and soul is out of order, disengaged and disconnected from God and others. It is as if some part of you is lost and frozen in time, and is inaccessible for love, relationship, grace, or the truth.

God did not design or create us to be disconnected from himself or the life he wanted us to have. He is not that way himself. In his deepest essence, God is connected to and is all about love. As the Bible simply puts it, "God is love" (1 John 4:16). We are created in his image—God intended that we be connected in love to him and to others. This connection was intended to extend to every part of our being. We were to be known and loved in our wants, needs, desires, loves, hates, sins, passions, and failures. God did not intend that any part of us be in the dark and out of relationship.

However, the reality of life is that, for various reasons, we do get hurt or wounded inside. When that happens, we often withdraw an injured part of ourselves without even being aware of it. This withdrawal protects the injured part, but it also prevents the injured part from receiving the love and help it needs to heal. It is as if you tore a shoulder muscle while lifting a heavy item the wrong way and then treated it by "favoring" that shoulder and not using it for a while. Yet lack of use alone isn't enough to restore your muscle. To heal properly it needs exercise, massage, and physical therapy.

Remember our discussion in Chapter 8 on loving God with every fiber of yourself, including your heart, soul, mind, and strength? God designed you with many aspects to yourself. You have many parts to your soul and personality. At the same time, parts of your soul can get "out of life." Perhaps you have no ability to grieve and let go of loves you have lost; that ability is then out of life. Or maybe you are unable to make emotional connections with others in the first place. If so, you may feel as if you are not part of life, or that you are almost like a ghost, seeing other people's warmth, love, and compassion for each other, but not being a part of it. You may feel as if you are looking at the real world of love and relationships through a window, but that you are unable to go into the room where it is occurring. You may never have had the ability to possess and own your own feelings and emotions; in this case your feelings exist out of life. Or perhaps you have never been able to be separate and clear about what you will allow and tolerate and what you will refuse, and thus, you may burn out and become depressed. When any of these things happen, these parts of your soul—parts that you really need—stay wounded or undeveloped inside you.

◆ THE SOUL'S CRY FOR HELP

God is eternal and lives in eternity, and he has also made us eternal. We do not cease to exist after we have died. Similarly, the parts of us with which we have lost contact become buried but they do not die. They remain in a stuck and wounded state, deep inside us, waiting to be revived from the outside by life and light. Yet when we do not have access to all of ourselves, and when those parts of us are not loved and in the process of healing and growth, then life does not work well for us. We are handicapped in our choices, in our ability to function at high levels, and in our ability to be deeply connected to others. It takes a great deal of energy to keep these parts of ourselves underground, although we may not be aware of it. Thus, handicapped and spiritually exhausted, we become depressed.

Depression is truly the soul's cry for help, and in this sense it is a blessing. Depression is an unmistakable signal that something is wrong inside and needs to be explored and understood, and to have God's healing resources brought to bear upon it. In a way that few conditions do, depression brings us to our knees—to the end of ourselves—so that we will seek God's answers and ways. Many people whom I have treated for depression have told me that they were grateful that God allowed the condition, for it caused them to look for his answers in a way that they had not been open to or aware of before: "It was good for me to be afflicted so that I might learn your decrees" (Psalm 119:71).

What, then, are the ways that God provides for you to deal successfully with depression?

◆ CONNECTING THE DISCONNECTED

If, instead of depression, you had a stomach ulcer, what is the first thing you would do? You would probably go see a specialist who would examine, diagnose, and treat you. The worst thing you could do would be to avoid talking to anyone about it and hope it went away.

The same is true with depression. No matter what is causing or driving your depression, in order for the depression to lead to life, you need relationship. Your soul needs to experience the depth and healing of love and grace. No one gets well on his or her own. Anyone struggling with depression will need to be connected, both to God and to people. As we describe in chapters 1 and 2, the best place to be in any situation is in relationship. Relationship is not a luxury, it is a necessity; and this is particularly true for you if you are depressed.

As I said earlier, a lack of connection and relationship helps give rise to the depression. The nature of depression requires that you be open and vulnerable to other, safe people. The presence and application of relationship will help to undo your depression, because the broken part of your soul is receiving what it has been lacking.

As you likely recognize, this can be difficult. People who care about you and love you can surround you, and yet the isolated parts of your soul may remain untouched because you can't open up and receive their love for you. It will take time for you to recognize and reach the part of your soul that you have kept from others. Initially, you may not be able to "reach out and touch someone" with the broken part of yourself because it may simply be too inaccessible, hurt, or undeveloped.

I have a friend, Dawn, whose depression had a lot to do with her inability to let others inside her heart. When she became a part of a therapy group to heal the depression, she could not make herself feel close to or trusting of the people in the group. In fact, she could not trust God or anyone with her heart. However, Dawn did do what she was able to do: She trusted God and his process enough to get involved in the group. She brought her inability, her fears, her lack of trust, and her emotional inaccessibility to the group, who then supported her, loved her, and, over time, earned her trust.

Dawn did this by first watching and observing quietly how the group interacted with each other. She kept a safe distance. Then, as she noted that the members did not condemn each other (Romans 8:1) and that they were vulnerable with each other, she began taking risks with them. She talked about her fears of opening up and being hurt, abandoned, or attacked. Then, as the members of the group proved safe, she revealed her own experiences of being injured by significant others, the losses she had sustained, and the things she had done to make things worse for herself.

Dawn did what people all through the centuries have done, and what you can do: Reach out to God and his people with whatever you have the ability to reach out with—your need, or your commitment, or your pain, or your awareness. That is, whatever you are in touch with about yourself, whatever is hurting, whatever you can talk about that deals with what is real in your life. God takes us in whatever state we are in, and wherever we cannot provide, he takes up the slack and goes the extra mile. One of my favorite stories in the Bible is the one about the father of the boy who was possessed by a demon. The father took his son to Jesus, who talked to him about the importance of belief in Christ himself: "Immediately the boy's father exclaimed, 'I do believe; help me overcome my unbelief!'" (Mark 9:24). I can so identify with the father's reaching out with all the belief he had, yet knowing what he had was not enough. At that point, he humbly asked Jesus for the rest of the belief he did not possess.

All you have to do—and I admit that this can be a lot—is reach out for relationship and connection with God and others and be committed to the process of healing, to God's path for you out of depression. You can bring yourself to relationship, even in a depressed state. The best you may be able to do is to reach out to a group, a pastor, or a counselor who can give you some relational structure and tell them, "I have an aloneness inside. As I am now, I can't let you inside where it is. But I want to be as vulnerable and honest as I can so that, in time, the disconnected parts of me can also come into the relationship." Be open with those parts of your heart that you can be open with, and allow God, his love, and his people to help the rest happen.

Remember that relationship, as God has designed it, is most of what life really is. Allow relationship to fill, guide, and comfort you. That is a large part of what begins to heal and resolve depression.

As you seek connection with God and others, you should also begin exploring the cause of your depression.

◆ REDEEMING WHAT IS LOST OR BROKEN

Depression can have more than one cause. Because of that, steer away from such simplistic explanations as "It is always poor self-image," or "It is always anger turned inward," or "It is always genetic and biological." Humans are more complex creatures than that, and depressed people need help to explore the origins of their depression from those who understand these matters: "The purposes of a man's heart are deep waters, but a man of understanding draws them out" (Proverbs 20:5).

As you ask God to help you identify the cause of your depression, remember that he always redeems his people who have lost their way or have lost some part of themselves. God is a redemptive God. This is why he is called "my Rock and my Redeemer" (Psalm 19:14), for that is who he is and what he does. He seeks out the lost, repairs them, and helps them reenter life to the fullest.

Here is a brief list of some of things that can cause depression. As you go over it, see if any of these resonate with you. Ask those who know you if any make sense for you. And ask God to open windows inside you to help you find what is true about you:

◆ *Inability to grieve losses.* This is a very common cause. When you do not have the capacity to experience your sadness over your losses in life and let go of those things you have lost, the "frozen losses" keep you stuck. That is why, when people become safe enough to feel sad about who or what they no longer have in their lives, they go through a period of grief and then the depression resolves. That is why depression and grief are so different and should not be confused. Actually, grief is the cure for many kinds of depression.

◆ *Lack of ability to need and depend on others emotionally.* Some people have been disconnected from love and comfort all their lives. Their inner world is an empty, isolated place where they cannot reach out to anyone for their needs.

◆ *Problems in responsibility and freedom.* There are times when a person has trouble taking ownership and control of his or her life, or does not feel free to choose what is right for him or her.

◆ *Burnout.* For some reason, some people give to others beyond their resources, and even have difficulty receiving what they need in order to continue.

◆ *Perfectionism.* The perfectionist will often become depressed as the reality of his or her failings and weaknesses becomes too much to bear.

◆ *Feelings of self-condemnation.* This is an individual's suffering from an unbiblical, overcritical, and harsh conscience that attacks him or her even when he or she has done no wrong.

- *Unresolved trauma.* When a person has experienced a catastrophic event or injury that is not processed, confessed, grieved, and worked through, it can contribute to depression.
- *Medical causes.* Some depressions are caused or influenced by a problem in brain chemistry, as we mentioned previously, or by other medical conditions that produce depression. Make sure you have adequate medical input here. A complete physical by a general practitioner and a psychiatric workup by a psychiatrist might be in order.

As you seek to discover which part of you has been lost, think of it as a part of you that you need in order to function well in life. Look at the preceding list. Why do you need the ability to grieve? Why is it important that you experience need? Why is it necessary to be clear about your responsibilities? Learn the value and purpose of the lost part of yourself. It will help you to see how much you need it.

Then, as that part emerges in the context of warm, safe, and loving relationships, begin allowing yourself to feel the feelings that go along with it. Experience the hurt that made that part disappear in the first place. Keep exposing it to the nurture and care of relationships. As it strengthens, take small risks with it. Learn to use it again in your life. Let it take its place in your world. Over time, allow that part of you to mature, grow up, and simply be a part of you that you again own, utilize, and experience.

Clearly, this will require a mentor. You will need someone who has good experience with depression, as there is a great deal to know about it. Follow their guidance, and God's, as the part of you that is lost becomes found.

Depression can be debilitating and frightening. However, God is right there with you in the black hole, as he fills it up with love and light and provides a way out, back into his world. Trust him for that.

18

GUILT AND SHAME

I (Henry) was talking to a woman one day who I did not know very well, and she asked me what I did. When I told her that I wrote books about relationships and the spiritual life, she looked at me a little funny. "What are you, one of those Bible thumpers?" she asked.

"Absolutely," I said, kidding her back. "Why? Aren't you?"

"No way," she said. "I gave up church a long time ago. Too much for me."

"Too much what?" I asked.

"Too much guilt," she said. "What did I need that for? All church ever did was make me feel bad for stuff that seemed pretty normal to me. I was just being a teenager, but when I hung around church, I just felt 'bad.' So I quit."

"Do you miss it?" I asked, not exactly knowing what to expect.

"I don't know what I believe anymore," she said, getting a little more serious. "I think that I would like to connect to my faith, but I don't want to go back to all that guilt. I just can't do that anymore."

Many people are like this woman. They associate guilt with a life with God. Nothing could be further from the truth. Jesus himself, the one who started Christianity and said he was God, hated guilt and judgment. In fact, he hated it so much that he suffered and died so that we would never have to feel it. His life was about forgiveness and freedom from guilt.

One of Jesus' strongest messages was that not only was he not going to judge us *but we were also not to judge each other*. He hates it when people begin to play holier-than-thou with each other.

One day some church people brought a woman who had been caught in the act of adultery to Jesus. Being good religious policemen, they were bringing her to judgment, or at least to the "judge." Here Jesus was, with a true, bona fide sinner. Here was his chance to "take a stand against sin," to let everyone know what he thought of such behavior. What did he do?

He turned to her accusers, and instead of saying they were right, he asked them if they were any different than she was. His first focus was not on the one who had sinned but on the ones who were judging her. It seemed that he was at least as concerned with their judgment of her as he was with her adultery. Could that be? Could the religious people's thinking that they were somehow better than the woman be as big a problem as the sin that she had committed? Take a close look at what happened:

> Jesus bent down and started to write on the ground with his finger. When they kept on questioning him, he straightened up and said to them, "If any one of you is without sin, let him be the first to throw a stone at her." Again he stooped down and wrote on the ground. At this, those who heard began to go away one at a time, the older ones first, until only Jesus was left, with the woman still standing there. Jesus straightened up and asked her, "Woman, where are they? Has no one condemned you?"
>
> "No one, sir," she said.
>
> "Then neither do I condemn you," Jesus declared. "Go now and leave your life of sin."
>
> —JOHN 8:6–11

To the ones who would condemn her, Jesus, in effect, said, "You are just as in need of what I am about to do for her as she is." Certainly some of those people had not committed adultery, and that made his message even stronger. Whatever their sin was, they were imperfect as well.

Jesus did not offer her guilt or condemnation, just forgiveness, compassion, and acceptance. He told her, "Neither do I condemn you." Then he showed his care for her by adding, "Leave your life of sin." He did not condemn her for her failure, but his lack of condemnation did not mean that he was denying the problem. He called her behavior what it was, destructive sin. The Greek word that is translated "sin" here means "to miss the mark, and so not share in the prize." Jesus told her that she was missing the point of what sex and marriage were about, and in doing that, she certainly would not share in the prize of the way it was intended.

In this example, we see how different Jesus was from the church people. That is why I want to scream when I hear people talking about church and guilt. I want to say, "I understand. I have seen that too. But please, don't blame God for that. He is not like that at all."

My question for you is, How do you see him? Do you associate God with guilt for your failure? Have you been the one that the church or other people picked on and proclaimed as "bad?" Do you have a chorus of accusing voices in your head who sing you song after song of guilt, telling you how bad you are and that you deserve the first stone? Or, by some miracle, have you felt the touch of acceptance that Jesus offered this woman, and do you know deep in your soul that you are totally forgiven and are free from guilt? That is the place we want you to be.

I was recently having lunch with a man with whom I do business, and it was an interesting contrast to the conversation I had with the woman described earlier. We were talking about church and faith, and I wished that I could have introduced him to this woman so that they could trade stories. He told me that he was excited to come back to God at age sixty. He said that he never thought he would see himself getting interested in doing "God things." I asked him why.

"Well, I used to go to church and I had to stop, because I felt so guilty. I knew that I had done some things that were really not the way you were supposed to live, and I wanted to be good; I just wasn't. I had not turned around at that time, and I was caught up in some things that I felt pretty bad about. I would go to church and hear about the very things that I was doing, and it was just too much.

"Then, a few years ago, out of desperation I went to the church where I go now. I knew that I had not been the person I should have been, but I just wanted to have God in my life. So I went, and the pastor talked about something I had never heard before. He said that it did not matter what you had done, that God would still accept you and forgive you, if you just asked him. I had never heard that before. I just did what he said, and my whole life is different. It is so good to know that God loves me and has forgotten all my past. I can start new every day. I wish everyone could know about this," he said.

"Well, that is pretty much why they call it 'good news,'" I said. "But I can't believe that you went to church before and never heard that that is what the Bible says. You did not know that God would forgive anything and everything if you asked?"

"No, I didn't. And the sad thing is that I don't think a lot of people are getting that message now either. I believe that when they think of Christians they think of people who are judgmental and will look down on them if they really know the truth," he said. "It is so different when you know that God really is forgiving and you can get rid of the guilt."

This man was now enjoying a relationship with God free from the fear that God was down on him. That is the message that Jesus came to bring to us. Yet, like him, some people have never understood the message of forgiveness. There are also people who *have* heard the message and still feel guilty. Why is that? Can you identify with either of these? Well, stick with us, for not only can God make a way out of guilt to total innocence, but he can make a way for the innocent who still feel guilty to be free as well.

◆ Guilty, As Charged

One of the reasons that we feel guilty in life is simply this: We are guilty. Every human is born with a capacity for knowing that there are standards in the universe and that we do not always live up to those standards. No matter what your belief system is, no matter what religion or lack of religion you adhere to, we have all failed to live up to that belief system. The content and the rules vary, but we all fail to meet our own standard. We all know that there are some things that we have done that we should not have done. We are all guilty.

We respond to our guilt in different ways. Some people try to do what the woman that I talked to did—just get away from it as best they can. They feel that if they get away from God, then they can get away from the problem. However, that never works, as the guilt just goes deeper and deeper into the mind and soul. It even affects us in other ways, such as making us feel like no one would really like us if they knew the truth about us.

Other people try to rewrite what they have been taught about right and wrong. In some cases, as we shall see, this is a good thing. Some of the things that we are taught are wrong are really okay. The need for a new perspective is one of the things that Jesus taught over and over. Yet, at times, just trying to believe differently is not enough, especially if we know we are just rationalizing our real guilt. No matter how many times we tell ourselves that something is okay, if it is really not, a part of us always knows, and the guilt remains.

Still others just live with their guilt and take on the identity of a "sinner." They know that they are "bad," and they adopt that way of thinking about themselves and try to accept it. I have talked with many teenagers who have been deemed the black sheep of the family, and they just come to grips with it, thinking that that is who they are and will always be. Sadly, I've also talked with many adults who still see themselves as black sheep.

Some give up the standard altogether and throw in the towel. They feel like they have already blown it, and there is nothing they can do about it anyway, so they may as well give up and just have a good time. Sometimes they will try to medicate the guilt with substances, sex, or something else, but it is always there.

Regardless of our response, we really are guilty. In fact, from the Bible's perspective, the problem is even bigger than that. From God's perspective, the problem is that we have all tried to live life apart from him and tried to be our own gods. We have all "gone our own way." We are guilty of rejecting God and his role in our lives.

Yet God has made a way for us out of our dilemma. He saw that we were separated from him, and he came to earth to win us back. That is why Jesus said that he did not come to judge or condemn the world. He came to find us, to tell us that he would forgive us if only we would come back to him. It is not about being good enough to outweigh all the bad things we have ever done. One bad thing is enough to make us guilty. (Even in a human court, if you break one law and keep all the others, you still have to face trial.) Nor is it about just blowing it off and saying, "No big deal." The things we have done are a big deal, as Jesus told the woman caught in adultery.

From God's perspective, our situation is very simple. We are all guilty, and there is a penalty for that guilt. Jesus paid the penalty—the death sentence—for our rejection of God and his laws. Since he paid our penalty, if we just put our faith in him and ask for forgiveness, it is a done deal. That is the end of guilt.

This is so simple that a child can understand it. Interestingly enough, it is that very simplicity that makes it sound too foolish for some people to believe. It is just too good to be true.

Yet it is true. Here is the way that Paul puts it:

> But now a righteousness from God, apart from law [God's rules], has been made known, to which the Law and the Prophets testify. This righteousness from God comes through faith in Jesus Christ to all who believe. There is no difference, for all have sinned and fall short

of the glory of God, and are justified freely by his grace through the redemption that came by Christ Jesus.

—ROMANS 3:21–24

Everyone has blown it, and everyone can be forgiven by just believing in him. The guilt is gone, forever. If you have put your faith in God, then the Bible says that you are totally forgiven—past, present, and future. As Paul says, "Therefore, there is now no condemnation for those who are in Christ Jesus" (Romans 8:1). If you believe, you are forgiven. Here are a few more verses just to let you know we are not making this up!

+ "Therefore, since we have been justified through faith, we have peace with God through our Lord Jesus Christ, through whom we have gained access by faith into this grace in which we now stand. And we rejoice in the hope of the glory of God" (Romans 5:1–2).
+ "He does not treat us as our sins deserve or repay us according to our iniquities. For as high as the heavens are above the earth, so great is his love for those who fear him; as far as the east is from the west, so far has he removed our transgressions from us" (Psalm 103:10–12).
+ "If we confess our sins, he is faithful and just and will forgive us our sins and purify us from all unrighteousness" (1 John 1:9).

God has made a way out of real guilt. By faith, you can stand in grace and acceptance from God. You can have peace because you've been forgiven and do not have to worry anymore. He has *removed* your transgressions from you, as far as east is from west. If you have agreed with him that you need forgiveness and confessed your need, then he grants it freely, no matter what you have done. Good news, indeed, isn't it?

Yet the message of forgiveness doesn't eliminate feelings of guilt for everyone. Some people have been forgiven but are still plagued by feelings of guilt. If you are in that situation, what can you do? There are some answers. In fact, the Bible talks about that problem: Our heart can "condemn us, but God is greater than our hearts" (1 John 3:20). Here are some ways and reasons that our hearts can condemn us, and what we can do about it.

◆ THE HEAD AND THE HEART

"I know that God says he forgives me, at least in my head," said Barry. "But I just can't feel it in my heart. I still feel 'bad.'"

Knowing something in our heads does not always translate to feeling it in our hearts, where our emotions live and breathe. This is because we know things in two different ways. One way is conceptual and informational. We *know* that we are forgiven. We know that from the information in the Bible, for instance, or from what someone tells us.

The other way of knowing is experiential. It comes from what we have experienced in relationships. If, for example, a lot of our significant relationships have not been very forgiving and have left us feeling bad or fearful of losing love and acceptance, then that is what our hearts *know,* even if our heads know differently. The gap between the head and the heart renders us unable to feel what we know to be true.

To close the gap, you have to talk to your heart in its own language, the language of experience. *You not only have to learn about forgiveness, you also have to experience it.* You do that by bringing your faults out into the light, confessing them to other people who are safe and loving, and then experiencing the love and forgiveness that they offer you in the name of God. In *How People Grow* (Zondervan, 2001), I told the story of a pastor who suffered from a recurring sexual compulsion and felt so guilty that he got very depressed. He knew that God had forgiven him, but guilt and fear still gripped him.

One day, I put him in a group and told him that I wanted him to talk about his struggle. At first, it was very difficult for him even to think about doing that. Yet he did. As he opened up, the group got teary-eyed and felt compassion for him. He was looking down and could not see the compassion and grace that they had for him. I interrupted him and asked him to look up.

When he did, and he saw their loving and compassionate faces, he broke like a reed. He fell forward and just sobbed and sobbed. That day, he came out of the prison of his guilt. He was a new person, and for the first time he felt the forgiveness that he had read and studied about for years. He realized the power of opening up to others and receiving the love that God gives to us through his people. He discovered that these words of Scripture were truer than he had ever imagined: "Therefore confess your sins to each other and pray for each other so that you may be healed. The prayer of a righteous man is powerful and effective" (James 5:16). He also experienced the blessing described in 1 Peter 4:10, which says, "Each one should use whatever gift he has received to serve others, faithfully administering God's grace in its various forms."

As we confess to each other, and receive the gift of love that others give, God's grace through them heals our hearts, and we know the experience that we might have never had and therefore have been unable to feel. The head and the heart come together.

◆ BEING IMPERFECT

One time I was leading a retreat of successful leaders, one of whom was an "up and comer." He was happy to be on a retreat with successful leaders whom he admired. The first night, I had them go around the circle and tell the group what was going on with them and what they hoped to get out of the retreat.

They went around the circle and told the group what they were dealing with, and some of them had some significant struggles. When it came time for the young star to speak, he said, "Man, I just feel better already. I am not as screwed up as I thought!" What he meant was that he had discovered something very, very helpful. He had found that *all of us struggle*. He had heard men who he idealized and placed on pedestals confess to imperfections and struggles. When he did, it was easier for him to accept his own imperfections, sins, and foibles.

You may feel guilty because you have some impossible standards in your head. You might feel like you ought to be perfect, or nearly perfect. Yet impossible standards can survive only in an isolated vacuum. When you get with others and begin to be real with each other, then you find that other people are just like you. We find that we are all sinners and subject to the same imperfections. Then, when we find that, we change our expectations. We become realistic by moving from expecting to be perfect to expecting to be really, really imperfect, which is reality.

The Bible shows us how God makes a way out of our perfectionism—he just nukes it. He thinks that we are pretty nutty, and he wants us to see that as well, so we can get better. He wants us to see who we really are and just face the truth. If we could see ourselves as imperfect, as he does, we would become humble and be a lot more comfortable accepting ourselves. Listen to what he says:

- ◆ "There is not a righteous man on earth who does what is right and never sins" (Ecclesiastes 7:20).
- ◆ "As a father has compassion on his children, so the LORD has compassion on those who fear him; for he knows how we are formed, he remembers that we are dust" (Psalm 103:13–14).
- ◆ "If we claim to be without sin, we deceive ourselves and the truth is not in us" (1 John 1:8).

We need to align our view of ourselves with God's view. We need to see ourselves as we really are: imperfect, prone not to get it right, and so on. Then, when we see our imperfections, we will not be so shaken up, and we can do what he does. We will be able to say, "Well, there it is again, that imperfection stuff. I missed the mark one more time. Thank you, God, that you love me like I am."

Again, we need both the information and the experience of being imperfect yet accepted to make this shift. The information comes from seeing what God says we are like, and seeing what others are like as well. Experiential knowing comes from getting together with others and talking about our faults and imperfections and being loved and accepted despite those things. We learn we are fellow travelers on the road of overcoming problems, failures, sins, weaknesses, hurts, and the like. We are a family of strugglers, and God loves us just the way we are. As Jesus said, he did not come to judge us for who we are. He came to seek and to save us, just as we are (Luke 19:10).

◆ CONFESSING AND MAKING AMENDS

Sometimes, we can be heartbroken over something we have done in a relationship. Often, to get through those feelings, it helps to go to the person we have hurt and ask for forgiveness. The Bible tells us to practice this principle, and it's one that people in recovery have also found to be healing. In fact, one of the twelve steps in traditional recovery programs involves making amends to whomever you have hurt, except when it is harmful to do so.

Jesus taught that our spiritual relationship with God is intertwined with our relationships with each other. One time he said that if we were worshiping and giving to God and we became aware that someone had something against us, we should put down our offering and go to that person and work it out: "Therefore, if you are offering your gift at the altar and there remember that your brother has something against you, leave your gift there in front of the altar. First go and be reconciled to your brother; then come and offer your gift" (Matthew 5:23–24).

Confession will do several things. In confession you go to the person you have wronged and ask for forgiveness. This allows you to receive that person's forgiveness. Many times the people we have hurt really want to forgive us. In addition, when we humble ourselves, it can disarm those from whom we are seeking forgiveness. In most cases your confession is a wonderful gift to the other person;

it validates his or her pain and feelings and lets that person know you care about him or her.

Furthermore, not only will you be forgiven, which is *huge,* but after your confession you may find that you have been carrying around something that the other person did not feel that hurt or angry about, or something that he or she had already forgotten about or forgiven you for. You will be relieved of unnecessary suffering.

Of course, there are times when the other person will refuse to forgive you. Yet, even in this situation, you can find resolution because you will know that you have confessed and asked for forgiveness. You can be at peace knowing that you have done all that God has asked you to do. It is up to the other person to work out how he or she will respond. As Paul lets us know, sometimes all we can do is all we can do, for there is only so much that we can control in any relationship. We can do only our part: "If it is possible, as far as it depends on you, live at peace with everyone" (Romans 12:18). The rest is up to that person and God.

◆ GETTING INTO REALITY

The Bible is not really that big on guilt. It sees it as a problem more than a solution. Jesus died to take guilt away. Yet, as we pointed out in the story about the adulterous woman, that does not mean that God just lets problems slide. Far from it. He addresses the reality of the problem and wants us to work on it, *instead of feeling guilty.* Have you ever known people who felt so badly about failing you that they seemed oblivious to how you were feeling? They were so focused on their own self-centered guilt that they couldn't look at you and how their actions were affecting you. This is one reason that God does not want us to feel guilty when we fail someone.

Instead, he wants us to feel sorry. He wants us to feel remorse. Guilt is all about me and how bad I am when I sin, and remorse is all about you and the effects of my sin on you. Love, not guilt, motivates remorse. In remorse I look at you and how I have hurt you and feel empathy and sorrow for what I have caused. Remorse motivates us to change our behavior when we see how it is hurting someone else. As Paul puts it, godly sorrow leads to real change (2 Corinthians 7:10). Guilt is often more about self-condemnation. That does no one any good at all.

So stop looking at how bad you are when you sin or fail someone. Instead, look at what your behavior is doing to the person you have wronged. That will lead you to the highest morality possible, which is the golden rule: "Treat others as you would want to be treated."

The same is true when you look at the reality of your behavior in your own life. Feeling guilty about your failures will never motivate you to lasting change. However, looking at the way that you might be wasting your life, your talents, or your health might motivate you. We all need wake-up calls to get us serious about changing.

God is not into guilt, but he is very much into reality. Jesus did not condemn the woman caught in adultery, but he did want her to face the reality of adultery and what it was doing to her. The apostle Paul, in the same chapter that he tells us that we are not condemned (Romans 8), goes on to say that if we sow to our fleshly indulgences, it will bring about death, and if we sow to the life of the Spirit, it will bring about life. No condemnation, but major concern about how we live (vv. 12–13). This is reality, and this is what we should be worried about.

◆ GROWING UP

Children feel guilty when they fall short of the standards that their parents have set. Since God has told us that he forgives us for not living up to his standard, we are free to "grow up" and be adults for the first time. We can get over the guilt that has kept us "down" and become the mature people he wants us to be. Mature people think about the reality of their problems. Yet, first, we have to take a step.

We have to come out of the "guilty child" syndrome in relation to other people. When you do not see yourself as equal with other adults, you will struggle with guilt to some degree or another. You will turn others into parent figures and try to "live up to" their standards for you, and consequently you will be subject to guilt messages from them.

Jesus didn't want us to turn others into gods or parent figures. He wanted us to be siblings—brothers and sisters—and to seek to please only God. That removes the potential of guilt from trying and failing to please others. If there is a person who you cannot please, God's answer is to stop trying. Don't try to please people. Realize that you are their equal and live for God instead. As Jesus said, "But you are not to be called 'Rabbi,' for you have only one Master and you are all brothers. And do not call anyone on earth 'father,' for you have one Father, and he is in heaven. Nor are you to be called 'teacher,' for you have one Teacher, the Christ" (Matthew 23:8–10).

With God as your parent, you can treat other humans as equal adults and stop being "under their law."

◆ GETTING ON THE PATH

As we have seen, God doesn't want us to focus on guilt but on forgiveness and dealing with reality. His path for getting rid of guilt is simple: confession, receiving forgiveness from him and others, and then facing the reality of the problem and dealing with it. By this we mean looking at how the problem is either self-destructive or destructive to someone else and getting into a path of growth that will do away with the problem. That is the path to freedom.

So, to review, when you fail, follow these nine steps to freedom:

1. Turn to God and ask him for forgiveness. Once you ask, it will be granted. He is not withholding at all. He promises it as soon as it is requested: "If we confess our sins, he is faithful and just and will forgive us our sins and purify us from all unrighteousness" (1 John 1:9).
2. Look at the reality of your failure and take it seriously. That is called *repentance*. See your sin for the destructiveness that it is, and do whatever you have to do to deal with it.

3. If there are others you have hurt, then go to them (unless it would be somehow destructive), ask for forgiveness, and be reconciled (Matthew 5:23–24).

4. Confess your failures (all of them) to another person who understands God's forgiveness and will administer it to you (James 5:16).

5. Work to make the false standards and messages in your head more realistic (Ecclesiastes 7:20).

6. Get in community with other people and open up with each other, so they know you and you them. As you join other strugglers who can identify with you, you will know that everyone is imperfect, and you can help each other with a humble and gentle attitude (Galatians 6:1). As they come to know you, you will internalize their acceptance and it will become self-acceptance.

7. Do an entire moral inventory of your life, as far as you can remember, and as completely as you can. Write down every sin that you can think of, and ask God to help you bring things to mind for which you need forgiveness (Psalm 139:23–24). Then, confess that sin to him, ask for forgiveness, and share it with someone safe. Finally, claim your clean slate and go on from there in freedom. If this is too painful, get some counseling or professional help to work through the things about which you feel guilty. Don't try to do it on your own.

8. When you have accusing voices in your head about your failure, remember, *they are lies.* Find their source and deal with it. As we said in chapter 14, combat these voices with Scripture. When they accuse you, quote the truth of Scripture, including Romans 8:1: "Therefore, there is now *no* condemnation for those who are in Christ Jesus" (emphasis ours). You are forgiven, so, tell the voices to be quiet.

9. Memorize Scripture. When Satan or others lied to Jesus, Jesus quoted the Bible. For you to do the same, you will need

to know the Word. David said that he had "hidden" God's Word in his heart, and you can do the same. Get flashcards and write down Scripture verses on forgiveness, and carry them around. Memorize them so you will be able to quote them. It really works!

◆ GOING ON IN FREEDOM

When Jesus encountered the woman caught in adultery, he sent her out to a new life of freedom—freedom from her past, her guilt, and her failures. He did it with his love and his word. Today, he offers that same freedom to all of us.

Sometimes it is difficult to believe, but it is true. He forgives everything for those who ask. So ask him, and believe what he promises: He will forgive. When it is difficult to believe or to feel, then do the things we have suggested here, and God will make a way for you to deal with guilt. Then, when he does, hold your head up high. Don't be shy. Act like the innocent person that you now are! God has pronounced you "not guilty."

19

WEIGHT LOSS AND HEALTH

Since I (John) hit my thirties, my weight has gone up and down within a certain range. It goes up when I eat too much or wrongly, or when I don't get enough exercise, or have too much stress. It's also gone up when I've felt distant from God or have had trouble experiencing his presence and grace. As I have reflected on this over the years, I have determined that weight gain often has to do with the need for love, not only from people but also from God. When we don't experience what we need, we sometimes use food as a substitute.

Most of us will struggle with weight during our lives, whether it be on a slight, moderate, or severe level. Being overweight can be annoying, or it can be life-threatening. So much has been written about weight control over the years that you might be tempted to think, *Here we go again, more of the same.* Much of the information available today is very helpful and well thought out. In fact, we hope you are using it. However, in this chapter we want to help you view weight problems within the context of all of life, especially within the life of God. We hope to help you understand that your weight is a part of your life and who you are; it's not an isolated part of you, disconnected from God, your relationships, your heart, and your growth process.

◆ A SPIRITUAL ISSUE

Perhaps you're wondering what God and his way have to do with weight in the first place. The answer is one we have threaded throughout this book, and that is that *all issues are spiritual issues, and all struggles are spiritual struggles.* There is no reality in your life that is not spiritual, as God is the Lord of all reality. He does not divide the universe into "God things" and "real life things," as we tend to do. He designed the human, physical, and emotional dimensions from within himself: "The earth is the LORD's, and everything in it, the world, and all who live in it" (Psalm 24:1). The universe, including that part of it which is your weight problem, is spiritual in nature.

God is also present and involved in all aspects of our lives. Our well-being and very survival are important to him. He does not provide "spiritual" answers for theological problems and leave the answers for "real life" problems to others. He has answers, a plan, and a path for all of this. "The LORD commanded us to obey all these decrees and to fear the LORD our God, so that we might always prosper and be kept alive, as is the case today" (Deuteronomy 6:24). He is concerned about all parts of your life.

Seeing the spiritual nature of weight issues often provides a great deal of relief and comfort. Believing that we are alone with our problems can be extremely discouraging. But when you see that God cares, is present, and has a way for you, you can share your burden with him—and his shoulders are extremely broad. As you make your journey into weight control, you can ask for his help, submit to him, seek his answers, and expectantly look forward to seeing results in your body.

This is good news. For one thing, it can free you to deal with the medical and physical realities that pertain to your weight. These matters are spiritual ones; so God is also present within them. So don't worry that looking at issues such as nutrition and exercise means that you are neglecting your faith. Actually, just the opposite is true. It is good and right for you to look for people and resources with the expertise and information that can help you. The Bible instructs us to discipline our bodies (1 Corinthians 9:27).

So as you seek truth about your body, ask God for his help and guidance. This goes hand in hand with trusting in him.

◆ Not doable without Grace

God's grace is a key factor in weight control, especially if you are one of those people who has tried and failed at previous weight control attempts. Grace provides you with the ally and resources you will need to undergo the process of weight control.

Grace, briefly defined, is *unmerited favor.* It means much more than that God has forgiven you and no longer has enmity with you. More than the absence of his wrath, grace is also the presence of his favor—favor that, because it is unmerited, is freely given to you. You cannot earn it. When God favors you, or graces you, it means he is for you. He is on your side. He wants your best. He is in an allied relationship with you. This means that discouragement, overwhelming problems, and even weight issues pale before your Ally: "If God is for us, who can be against us?" (Romans 8:31).

One of the hallmarks of people struggling with weight issues is that they are vulnerable to a "try harder to be good enough" mentality. Because of their weight, they feel unacceptable to God or others. So they exert their willpower and self-effort, disciplining themselves in order to lose the pounds and become acceptable. Some maintain the weight loss for a period of time, but then they gain it back. They may try different strategies and approaches, but their own efforts inevitably let them down.

This failure is due to the failure of the law, or the commands of the Old Testament, to transform us into acceptable people. Self-effort and willpower alone cannot do the trick. The law, while true and righteous, is insufficient to make someone lovable or acceptable. In fact, one of its very purposes is to show us our sin and need for God's grace: "Therefore no one will be declared righteous in his sight by observing the law; rather, through the law we become conscious of sin" (Romans 3:20). Many people do not understand this. Instead, they think, *If I work hard enough at it, I can be good enough.* This mentality is always destined to fail.

The realization that you can't be good enough can make you feel despair and discouragement. If you, on your own, cannot do what it takes to lose weight, then you are hopeless. Yet it is a blessed hopelessness, because when we come to the end of self-effort and give up trying to be good enough, we find God waiting on the other side, holding out his grace to us. Through Jesus, we are set free from the law of death to find his law of life: "Because through Christ Jesus the law of the Spirit of life set me free from the law of sin and death" (Romans 8:2).

This is where true hope lies, whether it be in weight control or a relationship problem. When we accept God's gift of grace through his Son's death for us, we can release the burden of being good enough on our own and embrace the reality that we have God on our side. He will help us, guide us, sustain us, and lead us. Living in grace is the only way to succeed in the difficult task of weight loss. When we allow God to remove the extra weight of self-effort, we open the door for him to help us lose the physical weight as well.

Go to him, surrender your willpower and attempts to try harder, and take the humble step of admitting you are powerless in your own strength. That humility and that confession are the keys to your future success.

♦ THE PRINCIPLE OF REFLECTION

A third significant principle for weight control is this: *That which is seen reflects that which is unseen.* Put another way, the visible can illuminate the nature of the invisible. We see this in the person of Christ, who illustrates and reflects the Father: "He is the image of the invisible God, the firstborn over all creation" (Colossians 1:15). We learn about God through observing Christ. However, on the negative side of things, people can suffer physically because of internal spiritual issues (1 Corinthians 11:30). The internal often is manifested through the external.

The body can reflect the state of the soul. Weight issues are often symptoms of something going on inside: a problem, a lack, or a brokenness. Yet as you begin to follow God's steps in dealing with the internal issues, you go a long way toward resolving the weight problem because the job of the weight has been accomplished. Your body no longer needs to send you a signal of the internal problem, and just as a fever goes away when the infection driving it is gone, weight often comes under control because the driving personal issues have been healed.

We're not saying that you should ignore the medical, nutritional, and exercise parts of weight control. They are also part of a whole-person growth plan. However, many people who have tried those three over and over again, without results, have often found great success when they not only kept their regimens but also began to deal with their inner lives. That's what happened for a friend of mine.

Ellen couldn't keep the extra weight off, no matter what program she was on. She was very discouraged about it. So we started talking about her life, not her weight. We discovered that almost her entire existence was taken up in taking care of others' problems: her husband's demanding nature, her kids' immaturity, her coworkers' slackness. She spent all her time enabling and rescuing them. This had two results: one was that she spent a lot of time in crisis situations, staying up late, and not being able to have regular, balanced meals. She would get in her car, grab a burger at a fast-food restaurant, and drive to a friend's house for help. The other was that she was on serious overload because she was giving so much and receiving so little in return. Naturally, food became a substitute for the grace of which she was deprived. As she began to set limits, to stop rescuing others, and to make use of good, supportive relationships, Ellen began to have more success with weight control.

◆ YOUR WEIGHT AND STATE OF YOUR SOUL

If you struggle with weight control, ask yourself, *What could my weight be telling me about the state of my soul?* As you reflect on this question, consider whether any of the following underlying problems could be the cause of your struggle with weight.

1. *You have a deficit or emptiness inside.* Rachel is one of the nicest, kindest people I know. She remembers to call people on their birthdays and really cares about their feelings and lives. No one understood why such a nice person had such a weight problem. Yet what they didn't know was that Rachel had great difficulty letting others know when she was down, lonely, or struggling. She felt that her needs were selfish and bad. Basically, Rachel was unable to request from others what she so readily provided for them. Finally, she began to take risks with people, letting them know she wasn't happy all the time, and letting them comfort her in her pain and sadness—and the pounds began melting away.

For Rachel, and for many others, food represents love and can compensate for a lack of relationships. It doesn't reject, it has a satisfying quality, and it is always available. From early on, some people make a strong correlation between food and love, because one of the ways that a mother shows her baby her love is by feeding him or her.

2. *You have control deficits or boundary problems.* God designed us to develop ownership and responsibility over our lives, so that we could be free to live and choose him and his ways. When we are free to make choices and be truthful and honest with others, we are living out the freedom Christ purchased for us with his death: "It is for freedom that Christ has set us free" (Galatians 5:1). However, many people struggle with problems in taking control and ownership over themselves. They may fear the rejection or anger of others. They may be saddled with guilt feelings that keep them from being honest, or they may have dependency needs that keep them in bondage to pleasing and complying with others. Whatever the cause, this type of restriction can also drive a person to eat. Food becomes the only

arena in life in which the person can make free choices, the only arena that does not involve pleasing others.

3. *You hate yourself and eat to medicate the pain.* Some people experience such severe and painful degrees of self-condemnation and self-hatred that they can't see themselves as having any good qualities. When they make a mistake, their conscience attacks them harshly instead of gently and realistically. Since you can't run from yourself, people who struggle with self-condemnation can't escape the self-doubt and self-criticism, and some use food as an anesthetic from the pain. Yet, as so many know, the self-loathing always comes back. All anesthetics wear off.

4. *You have a sense of entitlement.* Entitlement refers to feeling as if you should be able to have special treatment in life, or have no limits in life, by virtue of your existence. Some people take the view that they should be able to eat whatever they want, whenever they want, and it is an offense to take that right away from them. Often they are unaware of their weight problem, or they minimize it, because they have difficulty thinking they have any problems at all.

5. *You are uncomfortable with your sexuality.* Fear often drives this discomfort. Some people fear they won't be able to control their sexual desires. Others fear interacting with the opposite sex in romantic situations, because they might become involved with an unsafe person, or because they might turn off a person in whom they might be interested. The extra weight hides their attractiveness, ensuring that they will avoid any sexual and romantic scenarios. Of course, their sexuality is not gone; it is simply buried.

As you may know from experience, food does not ultimately satisfy any of these internal issues. Although God intended that we should enjoy eating, he did not design it to replace love. Furthermore, though eating may temporarily ease your pain, it also creates a cycle of insatiability. When you are separated from deep and abiding community with others, you are also separated from the life of God. This results in a continual lust for more of whatever you are using as a substitute for life (Ephesians 4:18–19).

However, God has not left us to wrestle with this alone. No matter the cause underlying a person's struggle with weight control, God's way includes a life of self-control over our bodies.

Let's look at some of the factors that can help you learn to eat the way you were designed to eat.

◆ ENTERING THE LIFE OF GOD

When we enter the life of God, we begin the process of loving him with all our heart, soul, mind, and strength (Mark 12:30). This means a couple of things. First, it means bringing yourself to his ways, so that you will be on his path; it means dedicating yourself to him: "Commit your way to the LORD; trust in him and he will do this" (Psalm 37:5). When you have begun fully loving him, you have started down the path of living life the way you were designed to live, which is the way that works best in this life.

We also allow God to be God in all of our life. Most of us have specific and disconnected parts of our heart and life that we compartmentalize as if they had nothing to do with our life with God. We may have one of the underlying internal struggles mentioned previously, or we may have an unreconciled relationship, a habit, a secret sin, or an unconfessed hurt that we have not integrated into our life with God. These parts of ourselves exist in darkness; they have no connection to God's warmth, love, grace, or protection. They live in a sort of suspended state, without love and hope, and they often manifest themselves in eating problems. As it has been said, "Sometimes it's not what you are eating; it's what's eating you."

Many people have found that their weight problems were highly related to these specific, disconnected areas. We encourage you to search your heart to see if there is anything preventing you from allowing God to be God of even the darkened parts of your life.

If this is your situation, we suggest that you pray for enlightenment about what part of you is lost: perhaps your sadness, your anger, your past, or your dreams. Make yourself vulnerable not only to the

Lord but also to people who can help you get connected to yourself through safe and intimate relationships, as relationships connect us to others and ourselves. Begin to grow and heal in those areas.

◆ MAKING THE LEAP TO RELATIONSHIP

Over and over again, research in weight control has proven what the Bible has taught about the necessity of having a community of support: "Two are better than one, because they have a good return for their work: If one falls down, his friend can help him up. But pity the man who falls and has no one to help him up!" (Ecclesiastes 4:9–10).

People who have sustaining, supportive relationships tend to lose more weight, and keep it off for longer periods, than those who don't. We were not built or designed to be alone. This reality manifests itself particularly in weight control, as it involves discipline, deprivation, and changing habits, all at one time and all stressful. When we are in these straits, we need the comfort and encouragement of relationship to see us through.

So ask your friends to support and encourage you as you seek God's way for you in the area of weight control. Yet choose your friends well. Look for those who incorporate both emotional presence and honesty, who are safe, compassionate, and loving, yet will confront you when needed. Avoid people who are one extreme or the other. Those who are loving but afraid to be truthful will keep you in comfort and won't challenge you to grow in those areas where you need growth. Those who are not very warm but are honest will make you feel condemned or beat up, which may produce good initial results, but, as the law always does, will fail over time.

It's essential that you bring more of your life into these relationships than just your weight. Be vulnerable, and confess your inadequacies to these safe people, that you might be healed (James 5:16). Bring in your weaknesses, sins, relationships, and fears. Be known. *The more known we are, the more healed we become.*

Tom was morbidly obese, and his weight was becoming a serious health risk. He tried many things to help but couldn't stick with it. Finally, he began working on his heart and found that he had a truthful, honest, sometimes angry part to him that underlay a lot of his nice-guy exterior. He was very frightened that his anger and truthfulness would be hurtful to others, and that everyone would leave him. However, he learned that God and good people stayed with him while he was getting to know this new part of himself. In time, Tom became comfortable being both nice and honest at the same time, and his weight issue improved greatly.

◆ FINDING A SAFE STRUCTURE

Most people who struggle with their weight need an external structure to help them. They lack the internal discipline to lose weight, so until that is developed, they need the discipline to come from the outside. That is the nature of any good discipline that is part of the life of God. It may not be pleasant, but it produces good things: "No discipline seems pleasant at the time, but painful. Later on, however, it produces a harvest of righteousness and peace for those who have been trained by it" (Hebrews 12:11).

Structure has to do with the ability to be disciplined and ordered, to tolerate frustration for a larger goal, to have patience and diligence, and to delay gratification. Many people have deficiencies in structure, often stemming from a lack of good parental structure in childhood, and they have little ability to rein in their impulses when they feel hunger. Like a small child or a drug addict, they live only in the now and have a hard time postponing something now for something better tomorrow.

If you have some of these tendencies, you will need to find or create a structure of relationships, love, and accountability that can build those things inside you. The type of structure you need depends upon what will work best for you. You may not need to be in a weight-loss group if you have a regular group of people with whom you can meet, open your life, and grow. As long as you can be vulnerable, be honest, give and receive truth, and talk about your weight issues, a growth context may be enough.

If you need more, an individual counselor can help you work through any underlying causes of your struggle with weight control. A great deal of healing can be gained when you are in therapy with someone who can work with both the emotional issues and the weight issues that are involved.

However, you may need something intensive, focused, and specialized that concerns weight alone, such as a formal weight-loss group. In these groups, the only subject is weight, including victories, defeats, tips, and advice. A client of mine tried everything but a weight-loss group because she really didn't want to think she had "that bad of a problem." So she kept struggling until she bit the bullet and attended a weight-loss meeting. There, she found some good people, a good program, and the missing piece in her weight-loss plan. We talked about the principle that God doesn't heal until we know we are sick: "It is not the healthy who need a doctor, but the sick" (Matthew 9:12).

A regular exercise routine can provide another necessary structure. Workout buddies, classes, and trainers can help you stay motivated and committed to consistent physical exercise. Left to ourselves, we tend to create our own worlds and distort our goals and values. However, when we make a commitment to someone else, and that person expects to see us at a certain time and place, it helps keep us in the world of reality, outside of our heads.

◆ A LIFE FULL OF GOOD THINGS

Another factor in controlling your weight is the ability to take pleasure in food, even when you have to monitor what you eat. Unlike those who have drug and alcohol dependencies, you cannot give up food even if you use it to medicate yourself. A substance addict can give up the substance and go through life without its presence. Not so with food. This makes it more challenging to gain control over an addiction to food. It's easier to rid something from your life than to manage how you use it.

God designed food as a good and necessary gift. Not only did he intend for food to sustain us, he also created it for our enjoyment and pleasure: "Go, eat your food with gladness, and drink your wine with a joyful heart, for it is now that God favors what you do" (Ecclesiastes 9:7). God has good things in mind for you, and food is one of those things.

Yet most dieters see food as a problem, not something that gives them pleasure. Meals become tasteless regimens that they dread, with portions so small that they feel very deprived. While exercising self-control over what we eat is a large part of weight control, it does not have to destroy our ability to enjoy what God has provided. Healthy diets should always incorporate good taste and a certain degree of satisfaction for you. Otherwise, you'll get discouraged and give up.

We can have the same attitude about our spiritual life, feeling that the life of faith is just as depriving as the strictest diet. We segment life into two choices: do it our way, and have a lot of fun; or do it God's way, and live in drudgery. It can certainly be painful to give up being a god unto ourselves—that's why we don't want to do it. Yet ultimately, the life God designed for us, because he did design it for us, is meant to be a good and meaningful one. "LORD, you have assigned me my portion and my cup; you have made my lot secure. The boundary lines have fallen for me in pleasant places; surely I have a delightful inheritance" (Psalm 16:5–6). I have found that people who have difficulty enjoying food also often have difficulty enjoying God. They oscillate from impulsive food binging and trying to forget God, back to a legalism of extreme deprivation and feeling obligated to God. The solution to this problem is learning to experience our relationship with God as a pleasant one, and food as a pleasant, enjoyable gift.

Begin to ask God to show you the pleasant parts of his life, which come along with the difficult parts. As you find rich, rewarding relationships and the freedom to make choices and be honest, and as you develop your gifts and talents and become increasingly close to God, you will have more resources to help you tolerate the deprivations you will encounter as you gain control of your weight.

♦ A Reality-Based Body Image

Ultimately weight control is about an alliance between you, your body, and God. You are the one who cares the most about God's finding a way for your weight. Because of that, your perspective and viewpoint will be critical factors in how your efforts bear fruit. This is especially true in how you view your own body. The term for this is *body image,* and it refers to the unique way you see and experience your body's size, weight, and look.

In general, the more reality-based your body image, the better equipped you are to deal with it. The Bible tells us to view ourselves with *sober judgment:* "For by the grace given me I say to every one of you: Do not think of yourself more highly than you ought, but rather think of yourself with sober judgment, in accordance with the measure of faith God has given you" (Romans 12:3).

In other words, God can help you see and experience your body as it really is—not better or worse. Some people have a catastrophic view of their bodies, far beyond how bad the case is. Their harsh assessment causes them to overreact or lose heart. Others minimize or deny the problem and miss the danger signs they need to heed. To a person with this issue, their body image is reality itself. So they need to be open to the feedback of others who are safe and balanced, in order to see themselves how they really are.

If you have a distorted view of your body, take heart in the truth that you can develop a new body image, based on how God and others see you. If you need to develop a new body image, begin by confessing to God, as well as to a safe and sane person, how you see yourself: "I am so fat," or "People who see me are turned off by my size." When someone hears and understands your confession, and then lovingly gives you reality-based feedback and information, your mind internalizes that view. As you receive the perspective of God and others who are more realistic, you can change your body image into something that can be dealt with effectively.

Some people don't see themselves as having a body; they are a body. They are not able to separate their body image from being the central identifying feature of who they are. Such *overidentification with the body* can disrupt the weight-loss process, as your body is not everything you are, in reality, nor is this how God sees you. Such overidentification with the body makes matters worse, because weight issues cannot easily be concealed from view. Unlike the person struggling with drugs, alcohol, or depression, the individual with a weight problem is exposed to the world.

Keep in mind, however, that while it is important to understand and deal with whatever your body is reflecting about the state of your soul, this is all it is: a reflection. You are much more than a body that makes you unhappy. You are a soul, with abilities, loves, and talents that can take part in the miraculous work of transforming your body into the shape and size that works the best for you. God's design is to integrate and mature you, body, soul, and spirit, as he planned from eternity past: "For he chose us in him before the creation of the world to be holy and blameless in his sight" (Ephesians 1:4). Therefore, if you overidentify with your body, you can experience great gains as you learn how much God and the people to whom you are close are able to see and value your other parts: your talents, gifts, emotions, passions, and heart. You begin to see those parts as they do, and you identify yourself as a whole person with all those aspects, not just a body.

◆ PUTTING LIMITS ON BLAME

Another critical factor for weight control is taking ownership of the problem. Those who do are able to move forward and learn how to control their weight.

Some people get stuck in looking at their genetics, their childhood years, or their significant relationships or losses as the reason for their weight. They become focused on what they have suffered at the hands of others, or what they have missed, and they blame their weight issues on that. They become unable to move forward, as they continually focus on the injuries done to them. While it is true that people can have genetic and relationship issues that highly influence their weight—and those realities should never be minimized—they need to be brought to the light, discussed, and worked out.

God models for us a life of letting go and forgiveness (Colossians 3:13). He lives in the present, unencumbered by the past. Learn to let go of blame, learn from the past, and take ownership in the present.

◆ THE REGIMEN ITSELF

Weight loss usually requires a specific regimen, or regulated system, that is designed to fit the individual and includes realistic goals and methods for achieving them. Think of your regimen as being not simply about weight loss but about health itself. People who are into weight loss alone sometimes run into health problems that are associated with a life out of balance. Healthy lifestyles lend themselves toward bodies that are within a healthy weight range.

Before you start an exercise program, check with your doctor to see if there is any medical reason for your weight gain. Your doctor can also advise you if you need to start the regimen at a lower level of intensity, due to your weight, cardiac conditions, respiratory issues, and so forth.

Most good plans involve nutrition and exercise. Nutrition has to do with what foods you can eat, and in what quantities. There are many ways to arrange this, from counting calories to planning portion sizes. Exercise burns off calories, increases muscle and decreases fat, and promotes general physical fitness. Read up on the reputable literature available, and ask someone who is experienced in these matters to help you develop the best approach for you.

Most of all, be patient with yourself. Research has shown that quick-loss diets have a roller-coaster nature: You lose it quickly and regain it quickly. Most people who have gotten the weight off and kept it off have done so a little at a time, at a reasonable rate of loss. This is reflected in the Bible's words that contrast diligence and haste: "The plans of the diligent lead to profit as surely as haste leads to poverty" (Proverbs 21:5). Your plan may involve months or years. The important thing is to be on it, stay on it, and keep God and your friends involved in it. You may fall off from time to time, but keep getting back on.

God will make a way for your weight to come into balance. Just as he helps you enter his life and his paths, as you live as he designed you, the more your mind, heart, and body will work together for a good result.

PERSONAL GOALS AND DREAMS

I (Henry) felt sad after my conversation with Jeremy. A friend of a close friend of mine, he was one of the most talented people that I knew. He was very bright, energetic, and personable. There was no reason that he could not be a success in life, but he had never really "made it." In his early forties, he had just had another false start with one more company, and his dream of building a career in that field had fallen by the wayside, one more time. Jeremy was disappointed, but he was also mad.

"I don't get it," he said. "I don't know what God is doing. It just seems like he won't allow me to break through. How long will I be punished for my past?" He was referring to some moral failures he had had in his dating life several years before, and he thought that God was not allowing him to be successful as some sort of "discipline" for his sins. Yet as I talked to him, I had another spin on what was happening. Although Jeremy was praying to God to help him in his career path, he was also violating a lot of principles that God had outlined regarding success and failure. As I listened to him, I began to see that if he continued on the same path, he was going to keep on failing. As smart and as talented as he was, *he was asking God to violate the very structure of work and success that God himself had set up.* That was not going to happen. I thought Jeremy had better take another path, and get in line with the laws of success that God designed. Then, I believed, he could indeed have a very bright future.

So I told him some of God's laws of success. Guess what? It didn't help. He did not listen. In fact, he was a little ticked at me for suggesting that if he were going to be successful, he would have to make some changes. He felt that if he had good intentions, talent, energy, and dreams, then he was doing "his part," and it was time for God to do his.

We parted, and I heard through the grapevine that he had other false starts. The pattern was continuing.

I ran into him again recently, and we greeted one another. Jeremy told me he had "found success." He was doing great in a brand-new career, and his future looked bright.

What interested me most, though, was how he got where he was. Jeremy had not become successful by "trying again" and finally hitting it. He had become successful by *changing the ways that he was pursuing success and his career.* As he aligned his life with God's principles, God had entered into his life and made a way to get him on course. God had not just "sent success," as Jeremy had been hoping. Instead, God had already made a way for Jeremy, and when Jeremy followed the laws and principles that God had established a long time ago, he found the satisfaction and fulfillment for which he had been longing. You can too.

◆ SUCCESS IS USUALLY NO ACCIDENT

Success does not just happen to people. It comes from following the design and laws of God, and at the same time, receiving the favor and blessing of God. This is so important, I'm going to say it again: *Success comes from following God's laws and from receiving his favor.* God doesn't offer us a guarantee that things will work out the way we want just because we follow his laws. This is not a magic formula. We do not control what God does. He is sovereign, and can direct our path in any way he chooses. As James tells us:

Now listen, you who say, "Today or tomorrow we will go to this or that city, spend a year there, carry on business and make money." Why, you do not even know what will happen tomorrow. What is your life? You are a mist that appears for a little while and then vanishes. Instead, you ought to say, "If it is the Lord's will, we will live and do this or that." As it is, you boast and brag. All such boasting is evil.

—JAMES 4:13–16

Each of us needs the favor of God in order to succeed. We need the same kind of favor that he promised long ago:

I will look on you with favor and make you fruitful and increase your numbers, and I will keep my covenant with you. You will still be eating last year's harvest when you will have to move it out to make room for the new. I will put my dwelling place among you, and I will not abhor you. I will walk among you and be your God, and you will be my people.

—LEVITICUS 26:9–12

Throughout the Bible we see God giving his favor and blessing to people. He is a giver of good gifts to us (James 1:17). All of our lives are in his hand, and it is always imperative for us to be seeking his blessing and favor. We need him to shine his favor upon us to reach any goal.

On the other hand, *while working in the ways that God has ordained does not guarantee our "success," if we don't follow his ways, we most likely won't achieve success.* We need to walk in God's ways. If you are not feeling fulfilled in your work or if you find that you have trouble achieving the things you want in life, it may be that, like Jeremy, you are not following God's path for success. Our prayer is that this chapter gives you insight into what you might need to change so that you can be on the path that God has for you.

◆ START WITH GOD

The path to reaching our goals begins with trusting God. Earlier we said that having faith meant seeing God as the source of all that we need. Faith is the conviction of things unseen and of things hoped for (Hebrews 11:1). Trusting God with your goals means *believing that he is the source of all good things, and that he can instruct you about what is good.*

God says that he will give you the desires of your heart, and that he "satisfies your desires with good things" (Psalm 103:5; see also Psalm 145:16, 19; 1 Timothy 6:17–18). God gives to those who ask, but he does not give to those who ask with impure motives (James 4:2–3). In other words, he wants to bless us, but for reasons that are good for us.

If your goals and desires stem from impure motives—such as greed, envy, materialism, or pride—then God will not give you what you ask. Goals that are based on impure motives are like dead ends. Even if you accomplish them, you will still be empty inside. They cannot fulfill your soul. There are a lot of miserable people who live in nice houses. They should be working on the real reasons behind their misery, instead of thinking that reaching one more goal or accumulating material things for their egos' sake will do the trick.

If, however, your motives are good, real, and truly satisfying, then God may be all for them. Even material goals can be motivated by good reasons. For example, you may want a new house because you want one large enough to entertain guests and exercise your spiritual gift of hospitality (Romans 12:10–13). Perhaps you want a new home because you feel that your kids would benefit from being in a different part of town. Maybe God has put the love of the outdoors in your soul, and you desire to be in the country. All of these are good reasons for wanting a new house. Remember, God loves to give people gifts. He just might honor your desire to move to the coast or to the mountains so that you can enjoy the beauty of his creation.

In order to check the motives behind your goals, you might ask yourself these questions:

- Is my purpose to find God's calling and role for my life so that I can serve him in the best possible way and also be the person that he created me to be?
- Do I believe that he is committed to the best path for me and that he will lead me and provide for me?
- Are my goals and desires based on good reasons and motives?
- Will it be really satisfying if I achieve these goals? Do these goals truly go deep enough into who I really am?

Begin by committing yourself and your path to God (Romans 12:1–2). Then, as he works in your life, you will be able to find out what he wants to do with, for, and through you. In other words, *if God is your primary goal, then you will reach your other goals,* for he will guide you in determining what they are and reaching them.

◆ SAY "YES" TO WHO YOU REALLY ARE

After beginning with God, the next thing that you have to do to reach your goals is to say "yes" to who you are and "no" to others' definitions and expectations of you. Have you ever really taken the time to find out who you are? Do your goals and desires really belong to you? Or are you seeking goals that other people—your family, your friends, or your culture—have defined for you?

It is helpful to get input from others, as we shall see in a moment. Yet, it's not good to allow others to define who you are and what you should be doing. Listen to the words from Romans 12:2: "Do not conform any longer to the pattern of this world, but be transformed by the renewing of your mind."

Being who you are may mean saying "no" and not conforming to outside pressures, like the expectations of your parents, your friends, or your church. Just recently I was talking to a woman who was in the middle of a career change because she had been depressed and miserable in her job. As she began to work through things, she began to see that she was in her career only because of her family, and she had been doing work that she did not even like. You should have seen the exuberance on her face when she told me about her new career choice. She had found herself by *first finding who she was not.*

Being who you are may also mean saying "no" to expectations that are the "pattern of this world." Our culture says that we will gain fulfillment by becoming successful, or wealthy, or by gaining the recognition of other people. It looks to temporal, passing values to make direction-setting decisions. Yet God says that our significance comes from being loved by him and significant others, from fulfilling our talents, and from leading a life of service to God and other people.

◆ IDENTIFY NEGATIVE PATTERNS

As we have seen, sometimes it is just not God's will that we reach a particular goal. We can all relate to that. Yet it is not God's will that you *never reach any of your goals.* If you have consistently not met your goals, then you may be doing something that gets in the way of your reaching them. If you are reading this and saying, "I have had great intentions and desires, but things have just never really worked," then stop. Do not set another goal. Do not try again to reach your goals. If you do, you are likely to fail at achieving them for one simple reason: *patterning.*

Patterning is what we do over and over again to try to gain the things that matter to us. We have patterns that we live out repeatedly, for good or bad, in our relationships, in our work, and when we try to reach our goals. Believe it or not, most of us have patterns to our failures. Our success or failure usually comes out of who we are as people—the way that our characters are wired. We are glued together to do things a certain way, and until we change, we will do those things the same way every time, probably with similar results.

So, as you look back over your dreams and goals and your attempts to meet those goals, ask yourself what happened. If you have consistently failed or have been dissatisfied to some degree, then you probably have a pattern of doing things that is getting in the way of what you want to do. See if you can relate to any of these patterns:

- *No defined goals.* You don't really know where you are headed until it happens.
- *Specific goals, but too unrealistic.* You want to be something that is totally, at least at present, out of reach.
- *Specific goals, but underresourced or underplanned.* You have good goals, but you do not make sure that you have the needed resources to achieve them, or you fail to plan strategically in other ways that would ensure success.
- *External motivation or definition.* Your plans are motivated from external sources and reward systems instead of internal ones, or you have been defined and your goals have been chosen by someone else.
- *Derailed by personal weaknesses.* Your weaknesses keep you from succeeding.
- *Start but don't complete or finish.* You begin well but do not carry on, persevere, and complete a goal.
- *Lack of discipline or structure.* You have goals but are not self-disciplined enough to follow through and do the things that are required.
- *Hit obstacles and not able to recover.* You are fine with moving forward but become defeated by obstacles or problems that arise.
- *Failure did you in.* You get too discouraged when there is a failure to a goal or to a single part of a goal.
- *People did you in.* You allow other people to keep you from achieving your goals, for a variety of reasons.

See if you can identify the patterns that may be holding you back so that you can safeguard against that weakness in the future. For example, let's say you have a pattern of lacking discipline and structure, but you want to lose some weight. Since you recognize that you don't have the internal structure to stick to a diet program, you shouldn't join another health club or buy a bunch of diet food, because these things aren't going to provide you with the structure you need. If you want to break your pattern, you should join an exercise class that meets at a regular time or sign up with a prepaid weight-loss program that requires you to attend meetings so that you are not left on your own.

If there is a pattern, that pattern is you. It will continue until you change, and you need to plan for it and make allowances for it so that it doesn't defeat you. You may need to work on some of the principles we talked about in the first part of this book.

◆ IDENTIFY YOUR STRENGTHS AND GIFTS

Another reason people don't meet their goals or find success is that they have never learned another truth of Romans 12:3–8:

> For by the grace given me I say to every one of you: Do not think of yourself more highly than you ought, but rather think of yourself with sober judgment, in accordance with the measure of faith God has given you. Just as each of us has one body with many members, and these members do not all have the same function, so in Christ we who are many form one body, and each member belongs to all the others. We have different gifts, according to the grace given us. If a man's gift is prophesying, let him use it in proportion to his faith. If it is serving, let him serve; if it is teaching, let him teach; if it is encouraging, let him encourage; if it is contributing to the needs of others, let him give generously; if it is leadership, let him govern diligently; if it is showing mercy, let him do it cheerfully.

In this passage, God is also asking us, in essence, "Who do you think you are?" because he wants us to have an accurate and realistic picture of ourselves. If we are thinking of ourselves "too highly," we may be thinking that we can do things that we are not equipped to do. We may be blind to our limitations, and this will keep us from reaching our goals.

Having a "sober" view of yourself means *seeing your real strengths and operating within them.* Don't try to build a dream or a goal on a strength that you do not have. Let me give you an example. I am the kind of person who envisions things, creates new ideas, thinks up new strategies, and launches new businesses. Yet when it comes to managing, organizing, and administrating, I am a nightmare. If I fool myself into thinking that I can do a good job at these kinds of tasks, I reap the consequences. The things that I create turn out to be a mess if I do not get help with organizing and managing. For me, seeing myself with "sober judgment" means taking my limitations to heart and planning for them. I need to put a good team around me in order to meet my goals, or I will create more than I can handle effectively. We all do not have the same gifts, and we need others around us to make up for our limitations.

Having a sober view of yourself also means that *you must not think things should be easy for you or that you should never fail.* All of us tend to look at others, see what they have accomplished, and think that it came easy to them and so it should be easy for us. Yet this isn't true. For most people, success is 1 percent inspiration and 99 percent perspiration. If you think that reaching your goals should come easy, or that your path should not be riddled with mistakes and failures, then you will never accomplish anything very significant. All great achievers fail along the way, but because they expect failure to be part of the process, they persevere. They do not think so highly of themselves that they get down on themselves when they are not perfect.

Humans can achieve incredible things, and in fact we were created to do so. Yet when we think that we should not make mistakes, aren't we expecting to be like God? We end up punishing ourselves for not being God, and we *never achieve the heights of human achievement that we were designed to achieve.* Give yourself a break and do not have unrealistic expectations. The result may be that you will achieve more than you ever dreamed. You just will not do it in the way that you thought you would.

Last, having a "sober" picture of yourself also means *having an accurate one. Find your gifts and claim them.* God gave you a set of gifts and talents. Every human has them. Find out what you are designed to do, and as the passage says, do it with the amount of faith you have—all of it—and with gusto.

There are many ways to identify your gifts and strengths. First, look at your history. What kinds of things have you done well? Look at what comes easily to you. What are you good at? What might be tough for others may be easy for you, which means you may be gifted in that area. Think back to times in your life when you were doing things that brought you pleasure or energy. This is a clue about what would truly motivate you.

In addition, you might want to take advantage of the many different assessment tools available for people who want help in making a good career choice. For example, if you work for an organization or business, ask your human resources director for the feedback tools that your company has. Most companies have review tools, even if they do not use them regularly. You might also want to go to a library or a bookstore and check out some books on career planning; many contain questionnaires to help you assess your abilities. You may also want to visit a career counselor. He or she will likely interview you and give you other tests and assessments. Many people find these kinds of tools very revealing, and they open the door to a new path.

Be sure that you also interview people who know you well. Call old bosses, coworkers, and close friends who will be honest with you about how they see you. Get honest feedback about your gifts, strengths, and abilities. Ask them about your weaknesses as well.

Then, look to your heart. What do you daydream about? Write the story of your ideal life, and then ask yourself what it would take to get there. Whose life do you find yourself wishing were yours? Why can't it be?

A dream that has no benefit to others is probably not a God-inspired dream. I am sure that God made performers and opera singers, athletes and musicians to pursue their dream so the rest of us could watch and enjoy their talents to the glory of God. Remember, God has given you gifts and abilities. Use them and develop them. As the Bible says, put them out there for all to see, so that you might be thankful to God for how glorious he is in making those talents and gifts of service to others (Matthew 5:14–16). How glorious he is in both giving you the gifts and empowering you to bring them to fruition in the service of others.

◆ COUNT THE COSTS

Before you set out to reach your goals, sit down and figure out what it is going to cost you. Many people have attainable goals, but they do not plan well for how they are going to get there in terms of allocating and releasing resources. Here are some helpful things to think about:

- ◆ How much money will it take to get to where I want to go? How am I going to save, raise, produce, borrow, or earn that amount? (Then increase it by 20 percent!) At what intervals am I going to have to release it?
- ◆ What kind of time commitment is it going to take to get there? What may I have to say "no" or "good-bye" to in order to achieve my goal? Am I willing to do that?
- ◆ What other losses may be required for me to reach my goal? Do I have competing goals that will interfere? What things that I love must I jettison to get there? Am I willing to do that?
- ◆ What relationship costs will there be? What relationship resources will I need in order to accomplish my goal? Who do I have to convince to "buy in" in order for this to happen? How will I get these people on board?
- ◆ What skills am I missing that I am going to need? Where am I going to get the help that I need for my weaknesses? Where will I get the missing structure that I need to get there? What group can I join? What team members might I need?

- ◆ What will this be like emotionally? Where will I get the support that I will need to get there?
- ◆ What knowledge am I missing that is needed to reach my goal? Where will I get it? Can I hire it? Can I borrow it?

Remember, to reach a goal you must spend resources: energy, time, skills, money, and others. These resources are finite, so to make sure that you have enough, budget for them. It is your job to go out and find those resources so that you will have them when you need them in the course of what you are doing.

◆ KEEP REALITY IN MIND

As you count the cost, keep reality in mind. By reality, I mean what truly is, and what truly will be if you do not reach your goals—not what you tell yourself *should be* or what you *wish would be*. If you look at reality and do not like what you see, then you may be more willing to do whatever it is going to take to change reality.

Look at your goals in terms of reality, and let reality motivate you. Let it hit you hard. If something is true now, and you do not do what it takes to change it, then that reality—or worse!—is going to be true this time next year. I know a woman who wanted to go to graduate school and get a better job. Yet when she found out that it would take her two years, she decided not to go—it would take too long. I told her, "Two years from today will come either way, whether or not you go to graduate school. Two years from now, do you want to be where you are today, or do you want to have a degree and a better job?" She enrolled in the program.

Look hard at what will be true if you do not pursue your goals or dreams. What do you see? How does that feel? Can you live with it? Is that what you really want your life to be?

I once worked with a father of four young children who needed to lose weight because his health was in danger. In order to help him look at reality, I suggested that he write about what his kids' lives would be like if he died of a heart attack while they were young. I told him to think about what their lives would be like growing up without a father—their junior high years, teen years, dating life, college years, and marriage choices. Then I suggested that he write about his wife's life as a single mother with four young children. Though this was difficult, I wanted this man to see the reality of what would happen if he did not lose weight.

Take a hard look at your life as it is today. Does the reality you see motivate you to pay the price? It may not; some goals are just not worth the effort or the cost, and that's why an exercise like this can be helpful.

Not only can this exercise help you paint a picture of what your life will be like if you don't pursue your goals, it can also help you dream of what your life may be like if you do. For that reason, I also asked the father to picture himself as healthy and enjoying those years with his kids as they grew up. I asked him to envision going to all those games, all those events, and going through all those wonderful stages with his children. I wanted him to think about walking down the aisle with his daughters and giving them away in marriage. This helped to motivate him to stick with the program.

God has done something similar for us. He has given us picture after picture of how it will be if we sow to the spiritual life and make the sacrifice to grow and serve him. We will enjoy banquets, rewards, joy, eternal life, and more. He posts those pictures on the doors of our minds so that we will constantly be motivated. As Paul says, "However, as it is written: 'No eye has seen, no ear has heard, no mind has conceived what God has prepared for those who love him'" (1 Corinthians 2:9).

Jesus speaks of paradise, and of the incredible life that lies ahead for those who follow him. He also has us look at what our lives will be like if we don't choose to follow him. He always gives us a choice, as is true for all of our goals. We can choose the positive, count the cost, and have one reality, or we can choose the other.

◆ WRITE OUT A PLAN

This goes without saying, as we have talked about it all along, but there is great value to writing down your goals, and writing out a strategic plan for how you are going to reach those goals. Make commitments to resources and to specific dates and times, and build in accountability. Share your plan with someone who will hold you to it. In a business, the CEO is accountable to the board, to whom he or she must present a plan and then proof of its execution. You are the CEO of your life, and you should have a board of directors in the form of an accountability group overseeing you. Present your plan, get feedback, and then have this group hold you to your plan. It will bring you one step closer to making it happen.

◆ MAKE LITTLE CHOICES

Goals are reached in little steps. We did not write this book in a day. We wrote it in a lot of little steps, and all of those were choices: the choice to write one section one night instead of going to a movie, the choice to get up an hour earlier one morning instead of sleeping in. There are many, many choices that go into reaching any goal.

Look at each little choice you make as either getting you closer or moving you further away from the goal. If your goal is to have more intimacy with your children, refusing to take on that extra project is a choice that helps you to reach your goal. If your goal is to get a degree, choosing to take a class on the weekends instead of going out with friends is a choice that takes you closer to your goal. Little choices like these make big goals become a reality. As my mother used to say, "Save your pennies. They become nickels, and they become quarters, and they become dollars. Then, dollars become bicycles." To save a penny is a little choice. To get a bicycle—now that is a big deal!

This is what the Bible refers to as "diligence." It means to be incisive, decisive, determined, eager, continuously attuned, committed, careful, industrious, thorough, and disciplined. Diligence is not easy, but we can't reach our goals without it. That is the law of the universe that God set up, and that we live in. Listen to all the great things that are promised to those who are diligent:

- "Lazy hands make a man poor, but diligent hands bring wealth" (Proverbs 10:4).
- "He who works his land will have abundant food, but he who chases fantasies lacks judgment" (Proverbs 12:11).
- "Diligent hands will rule, but laziness ends in slave labor" (Proverbs 12:24).
- "The sluggard craves and gets nothing, but the desires of the diligent are fully satisfied" (Proverbs 13:4).
- "The plans of the diligent lead to profit as surely as haste leads to poverty" (Proverbs 21:5).
- "He who works his land will have abundant food, but the one who chases fantasies will have his fill of poverty" (Proverbs 28:19).

When it comes to reaching your goals, God has already made a way. It is the path of diligence and all the things we have discussed. If we do things according to his plan, then the chances are certainly greater that we will succeed. Yet, in other ways, it is true that we need God to make a way.

◆ Fears and Obstacles Help You Grow

We need to be realistic. Just because God has made a way, it doesn't mean that we won't encounter challenges and problems. The Bible teaches that we will hit obstacles on the way to any goal. Whether it is a spiritual, relational, material, career, or other kind of goal, you can expect to "fight the good fight." You will encounter many obstacles. As Jesus said, "In this world you will have trouble. But take heart! I have overcome the world" (John 16:33).

The people who accomplish their goals are different than the ones who don't, in that they prepare for difficulties, face them, and solve them. Here are a few of the roadblocks that you can plan on facing:

- Fear and other difficult feelings
- Conflicts with people
- Failure
- Lack of resources
- Lack of abilities
- Discouragement
- Doubt
- Distance from God
- Second-guessing
- Criticism

So, what is the best thing to do? Remember and put into practice the principles that we have talked about here. When you follow them, they will guide you through the difficult times. As you begin with God, exercise faith, find good traveling companions, embrace problems as gifts, gain wisdom, and leave your baggage, reaching your goals will take on a whole different meaning, for reaching your goals is always secondary. *The process of who you are becoming with God and others in that process is what's important.* A path toward a goal is primarily a context or a road along which God is changing you into a much better person. He wants you to reach your desires and goals. Yet he is more concerned with who you are becoming as you do this, and how your relationship with him is going. So, in that sense, the obstacles that you find along the way are some of the best parts of the process. They help show you where you need to grow and how you need to change.

As you seek him and do the difficult work of changing into who he wants you to be, you will find that you are getting closer to your goals at the same time. For you will become the kind of mature person who is able to reach goals. That is the secret. As Jesus said, "But seek first his kingdom and his righteousness, and all these things will be given to you as well. Therefore do not worry about tomorrow, for tomorrow will worry about itself. Each day has enough trouble of its own" (Matthew 6:33–34).

So, as Jesus said, plan for the task. Consider the costs. Answer the following questions before you begin:

- What is the most difficult thing that I am going to encounter along the path of reaching this goal? What will I do then?
- What is the biggest loss that I will endure?
- How will I deal with it?
- How will I feel when things do not go well?
- What will I do?
- What if I fail?
- What will I do then?
- How will I stay connected to God each and every step?

If you think about it, you will probably be able to ask yourself some other questions that apply to the obstacles that you will encounter. Go ahead and face them now, not later. Prepare for them in advance, and ask God to help you. If you have your supports in place, then when the problems and fears come, you will be ready. You will pray. You will pick up the phone, or go to your support system or group. Or you will just exercise the plan you have in place. Yet you will be ready, with a plan, and with the right people to call and places to go. You have to have a plan that prepares you for the tough moments ahead of time.

◆ Go for It

You've likely heard it said that failure is not the worst thing that can happen to us; not trying and wasting our lives is. The Bible never calls us to succeed, but instead it calls us to be faithful. We are not called to be perfect either. Just faithful.

We are called to take what we have been given and add to it. We are to develop our talents, invest them, and get a return for our effort in life. To that end, we hope and pray that you will take the hand of God, seek him diligently with all your heart, dream big, and reach your goals. Ask him to show you who you are and what you are to do—and then trust him to make a way.

Conclusion:

Begin Your Journey Today

God's way always works. When you are at some crossroads in life, *when you don't know what to do,* God does. His grace, his leading, and his principles never fail, for he himself cannot fail in his purposes for us: "Do not be afraid or discouraged, for the Lord God, my God, is with you. He will not fail you or forsake you" (1 Chronicles 28:20). His way may not always be the same as the one we would have imagined, but it will ultimately be the best way for us.

God's way is not always the easiest way, and often it is not the way we are familiar with. It involves admitting we are powerless and in need, walking in faith, taking risks, and being able to face the truth. Yet his way is truly the only way that helps and heals us. As Jesus said, "Enter by the narrow gate; for the gate is wide, and the way is broad that leads to destruction, and there are many who enter by it. For the gate is small, and the way is narrow that leads to life, and few are those who find it" (Matthew 7:13–14, NASB).

Throughout the ages God has made a way for his people—a way that is based on his nature, his resources, and his Word, which are eternal and never change. History is filled with the stories of people who have sought and followed his path, and in doing so have found hope, healing, transformation, and much more.

Today is no different. God lives and moves among us as he always has, transforming those who earnestly seek his way. As you have been reading this book, you may be considering how God can make a way for you in your areas of struggle. In order to help you develop your own vision for what God can do in your life, we want to take you step by step through Beth's journey. She, like you, wanted a better life, and she entered the process of growth we have been describing in this book. Over time, God changed her—and her life—in ways she had never even imagined. As you read Beth's story, ask God to show you how you can implement these principles so they can begin working for you today, tomorrow, and for the rest of your life.

As we follow Beth's life and choices, we will note which of the principles she was following at each point. They appear as they occurred in her life. Some of the principles came into play at the same time as others; some appeared much later in her growth process. It's important that you understand that God's way is for *all* of these principles to be at work in our lives. Each one reflects a necessary concept. When all of the principles are present, we begin to see true and meaningful change. Just as we need to take all the correct medicines for an illness, we need to make sure that we are utilizing all parts of the way of God.

◆ TOO LITTLE, TOO LATE

When I (John) met her, Beth's marriage to Don was almost dead. She was an accountant, he a marketing executive. They were in their late twenties and were childless. They came to me because their marriage was in crisis. Don was not sure he wanted to stay in the marriage, and he admitted to having an affair. Beth was also unhappy, but she loved Don and wanted to work things out.

It didn't take long for me to understand why Beth and Don were so unhappy. They were involved in an ineffective dance, and their marriage was severely ailing. Beth was detached from her feelings and had difficulty opening up emotionally. She had trouble being honest about her feelings and opinions, particularly when she disagreed with someone. Don, on the other hand, was very much in touch with his emotions and had no problem expressing his negative opinions and feelings toward others. He also tended to be demanding and controlling toward Beth. He felt she should empathize and agree with everything he said and did. When she didn't respond the way he thought she should, he would be hurt. Then, to retaliate, he would distance himself or leave and hang out with his buddies. Beth, in turn, would try to keep him happy, but she could never do enough to please him. Finally, Don's affair came to light, and that's when they called me for counseling.

We had sessions for a while, but it was too little, too late. Though Beth did everything she could to hold on to the marriage, Don finally admitted that by the time they started counseling, he had already decided to leave. He had agreed to seek help only in order to mollify Beth. Don divorced her and ultimately married the woman with whom he'd had the affair.

Beth had really wanted the marriage to work. Though she and Don had never done well, the covenant and institution of marriage meant something very important and sacred to her, and it was as if a foundation of her life had been jerked out from under her. Don's decision to get a divorce devastated Beth, and she continued to make attempts to reconcile with him, up until the time that he remarried. Throwing her pride to the winds, she humbled herself to let him know she wanted things to work out between them.

This was an early indication of the depth of Beth's character, and it was one that I felt gave great promise for future growth and healing by God. Beth never resorted to the usual position of the law: *If you don't want me, I don't want you.* She wanted reconciliation and the restoration of love. Because of this attitude of love over law, I knew that whatever happened between Beth and Don, ultimately she would put her feet on God's path, and she would be okay. This proved to be true.

CONCLUSION

◆ Beginning a Journey with God

After the divorce, Beth wanted to stay in counseling, but her story is not about her counseling. Therapy was only one piece of the puzzle for her; Beth did many other things to allow God to make a way for her. She wanted to do whatever she could to become the person God wanted her to be for the rest of her life. She came to see God's role as the Source and Designer of life and began depending on him and incorporating his designs into her values and behaviors. *Her journey with God had begun.*

This new stance was pivotal for Beth. Before her problems with Don, she had oriented her relationship with God around her marriage. She had sought God's help, prayed, and asked his support in guiding her to the best ways to heal the relationship. Yet after the divorce, though she still wanted to be remarried someday, that hope was no longer the central desire in her life. When she lost what she wanted most (her marriage), her world crumbled. This loss, as so often happens, created room in her heart for God. Beth was beginning to grasp the truth of Jesus' words when he said: "For whoever wants to save his life will lose it, but whoever loses his life for me will find it" (Matthew 16:25). For the first time in her life, she began to understand that having a good marriage was not the most important thing in life. As she discovered a hunger and thirst for God, Beth slowly and thoughtfully came to the conclusion that even if God meant for her to be single for the rest of her days, that was preferable to being married if this wasn't his plan for her. In other words, Beth placed God's ways over her desire for marriage.

In the process she realized that following God's way does not mean living in deprivation and emptiness. Beth wanted a rich life here and now, and she realized that the surest way to such a life was to follow God's path. As a result of this new insight, Beth began to bring God from the periphery of her life into the center. She developed a regular devotional life and began reading and studying the Bible, something she enjoyed and began to depend on for insight about her choices and decisions.

◆ Choosing Wise Traveling Companions

As her love for God grew, Beth found a healthy church in which she explored the areas of worship, community, and service. Up until the divorce, her personal relationships had been her family and a few close friends. These people had always been helpful and meaningful to her. Yet they did not share her hunger for God and his ways, and Beth began to feel a need to connect with people who were also on a journey with God.

Along the way, Beth encountered many kinds of people, a number of them religious or spiritual. Some were pretty judgmental or legalistic. Beth would be drawn to their devotion to God and feel like she was "home." After a little while, however, they would start getting weird. One day when Beth was sad and depressed over losing Don, a woman told her, "Those feelings have no place in faith. You have the victory in Christ, so replace your emotions with victorious emotions." This woman didn't understand that while we do have the victory in Christ, there are still painful battles going on in our lives. Beth learned a lot about God, but not much about authentic connections with these folks, and she couldn't open up to them. She also met some good people of faith, but despite their care for her, they had no knowledge of what struggle, heartbreak, and dysfunction were about. They could not relate to what she'd been through and was going through.

Beth did not give up, however, and continued to search for a balanced and healthy support network. She kept going to meetings and groups at church and introducing herself to people. It took a while, but finally she developed some close relationships with people who, while certainly not perfect, loved God, each other, and her, and they understood brokenness. She began to open up to them, and they to her. Beth had found her *traveling companions*. What an impact these new friends had on her emotions, her values, and her day-to-day life! They gave her the freedom and motivation to keep on growing. She said to me, "For most of my life, I feel like I have been asleep. Now I'm waking up to what is going on inside me and in my relationships."

◆ LOVING GOD WITH ALL HER HEART

Beth literally started to *love God with all her heart, soul, mind, and strength*. All, not just part, of her began to love and follow him. Parts of her that she had not let God handle began coming to a relationship with him. For example, she was able to be honest with him about her anger toward him about the divorce. She said, "I was afraid to let God know I was mad at him about the divorce. Yet when I finally told him, I could feel how safe he was, and the anger began to go away." Beth also began to bring her dreams and goals in life to God, and to let him work on them. She told me, "I always hesitated to bring the dreams to God, because I thought he would take them away, and then where would I be? But it looks like he is giving me new dreams that fit me a lot better." She was referring to the changes she was making in career, friendships, and the direction of her life. Bit by bit, Beth began to love God with all of herself. In turn, God put her life together for her.

◆ OWNING HER FAULTS AND WEAKNESSES

In the early weeks after her divorce, Beth had a lot of anger toward Don, and she criticized him for his selfishness and his hurtfulness. In doing this, she was sorting out what had happened in the relationship—what was her fault and what was his. Her blame initially helped her identify who had done what, so that she could clarify what to work on in herself and what she needed to forgive in Don.

Yet then Beth continued to talk about Don's failings, over and over again, for no apparent purpose. Finally, I gently confronted her, saying, "Until you are more concerned about your part in what went wrong with your marriage than you are about Don's, you will always be in jail emotionally to this divorce." My words stunned her a little, but as she thought about it, she saw that she had been blaming Don in order to avoid taking ownership of their problems. When she admitted what she had been doing, she stopped blaming him and began shouldering the burden of her own contributions.

As she began *owning her faults and weaknesses,* Beth began to see that she had been afraid to confront Don about things and that she had let them go as a result. She had also let him control things because she had been afraid of making mistakes. She had lost her heart and life in the marriage, allowing the marriage to be about only her husband, rather than about both of them.

Beth had lived her life in a ghostly fashion, floating in and out of her connections with people. It was no wonder she had felt so alone for so long. Yet as she began to take ownership in her life, she started to work on her fears of rejection and intimacy and began experiencing life, instead of just surviving or existing. She began to risk being emotionally vulnerable with her friends in her support network, and she began to depend on them for love and understanding.

◆ Embracing Problems as Gifts

At about the same time that God began to do surgery on her heart about taking ownership of her faults, Beth also began *embracing her problems as gifts.* She started to see that despite all the heartache and pain that she had been going through over her divorce, she was learning valuable lessons.

This was a major growth step for Beth. When she began this growth journey, she had just wanted to feel better inside, to deal with the pain, to get her life back on track, and to be with her friends. She was a little like nine of the ten lepers whom Jesus healed. They were excited and glad to be healed, but they never returned to thank him for what he had done for them (Luke 17:12–19). However, a friend encouraged and challenged her to change her viewpoint and to focus instead on what she could learn from what had gone wrong in the marriage. This required her to go back into the years of problems with Don, which was very difficult. It was also difficult to even think that God wanted her to learn anything except how to avoid Dons in her future.

When she did, however, she did so with the same searching, humble, and teachable attitude that the prophet Eli taught the boy Samuel: "Speak, LORD, for your servant is listening" (1 Samuel 3:9). As a result, God showed her things about himself and his love for her that she had not expected. She learned about grace, faith, trust, honesty, patience, and responsibility, and finally realized that though Don had done evil to her, and she herself had done her share of evil, "God intended it for good" (Genesis 50:20). Beth knew that she had really grown when she realized that she felt gratitude for what she had learned in the ordeal. She might never have learned the important lessons she was learning or made the changes she had made, had it not been for her divorce. As she saw the gifts God had given her through what she had been through, gratitude gradually replaced the bitterness and hurt she had felt for so long. Beth ran across Don a few years after the divorce. I asked her what that experience was like for her. She told me, "It was really strange. Don was pretty much Don. But I didn't feel all the crazy stuff I used to with him. I felt more in control inside. I never thought I would think what happened to me was a gift, but I like what I felt the other day."

◆ LEAVING BAGGAGE BEHIND

Then there was the *baggage to leave behind,* let go of, and forgive that Beth had realized. Over time, she discovered, for example, that it felt safer to wish for Don and what they had had than it did to reenter life and find new people. She had been holding on to what had been, instead of letting go and moving on to a new existence. In order to move forward, she had a lot of forgiving to do. Initially she had resisted this by staying angry with Don, arguing in her head about the unfairness of it all, and hanging on to the sadness and longings that that had emerged from her grief work. Yet Beth was determined not to let baggage from the past hinder her present and future life with God, so she continued to accept reality as it was, and let go of what she could not have.

She knew she was beginning to let go when she went out on a date with a man who later complimented her by saying, "You are the first divorced woman I've been out with who didn't obsess on how bad her ex was." Beth had grown to the point that she was much more invested in what God and she were up to, in the here and now.

◆ PLACING A HIGH VALUE ON WISDOM

People often find that some of these principles come with great effort, while others come easier. This was true for Beth. One of the aspects of her character that I liked a lot was that she had no investment in appearing to have it together. She knew what she didn't know, and she wanted to know what she needed to know. Beth was a learner, and so she was very motivated to *place a high value on wisdom*. She became an information junkie, first in the area of divorce and recovery, then in the Bible and theology, and finally in personal and spiritual growth. She understood the clarity and guidance that information brings to people. Beth was always bugging me to give her references for books to read on various growth topics, as well as people to whom she could talk. Much to my surprise, she would then read the books and meet with the people I had suggested. I was impressed with her hunger to learn.

Beyond information gathering, however, Beth wanted the skill in living that comes with wisdom. She constantly sought out people who had experience and competence in the areas about which she wanted to know more. She spent time with these people, opened her life up to them, and asked them many questions. She wanted to make sure that she was armed with whatever she needed in order not to make the same mistakes. Wisdom was a prized part of her search, as she lived out this verse from Proverbs: "Get wisdom, get understanding; do not forget my words or swerve from them. Do not forsake wisdom, and she will protect you; love her, and she will watch over you. Wisdom is supreme; therefore get wisdom. Though it cost all you have, get understanding" (4:5–7).

One of the side benefits of Beth's quest for wisdom is that since that time, she herself has had much to offer people who are hurting not only from divorce but on a much broader level. Using the wisdom she sought and made part of herself, Beth is now helping others move into personal, emotional, and spiritual maturity.

◆ TAKING LIFE AS IT COMES

While Beth naturally placed a value on wisdom, she had difficulty with the idea of *taking life as it comes.* She saw life in pretty straight lines (A leading directly to B), and it did not make sense to her that there would be times of long waiting, periods of regression and failure, and then a season of harvesting and good fruit.

Though Beth did place the prospect of remarriage into God's hands, she thought she was ready a long time before God did. So she had a few relational shipwrecks, and she went out with men of questionable character or spiritual maturity. She even went out with a good man, but unfortunately she was not mature enough to handle the health of that relationship, so she unwittingly sabotaged it. As she phrased it, "I did him a favor. He didn't know how crazy I was at the time."

After each failure, however, Beth went back to the drawing board of God, her friends, and the principles. Each time she did, she learned and grew a little more. She sowed more grace, love, and truth into her heart from her resources, and allowed herself to have another season of growth.

Finally, much later than she would have ever accepted in the days when she was a control freak, she met Carl. He was the right guy, she was the right girl, and it was the right time. Their courtship was exciting, exploratory, and full of good friends, good experiences, and God.

Carl was just as much into God's ways as she was. He appreciated the work she had done on herself, and had been actively growing himself. They are now happily married, and have children of their own (and they are busy helping others find God's way for them).

God made a way for Beth. She did not receive her first heart's desire (Don never returned to her), but she submitted her heart and soul to God's plan and path. Because she did, she not only got a new life in God, she got a second chance at a good marriage. God's work has borne fruit at his time. Beth feels grateful and is much better off than she was before her marriage fell apart, because now she is closer to God and more spiritually and emotionally whole. In fact, Beth believes that had she not gone through God's process of growth before meeting Carl, the "old" Beth would not have even been drawn to him. She told me, "There is no way he would have gone for me. He would have been way too healthy!"

◆ As You Enter God's Way for You

We hope you have been encouraged by Beth's story, even if your own journey isn't about marriage. Whatever your journey (whether it concerns your family, a habit or addiction, your career, or your kids), God will make a way for you, as he did for Beth, if you are willing to step out and live according to the principles in this book. You may not receive your first desire . . . or you may. That is up to God and what is best for you. Perhaps you are already working on some of the principles, but weren't aware of some of the others. At any rate, these concepts work because the One who makes a way for us designed them, and he will accomplish his purposes in you as you allow him to.

God bless you and keep you, as you enter the way that he has for you. We want to encourage you, in the words of the apostle Paul, that we are confident "that he who began a good work in you will carry it on to completion until the day of Christ Jesus" (Philippians 1:6).

Embark on a Life-Changing Journey of Personal and Spiritual Growth

DR. HENRY CLOUD   **DR. JOHN TOWNSEND**

Dr. Henry Cloud and Dr. John Townsend have been bringing hope and healing to millions for over two decades. They have helped people everywhere discover solutions to life's most difficult personal and relational challenges. Their material provides solid, practical answers and offers guidance in the areas of *parenting, singles issues* and *personal growth*. Each week Dr. Cloud and Dr. Townsend host a unique event called **Monday Night Solutions** in Southern California. They deliver a powerful message of God's love and truth on a wide variety of topics. These compassionate and often humorous presentations are recorded and comprise their extensive audio library. For a complete list of all their books, videos, audio tapes and small group resources, visit:

www.cloudtownsend.com or

800-676-HOPE (4673)

ALSO AVAILABLE from Cloud-Townsend Resources

Dr. Townsend has been conducting popular and life-changing seminars for many years on a wide variety of topics such as *Boundaries in Marriage, Boundaries with Kids, Safe People, Hiding From Love, How People Grow* and *God Will Make a Way*. For information on scheduling a seminar or becoming a seminar partner call **800-676-HOPE (4673).**

Cloud-Townsend Resources
Solutions for Life
www.cloudtownsend.com

DR. HENRY CLOUD
Answers for Life

Now you have even more opportunities to learn from Dr. Henry Cloud!

Attend a daylong seminar led by **Dr. Cloud and Answers for Life**. Seminars include such topics as *Boundaries, Boundaries in Marriage, Boundaries with Kids, Winning at Life* and *How People Grow*.

Dr. Cloud's ability to connect with all audiences makes attending his seminars non-threatening, entertaining and life-changing!

Also available from Dr. Henry Cloud and Answers for Life:

- Character-based Leadership Seminars
- Training to Lead a Small Group
- Small Group Curriculum Resources
- Seminars via satellite
- Leadership workshops for companies
- Other Cloud-Townsend materials
- Dr. Cloud on live radio in more than 100 cities

For more information about attending a seminar or how you can be involved partnering with us to impact your church, community or company, call us at **1-866-DrCloud** or visit **www.drcloud.com**.

Dr. Henry Cloud-Answers for Life is a ministry of Campus Crusade for Christ. We exist to connect people to the life of God (Ephesians 4:15-18).